THE RISE OF
MODERN INDUSTRY

by the same authors

**THE VILLAGE LABOURER
THE TOWN LABOURER
THE SKILLED LABOURER**

The Rise of
Modern Industry

J. L. Hammond
and
Barbara Hammond

With an Introduction by

R. M. Hartwell
Fellow of Nuffield College, Oxford

METHUEN & CO LTD

11 NEW FETTER LANE EC4

First published November 26th 1925
Second edition 1926
Third edition 1927
Fourth edition 1930
Fifth edition 1934
Sixth edition 1944
Seventh edition 1947
Eighth edition 1951
Ninth edition 1966
Printed in Great Britain by
Butler and Tanner Ltd, Frome and London

PREFACE

IN preparing this book the writers have received great help from friends, among whom they must mention specially Professor Henry Clay, Mr. G. D. H. Cole, Mr. H. J. Laski, Mr. H. B. Lawson, Mr. Reginald Lennard, Mr. C. M. Lloyd, Mr. R. H. Tawney, Mr. Arnold J. Toynbee, and Mr. G. M. Trevelyan. They had the good fortune to benefit in their work on this book, as on other occasions, by the suggestions and criticisms of the late Professor George Unwin, who was known to all who came under his influence as the most generous and stimulating of teachers and friends.

This book is written for the general reader and not for the specialist. It is an attempt to put the Industrial Revolution in its place in history, and to give an idea both of its significance and of the causes that determined the age and the society in which it began. The scope and intention of the volume will perhaps best be made clear by means of a short synopsis of its contents. The book is divided into three parts.

PART ONE

In this part the authors discuss the development of commerce before the Industrial Revolution. The argument runs as follows: The reader who turns to Roman history, or to the history of Italy in the days of the ascendancy of Venice, will recognize several of the features of our modern industrial civilization; for example, capitalist organization and large scale production. There is, however, a very important difference. In those days the needs of the ordinary man were supplied either by himself or by his neighbours, whereas to-day they are supplied by a world-wide economy of production and exchange. For the beginning of this new system we have to go back to the commercial revolution that followed the discoveries of Columbus and the other great explorers of his time. For that revolution was a revolution in the character, as well as in the scale, of commerce: shipbuilding was greatly improved, more capital was used, and in time commerce came to supply things like tea for popular consumption, whereas in earlier days it had mainly carried silks and spices for the rich. This commercial revolution was a necessary precursor of the Industrial Revolution, for it is a mark of that revolution that industry, which at one time was mainly confined to the manufacture of articles used by the well-to-do, came to supply clothing for the poor. Mass production demands popular consumption.

Why did this revolution come in England in the eighteenth century ?

For the new commerce the Atlantic was as important as the Mediterranean had been for the old. The most active trading peoples, after the discoveries of Columbus, were those who looked out on the Atlantic. Of these peoples the English were in a specially favourable position, in the middle of the eighteenth century, as a result of their geographical situation, their climate, and their history. The Spaniards used their control of the New World for politics, and the wealth they drew from the American mines was spent, in the main, in ways that discouraged industrial expansion. The English colonists in America, on the other hand, settled where there was little gold and silver, and they grew into communities which needed British goods for their own consumption, and sent home products that were useful for industry.

Events in Europe also favoured the more rapid expansion of English industry, for the European wars of the seventeenth and eighteenth centuries did more harm to industry on the continent than in England, and the religious and political strife of the seventeenth century left England with a constitution and government more favourable to commercial development than those of France. Among other advantages which a comparison of the state of England with that of France discloses are the supremacy of the common law, internal free trade, an aristocracy interested in commerce, a mistrust of State regulation, fostered by memories of the Stuarts, and toleration in religion. The stagnation of politics, religion, and local life in the eighteenth century encouraged the concentration on industry, and this concentration drew to mechanical invention all the ardour and imagination that had been fired by the revival of mathematics, and the discoveries of physical science. For these reasons England was the most likely theatre for the Industrial Revolution.

Part Two

In this part the writers attempt to give some account of the Industrial Revolution, describing the changes in transport which preceded the railways, the dissolution of the peasant village, the destruction of custom in industry, and the free play that capital found in consequence. One chapter is devoted to the invention of the steam engine, and separate chapters to the changes that took place at this time in iron, pottery, and cotton. It is obviously impossible to cover the whole field of English industry in a book on this plan and scale; these industries have been taken because they illustrate different aspects of the revolution.

Part Three

In this part the writers examine the first social effects of the change from a peasant to an industrial civilization. One chapter discusses the influence of the tradition of the Slave Trade on the early industrial system, and calls attention to the resemblance between the arguments by which that trade, and those by which child labour, were defended. The next chapter, "The Curse of Midas," seeks to show that the spell of production overpowered the age, making it indifferent to all other aspects of life, beauty, culture, and pleasure.

The last two chapters describe the struggle between this passion for production and the deeper instinct to make a society. This struggle is put into its perspective by a comparison with two other ages of disorder: (1) the period of pillage that followed the Roman seizure of the Mediterranean and its wealth, and (2) the violence and confusion which followed the discovery of America. Just as in these other cases mankind had made a recovery from its first lapse into chaos, so the English people began to devise constructive institutions, such as the Civil Service, the Trade Unions, and the system of Factory Law. An attempt is made to estimate some of the influences that helped the English people to create a new society.

HEMEL HEMPSTED
August, 1925

NOTE TO SECOND EDITION

SOME critics have suggested that the picture of town life given in the chapter called " The Curse of Midas " is drawn from exceptional cases. That this view is not well founded will be clear to anybody who studies the most important public documents of the time: the Report prepared by Chadwick and other Poor Law Commissioners in 1842 on the Sanitary Condition of the Labouring Population and the Report of 1844 of the Commission on the State of Towns. This Commission examined fifty large towns and reported that there was scarcely one in which the drainage was good and only six in which the water supply was good: in seven the drainage and in thirteen the water supply was indifferent: in forty-two the drainage and in thirty-one the water supply was decidedly bad. It would have been possible to illustrate the argument of that chapter from the conditions of almost any large industrial town, though for reasons given in the text some towns were worse than others. A description of Leeds for example may be cited. The Commission after stating that the contractor for street sweepings rented a vacant plot of land in the heart of the poorest and most populous ward of the town, where he piled up all the refuse he could find and kept it to sell as manure, gave this further picture of slum life. "In one cul de sac there are thirty-four houses, and in ordinary times there dwell in these houses 340 persons or ten to every house: but as these houses are many of them receiving houses for itinerant labourers, during the period of hay time and harvest and the fairs, at least twice that number are congregated. The name of this place is the Boot and Shoe Yard in Kirkgate, a location from whence the Commissioners removed in the days of the cholera seventy-five cart-loads of manure, which had been untouched for years, and where there now exists a surface of human excrement of very considerable extent, to which these impure and unventilated dwellings are additionally exposed." The passage concluded with a sentence which may be said to sum up the argument of the chapter. "This property is said to pay the best annual interest of any cottage property in the borough."

HEMEL HEMPSTED
February, 1926

NOTE TO THIRD EDITION

SINCE the last edition was prepared M. Rostovtzeff has published his important work on the *Social and Economic History of the Roman Empire*. The writers have amplified and recast a few passages in the first chapter in the light of information they owe to his volume.

HEMEL HEMPSTED
February, 1927

PREFACE TO FIFTH EDITION

THIS edition contains a new chapter discussing the world economic crisis in its relation to the Industrial Revolution. This chapter glances at the history of that revolution in the nineteenth century and the rise and fall of Free Trade as a remedy for the problems that were created by the spread of industrialism, first in Europe and America, and then in the East. Only once before in the history of our Western society has there been a world economic order, and the authors have examined the condition of the world during the first two centuries of the Roman Empire to see what light that example throws on our present problems. The chapter is partly based on a series of Broadcast talks that one of the authors gave in 1932 in collaboration with Professor Arnold Toynbee. The authors are under a great debt to Mr. Toynbee who has been most generous in allowing them the full benefit of his wide knowledge and his large and philosophical outlook. They wish also to thank Dr. H. D. Henderson, Dr. C. Delisle Burns and Mr. A. P. Wadsworth for valuable help in preparing this new edition.

HEMEL HEMPSTED
March, 1937

CONTENTS

Prefaces		*page* v
Introduction by R. M. Hartwell		xv
Note on Further Reading		xxix

Part I
COMMERCE BEFORE THE INDUSTRIAL REVOLUTION

I	From the Levant to the Atlantic	1
II	England as an Atlantic Power	24
III	The Effect of the Wars of Europe	38
IV	The New Prestige of Commerce	50

Part II
THE ENGLISH INDUSTRIAL REVOLUTION

V	The Revolution in Transport	66
VI	The Destruction of the Peasant Village	81
VII	The Destruction of Custom in Industry	97
VIII	The Steam Engine	110
IX	The Revolution in Iron	131
X	The Revolution in Pottery	162
XI	The Revolution in Cotton	178

Part III
THE SOCIAL CONSEQUENCES

XII	The Shadow of the Slave Trade	190
XIII	The Curse of Midas	210

XIV	A World in Disorder	233
XV	The Beginnings of a New Society	245
XVI	The World Economic Crisis of the Twentieth Century	263
	Index	285

INTRODUCTION
by R. M. Hartwell
Fellow of Nuffield College, Oxford

" A work of synthesis in which the industrial capitalism of the opening decades of the nineteenth century is displayed against the background of earlier economic civilizations, it remains at once the most instructive and the most original introduction to the social and economic aspects of history available in English." (R. H. Tawney on *The Rise of Modern Industry*.)

I

Historical best-sellers, which both excite the general public and satisfy the professional historian, are rare ; so, also, are successful wife-husband writing teams. John Lawrence and Barbara Hammond were remarkable for their cooperation in research and writing, for their combination of " a gift for original work in history with unusual literary power," and for their productivity. They wrote, between them, seven important books (six research monographs and one general history) on late eighteenth- and early nineteenth-century England, which imprinted on a generation of readers their vivid and tragic interpretation of the social consequences, for the workers, of the industrial revolution. This they achieved, in particular, by three widely-read volumes. *The Village Labourer*, the most famous, was published first in 1911 and reprinted ten times (1912, 1913, 1919, 1920, 1920, 1924, 1926, 1932, 1936 and 1948), with four editions and a total printing of 66,500. *The Town Labourer*, published in 1917, had two editions, eleven reprints (1917, 1918, 1919, 1920, 1920, 1925, 1928, 1931, 1936, 1941 and 1949), and a total printing of 43,750. *The Skilled Labourer*, published in

1919, had only three reprints (1920, 1920 and 1933) and 6,000 copies. In 1920, *annus mirabilis* for the Hammonds, each of these books was reprinted twice, throwing onto the market in one year 18,500 Hammond volumes, of which at least 6,500 were sold in that year. Even so, the largest reprints came after the Second World War—50,000 copies of *The Village Labourer* in 1948 and 26,000 of *The Town Labourer* in 1949; a massive tribute to the lasting worth and popularity of the Hammonds' books. The record of *The Rise of Modern Industry* is modest only in comparison with these two; it was first published in 1925 and the eighth reprint was in 1951, to make a total printing of 13,500. Their other important books about the same period of English history were *The Age of the Chartists* (1930), with a revised version *The Bleak Age* (1947), and a biography of *Lord Shaftesbury* (1923), which ran through four editions by 1936.

With this formidable publishing success, it is little wonder that the Hammonds were, and are, so influential; indeed, their major theme that the working classes of England suffered increasingly during the industrial revolution is still widely accepted. But popularity did not ensure immediate academic approval. *The Village Labourer* was reviewed very critically by J. H. Clapham (a Hammond critic throughout his life) in *The Economic Journal* of 1912, and the first two labourer volumes were ignored by the leading historical journal, *The English Historical Review*. After 1919, however, with the completion of the labourer trilogy, the Hammonds' importance was established, and although criticism continued, all historians since then, who have written about the social history of the period 1750 to 1850 in England, have done so partly in reaction to, or in sympathy with, the Hammonds' interpretation of this century. Thus, for example, J. H. Clapham in the first volume of *An Economic History of Modern Britain. The Early Railway Age 1820–1850* (1926) attacked " the legend that everything was getting worse for the working man, down to some unspecified date between the drafting of the People's Charter and the Great Exhibition." And over thirty-five years later G. Kitson Clark in his *The Making of Victorian England* (1962) wrote of the Hammonds that " no one interested in nineteenth-century studies should refuse to be grateful to them," but that " their very strong feelings have too often led them to see the classes they disliked as odious stereotypes with few individual and no mitigating characteristics." On the other hand E. P. Thompson, in *The Making of the English Working Class* (1963), argued that " a defence of the Hammonds need not only be rested upon the fact that their volumes on the labourers, with their copious quotation and wide reference, will long remain among the most important source-books of this period," but also upon the fact that " they displayed ... an understanding of the political context within which the Industrial Revolution took place." Similarly E. J. Hobsbawm, in an article about living standards during the industrial revolution in *Labouring Men* (1964), has dubbed the Hammonds, approvingly, as " the classical exponents of ' pessimism.' "

The appeal of the Hammonds is many-sided : their passion and literary skill, their breadth of learning and research, their relevance to contemporary problems. The Hammonds' history was not only felt by its readers to be topical, it was the clear intention of the authors to make it topical. *The Town Labourer* was published, they wrote in the preface, because " the subject it discusses has a direct bearing on problems that are beginning to engage the attention of the nation " ; in particular, it explained how the industrial revolution had divided the people of England into " two nations." *The Village Labourer* was but one of many books about agriculture published in England in the decade after 1900 when the agricultural depression had finally run its course ; it reflected naturally a revival in interest in the last major reorganization of agriculture, in the eighteenth century, which had set the pattern of English farming and rural life. Indeed, the Hammonds believed, and demonstrated, that the great social problems of the twentieth century had their origins in the industrial revolution—in the Great Divide, as R. H. Tawney called it—in the transformation of social, political and economic life by industrialization and urbanization. The economic results, as the Hammonds saw them, were described in *The Rise of Modern Industry* : " Its men and women, in Mr. Hardy's phrase, serve smoke and fire rather than frost and sun; they produce for commerce and not merely for subsistence ; they use in their daily lives the products of different countries for which they make payment by an elaborate system of exchanges ; they live by an economy in which occupations and processes are sharply specialized ; they rely for most of their production on the help of machines ; the mass of the persons taking part in this production have no property in the land, the capital, or the instruments on which it depends."

If this description of the new society was economic, the Hammonds' emphasis, usually, was social ; they probed the early history of the social problems inherited by their own generation from the period of the industrial revolution. They were influential, however, not only because they were topical, but because of an increasing interest in economic and social history, an interest which they partly created and from which they certainly benefited. They were influential also because their scholarship was convincing ; they worked through an impressive pile of printed material (including parliamentary papers) and a mass of manuscripts hitherto little used, especially the Home Office papers in the Public Records Office. It is surprising that the Hammonds did not use industrial records—here the pioneering was done in Manchester—but it was nevertheless evident to their readers that the Hammonds' ideas and generalizations were based on conscientious and comprehensive labour on original sources.

Nevertheless, it is now generally realized that these sources gave a pessimistic bias to the Hammonds' views ; in the words of J. H. Clapham they " cast a shadow over the constructive energies of the industrial revolution " and it was for this reason that Clapham was determined " to lighten the darkness " and " to put the Home Office papers in a subordinate place as a source in the economic history of the industrial revolution." Equally important in a re-assessment of the Hammonds has been a fundamental switch in the interest of economists and economic historians; to-day problems of inequality and unemployment attract less attention than the problems of economic growth. On the forces which led to economic growth in the eighteenth century, however, the Hammonds, except in *The Rise of Modern Industry*, said very little; their preoccupation was almost exclusively with the social results, not the causes, of growth. To-day, however, the industrial revolution in England is seen as the first, and as a successful and novel example of economic growth, and historical judgment on it tends in consequence to be favourable. In method, also, the Hammonds now seem inadequate, particularly in their failure to reinforce their generalizations with statistics. They claimed, in reaction mainly to J. H. Clapham, that " on what men enjoy and what they suffer through the imagination statistics do not throw a great deal of light "; nevertheless they failed to realize how much their case for the immiseration of the English workers was weakened by tamely accepting Clapham's statistics, and by admitting that " as far as statistics can measure material improvement, there was improvement." At the very least, their generalizations based on literary evidence should have been reconciled with other generalizations based on statistical evidence which conflicted directly with them; the battle was not won, or lost, by switching the attack to social indices and by leaving the statistical optimists unchallenged in their own field.

The Hammonds were Liberals; nevertheless their works stand together as a massive indictment of the English ruling classes for not governing. They believed that, in the words of R. H. Tawney, " in an industrial civilization, the welfare of the majority of its members depends on the existence of conditions, physical and moral, which only collective action can create." The sub-title of *The Village Labourer* was " A Study in the Government of England before the Reform Bill," and its aim was to show " what was in fact happening to the working classes under a government in which they had no share." According to them fundamental changes in industry and agriculture produced social " chaos " —the result of the play of unfettered market forces which " gave to capital a much wider control of the life of men and of States " and which ensured that " restraint of every kind on the acquisition and use of wealth was discredited." " The problem of bringing into harmony and discipline those rude forces that either destroy a civilization or give it new power " was eventually solved and the English pioneered in the formation of a new industrial society. But success was achieved slowly and should have been achieved at less social cost.

This is the Hammond thesis, about which two general criticisms can be made. First, the Hammonds exaggerated the indifference and failures of English government; and they underestimated both the difficulties of government in a society without a skilled bureaucracy, and also the inevitable gap between the formulation and execution of public policy. It cannot be claimed, seriously, that the statesmen of early nineteenth-century England neglected their social obligations, that they were indifferent to the welfare of the masses, that they were unwilling to exercise the power of the state to regulate economic and social life. The new ideals of public policy, the philosophic justification of the welfare state, were formulated in this period, and, indeed, the Tories provided the widest and most constructive thought in the pioneering of new attitudes. The wealth of literature and the range of social legislation was impressive even by 1840, as J. B. Brebner has demonstrated.[1] And, given the prevailing social ethos, given the undeveloped state of central and local

[1] " Laissez Faire and State Intervention in Nineteenth-Century Britain," Supplement, *Journal of Economic History*, vol. XIII (1948).

government administration, given the composition of political parties and the electoral procedures, and, finally, given a twenty-year war, could government have done much more? It was unrealistic of the Hammonds to have expected the men of the industrial revolution to have controlled more firmly the forces let loose by industrialization. It is surprising, rather, that they exercised as much control as they did and solved, or began to solve, so many problems as soon as they did.

The second general criticism concerns estimations of the relative importance of the " hidden " and the public hands. As J. H. Clapham wrote: " To some of us ' unconscious ' forces at work in the ' chaos ' itself seem as important as acts of will in the governing human spirits that brooded over it." To a large extent the problems caused or inherited by industrialization were solved by industrialization, by the productivity of the new industrial system. As C. P. Snow, in a famous lecture, argued: " Industrialization is the only hope of the poor." Who could doubt, he wrote later, " that the industrial revolution had not brought us in 3 or 4 generations to a state entirely new in the harsh, unrecorded continuity of poor men's lives."

The Hammonds' main concern was with the social consequences of the agricultural and industrial revolutions, and their criteria were humane rather than economic: the effect of industrial change on the way of life and the status of the English workman rather than the effect on industrial production and national income. Thus " the decline of the village " and " the rise of the great industry " were seen as social tragedies for the humbler participants: freedoms and skills were lost, an " intellectual and moral chasm " divided rich and poor, personalities were dehumanized by factory discipline, and life was made ugly and brutish by town living. The sub-title of *The Town Labourer* was " The New Civilization." To the Hammonds the criteria of civilization could be posed in one question: " In what surroundings, and with what opportunities for the enjoyment of nature and art, does the population in question live and work?" Their criteria of morals and social conduct were derived from the ancient world. J. L. Hammond once said that an historian "requires an intellectual and moral base outside the prevalent assumptions of his day and his special sphere of work." It was a devotion to the literature and values of classical antiquity that gave the Hammonds their frame of reference. *The Village Labourer* is dedicated to Gilbert and Mary Murray. It was the influence of the classics, according to the Hammonds, which redeemed the statesmen of the eighteenth century. "For it was from the classics that men of liberal temper derived their public spirit, their sense of tolerance, their dread of arbitrary authority, the power to think of their nation in great emergencies as answering nobly or basely to some tremendous summons." And when J. L. Hammond came to write his greatest book, *Gladstone and the Irish Nation* (1938), he found Gladstone's strength and inspiration to have been derived largely from the classics. He believed, with Gladstone, that "politics was the noblest field for the mind and energy of man" and that the Greeks were "the pioneers of great politics in respect both of order and liberty." Hence the Hammonds' probing, in their examination of industrial society, not only of the material but also of moral consequences of the new economy and its social relationships. Hence their belief that working-class protest was not just a reaction against intolerable living conditions but, as in the case of Chartism, "a moral revolt against a conception of society." And when the framers of a new society came to do their work they did not face their problems "without help or guidance or warning from the wisdom or experience of the past." In the task of "erecting a society out of this new chaos" the governing class of England were guided by "the humanism of Cicero and the compassion of Christian teachers."

II

The aim of the Hammonds in writing *The Rise of Modern Industry* was to explain the modern world as it had developed from the industrial revolution. "This book is written," they wrote in the preface, "for the general reader and not for the specialist. It is an attempt to put the Industrial Revolution in its place in history, and to give an idea both of its significance and of the causes that determined the age and society in which it began." The main thesis was that in the nineteenth century, for the second time in history, there developed "an economic system so extensive and all-embracing as to make the term world-wide appropriate." The Roman Empire, based on "Peace, Free Trade and Disarmament," was the first world economy; nineteenth-century industrial Europe, based on mass production for popular consumption and "a world-wide economy of production and exchange," was the second. But whereas, the Hammonds alleged, great importance was given in Roman civilization to public beauty and to common enjoyment, so that all citizens of Rome, poor and rich, could share in the goods of the age, at first no such distribution of the fruits of the industrial revolution occurred. In England, for example, "the spell of production overpowered the age, making it indifferent to all other aspects of life, beauty, culture, and pleasure." There was a neglect, by both rulers and employers, of social obligations and, in consequence, the lot of the working classes in England became intolerable. Nevertheless, Rome declined, as did Venice and Holland, because of "the failure to develop production." England, in contrast, survived; having provided, by industrialization, the basis of a good life, she averted the chaos which threatened in the early nineteenth century by devising by mid-century "constructive institutions, such as the Civil Service, the Trade Unions, and the system of Factory Law," which contributed successfully to the creation of a new society.

This was the main thesis, but there were important related

and explanatory theses. The first of these attempted to explain why the Industrial Revolution occurred, and why it occurred first in England. The Hammonds insisted on a commercial explanation of industrialization. "The commercial revolution of the fifteenth and sixteenth centuries was an essential preliminary to the industrial revolution of the eighteenth and nineteenth centuries." As commerce changed its character, from luxuries for the rich to articles (sometimes former luxuries, like tea, sugar and tobacco) of general consumption, it increased in size and encouraged the application of capital to large-scale production. And as England "learnt how to make greater fortunes from clothing the poor in the simple fabrics of Manchester, than had ever been made from clothing the rich in the gorgeous fantasies of Babylon or Damascus," so the scale and mechanization of industry increased. "The day when more profit was to be made by carrying tea for the poor from India, than by carrying pepper for the rich from Java, marked an important stage in the progress of the world to the modern system." The main reason for this expansion of trade, and its new character, was the discovery of America, which also partly explained England's leadership. But "Watt invented in an England that had accepted and adapted the Reformation, established an oligarchy in power, achieved a unity of law and government, created a constitution more flexible and liberal than those of its contemporaries, acquired an empire in distant seas." In explaining the transfer of power from the Mediterranean to the Atlantic, and in explaining the changes in the relative importance of the northern countries, the Hammonds attributed great importance to the wars of the seventeenth and eighteenth centuries and to the Napoleonic Wars. Because of these "the English people were flung into the modern system, while war tended to keep the Continent in the habits and methods of the past." A second thesis concerned "the power of capital." As agriculture and industry ceased to be regulated by associations of producers, as the range of commerce extended, "the dissolution of the peasant village, and the destruction of custom in industry " allowed " the free play of enterprise " and freedom to " the power of capital." A third theme was that as customary restraints and obligations disappeared, there was no brake on exploitation. Because of " the shadow of the slave trade " (which had already hardened men's hearts) and " the curse of Midas " (which resulted from the belief that " the man who seeks private gain finds the public good " and, therefore, that " the restraints of custom, tradition and religion had never been so frail over the classes that held power "), the world lapsed into social disorder, and chaos threatened. A final theme dealt with " the beginnings of a new society " through the agency of new laws and new institutions.

These, in broad outline, were the Hammonds' conclusions in their study of *The Rise of Modern Industry*. In presenting them they divided their book into three sections : the first sketched the development of commerce from Rome to the eighteenth century, the second anatomized the industrial revolution, and the third its social consequences. Part I compressed so much in four chapters that there was, inevitably, some " oversharpening of contrasts." For example, in emphasizing, rightly, the mass-consumption character of modern trade, in contrast with the luxury character of ancient and medieval trade, the Hammonds were led to unsupportable, if striking, generalizations. For example : " Almost all that was brought up the Tiber was tribute rather than commerce." But, as M. Rostovtzeff showed (and whose *Social and Economic History of the Roman Empire* is acknowledged by the Hammonds in a note to their third edition, 1927), there was an elaborate network of international markets and trade in non-luxury goods in the ancient world. Similarly when the Hammonds claimed that a medieval " traveller would rarely have travelled with merchandise that was to satisfy the wants of the mass of mankind," they ignored, for example, the large-scale movement in the middle ages of grain and cloth. Again, one could question the Hammonds' emphasis on the importance of war, in explaining, for example, the changing fortunes of the countries of northern Europe. The wars of economic nationalism from the seventeenth to the nineteenth century may have helped Britain, but resource endowments, mentioned but not stressed by the Hammonds, were probably more important. And whether or not those wars gave " an unwholesome stimulus to industrial development " is still an open question ; indeed J. U. Nef has written a large book (*War and Human Progress*, 1950) to demonstrate that it was not war, but limitations on war, which made possible the industrial revolution. In spite of these criticisms, however, this section of the book, and especially Chapter IV, convincingly demonstrated the commercial origins of modern industrialization, and showed how it was in England " that invention achieved its greatest triumphs."

Part II, in addition to accounts of various industries and an excellent chapter on the steam engine, treated two major themes which were first dealt with in the labourer volumes. These are found in Chapter VI and VII, entitled " The Destruction of the Peasant Village " and " The Destruction of Custom in Industry." On the enclosures of the eighteenth century the Hammonds wrote in *The Village Labourer*: " We are not concerned to corroborate or to dispute the contention that inclosure made England more productive, or to discuss the merits of inclosure itself as a public policy. Our business is with the changes that inclosures caused in the social structure of England, from the manner in which they were in practice carried out." The results were, they reckoned, rural depopulation and the downgrading of the peasant to " an agricultural labourer " or " a kind of serf." As with the changes in industry, the main economic consequence of enclosures for agriculture was freedom of enterprise. " England emerged from this revolution as an agrarian society without peasants or the obstacles that a peasant economy presents to an industrial system based on concentration of power and specialization of tasks."

But free enterprise in agriculture did not work quite as the Hammonds claimed. For example, the figures of poor rates shows no close correspondence between enclosure and rural poverty, and, in any case, poor rates near large commons were abnormally high in many cases before enclosure. Again there was no rural depopulation before 1800, and, indeed, very little before 1850. In nineteen counties of England there was no possibility of deserted villages before 1800, either because of little or no enclosure, or because the land enclosed was mainly waste; in six counties enclosure was of such character that it could hardly have affected population; nowhere up to 1800 does there seem to have been any close correlation between the growth of population and the amount of enclosure; after 1800 those counties with large unenclosed fields did not have a more rapidly growing population; and the enclosed eighteenth-century parishes were usually the most densely populated ones before enclosure.[1] Certainly the Hammonds were right to have underlined the sufferings of those hurt by enclosure, but the implications that enclosures were in no way desirable and that but for avarice agriculture could have gone on as it was, were not matched with suggestions as to how common field agriculture could have coped with the food needs of a rapidly growing population.

Similarly, with industry, where the Hammonds claimed that the triumph of free enterprise, " the victory of capital," was complete. " The upper classes divided their world into capital and labour and they held that the struggle was between custom and initiative, between the prejudices of the poor which hampered industry, and the spirit of acquisition and adventure in the rich which encouraged it." But as against the Hammond thesis that in the eighteenth century " custom was the shield of the poor," J. H. Clapham has argued that " more than seventeen theses might be defended against this text, but it would be pedantic to

[1] All this information can be gleaned from E. C. K. Gonner's *Common Land and Inclosure* (1912).

propound them." For example, in some industries before the industrial revolution, justices of the peace occasionally carried out their statutory duty to regulate hours of work and rates of wages, but this was rare after 1700. Indeed in the eighteenth century appeals to enforce the wage clauses of the *Statute of Artificers* (1563) were generally unsuccessful; prohibitions of worker combinations were frequent, as was legislation directed against embezzlement (of raw materials being processed); and the common custom of hiring by the year, with penalties for breaking the contract, put masters in a strong employer position. It was the industrial revolution, as T. S. Ashton has pointed out, that finally led, for the first time, to " the emergence of an independent, self-respecting class of wage-earners." [1]

Part III began with the interesting but unproven hypothesis that the slave trade had hardened the hearts of Englishmen *generally* " to think of men as things." This thesis can be compared with that of E. E. Williams in *Capitalism and Slavery* (1961), attempting to show that the slave trade also provided the capital for the industrial revolution. Apart from other objections, the timing is wrong: William Murray, Earl of Mansfield, established the doctrine " amid general applause " that slaves were free in England in 1772; and the slave trade was banned finally in 1806, the result, according to J. S. Watson, " of the new evangelical conscience allied with Fox's advocacy of depressed minorities." [2] In the chapter dramatically headed " The Curse of Midas " the Hammonds pointed out that " the problem of arranging and controlling the expansion of the towns was thus the most urgent of the problems created by the Industrial Revolution "—a problem still not solved in the mid-twentieth century—and contrasted the common life of the ancient and medieval worlds with that of industrial

[1] T. S. Ashton, *An Economic History of England. The 18th Century* (1955), p. 216.
[2] J. Steven Watson, *The Reign of George III, 1760–1815* (1960), p. 441.

England. But "public beauty" in Rome did not prevent proletarian unrest, and lack of it in England did not deter the transition from proletarian violence, as seen in the Gordon Riots of 1780, to more peaceful and more democratic forms of protest in the 1840s, as demonstrated by F. C. Mather in *Public Order in the Age of the Chartists* (1959). Factory towns at first certainly made little or no provision for common enjoyment or common culture, but the provision of such facilities has always been negligible for the mass of rural workers; only town life and increasing wealth would provide civilization for the masses. As the Hammonds admitted, important contributions to a new social order were made by mid-century—Factory Law, Civil Service and Trade Unions—but, equally important by 1850, was the general establishment throughout England of an industrial system whose productivity increasingly ensured goods for all. The Hammonds failed to understand the full significance of their own generalization: " Mass production demands popular consumption."

NOTE ON FURTHER READING

Since the Hammonds wrote *The Rise of Modern Industry* in 1925 a large and important literature on the industrial revolution has been published. The most important single volume is perhaps J. H. Clapham's *An Economic History of Modern Britain. The Early Railway Age, 1820–1850* (Cambridge, 1926). Other general works of importance are: C. R. Fay, *Great Britain from Adam Smith to the Present Day* (London, 1928); H. L. Beales, *The Industrial Revolution, 1750–1850* (London, 1928; new edition, 1958); T. S. Ashton, *The Industrial Revolution* (Oxford, 1948); W. H. B. Court, *Concise Economic History of Great Britain, From 1750 to Recent Times* (Cambridge, 1954), and L. S. Pressnell (ed.),

Studies in the Industrial Revolution (London, 1960). On commerce before the industrial revolution see G. D. Ramsey, *English Overseas Trade during the Centuries of Emergence* (London, 1957).

On the various topics in Part II, see: C. I. Savage, *An Economic History of Transport* (London, 1959), and a new edition (1960) with an introduction by W. H. Chaloner of W. T. Jackman, *The Development of Transportation in Modern England* (Cambridge, 1916); B. H. Slicher van Bath, *The Agrarian History of Western Europe, A.D. 500–1850* (Oxford, English translation, 1952), and a new edition of Lord Ernle, *English Farming Past and Present*, with introductions by G. E. Fussell and O. R. McGregor (London, 1961); H. W. Dickinson, *James Watt, Craftsman and Engineer* (Cambridge, 1936) and *A Short History of the Steam Engine* (London, 1938); H. R. Schubert, *History of the British Iron and Steel Industry from c. 450 B.C. to A.D. 1775* (London, 1957); R. H. Campbell, *Carron Company* (Edinburgh, 1961), and M. W. Flinn, *Men of Iron* (Edinburgh, 1962); N. J. Smelser, *Social Change in the Industrial Revolution. An Application of Theory to the Lancashire Cotton Industry, 1770–1840* (London, 1959), and E. M. Sigsworth, *Black Dyke Mills. A History* (Liverpool, 1958).

On Part III, see: R. M. Hartwell, " Interpretations of the Industrial Revolution," *Journal of Economic History*, XIX (1959); E. J. Hobsbawm, *Labouring Men* (London, 1964); F. A. Hayek (ed.), *Capitalism and the Historians* (London, 1954); G. Kitson Clark, *The Making of Victorian England* (London, 1962), and E. P. Thompson, *The Making of the English Working Class* (London, 1963). On topics of importance which are touched on only lightly by the Hammonds see: P. Deane and W. A. Cole, *British Economic Growth, 1688–1959. Trends and Structure* (Cambridge, 1962); B. R. Mitchell and P. Deane, *Abstract of British Historical Statistics* (Cambridge, 1962); L. S. Pressnell, *Country Banking in the Industrial Revolution* (Oxford, 1956); T. McKeown and R. G. Brown, " Medical Evidence related to England

Population Changes in the Eighteenth Century," *Population Studies*, IX (1955); J. D. Chambers, *The Vale of Trent, 1670–1800* (Economic History Review Supplement, 1957). For the latest research, and for a systematic review coverage of published work, the following journals should be consulted : *The Economic History Review, The Journal of Transport History, Business History* and *The Agricultural History Review*. For an excellent collection of journal articles see E. M. Carus-Wilson (ed.), *Essays in Economic History*, 3 vols. (London, 1954 and 1962).

PART I

COMMERCE BEFORE THE INDUSTRIAL REVOLUTION

CHAPTER I

FROM THE LEVANT TO THE ATLANTIC

THE Industrial Revolution has created societies in which the plainest lives are ruled by forces that are as wide as the world. In the Middle Ages a man's neighbours were those who lived near him ; his outlook was bounded by his village ; he could watch the growing of his food, and the spinning and weaving of his clothes. This life, with the charm and the danger of its simplicity, was extinguished by a series of changes, of which the most dramatic were the great mechanical inventions that began in the eighteenth century and have succeeded one another with extraordinary rapidity from that time to this. The new industrial system has been associated throughout the world with the name of England, because the English people played the leading part in making and using the first discoveries. It was from England that the new processes, the new machinery and the new discipline passed to the continent of Europe.

This volume does not follow the fortunes of the revolution beyond the middle of the nineteenth century. This is not an arbitrary limit. England, unlike Germany and the United States, passed through a revolution of great importance before the introduction of the railway. That revolution was marked by the dissolution of the old village, by the transformation of the textile industries, by changes of a different kind in the Pottery industries, and by a great concentration of capital and power in the industries connected with iron, steel and coal. Its effects were important enough, and decisive enough, to alter the character of English life. It is this revolution that is the subject of this study.

There is another reason for taking this period as a unity. By the middle of the century it is possible to discern the contributions that England was to make to the solution of the problems created by these new conditions. The immediate confusion has passed; society makes its first efforts to adapt its arrangements to its new life; the distinctive features of a new civilization are emerging from the shadows. Decisions have been taken, institutions have been created, a temper has been formed, beliefs have assumed solid shape that are to influence, for good and for evil, throughout the nineteenth century, first the life of the English people, and later the life of all the most active of the races of mankind.

Moreover, by the middle of the nineteenth century, records have been drawn up that enable the historian to review the social consequences of this revolution. The tradition of the eighteenth century gave a very definite and limited purpose to government. The politicians of that age did not cherish or pursue great constructive aims, for they held that a nation, which had a governing class distributed over the countryside, needed little in the way of leadership or initiative from the centre. The business of Parliament was to redress grievances, rather than guide development. With this view of their duty Ministers were ready to inquire into allegations, and statesmen, who contributed singularly little to the reform or readjustment of their institutions, introduced a custom of signal importance, the custom of Parliamentary investigation. When the reform of Parliament brought to the House of Commons men who took a less modest and leisurely view of the scope of government, inquiry on behalf of Parliament became a regular stage in constructive reform. Thus in the first twenty years of the life of the reformed Parliament, Commissions and Committees examined one industry after another, one aspect of social life after another, and the reports they published throw a powerful light on the society that was leading the way in the Industrial Revolution. For these reasons it is possible to take the first phase of the Industrial Revolution, the phase that was peculiarly and predominantly English, and to attempt to construct a picture of its effects.

The Industrial Revolution was in one sense catastrophic, since it had effects that were immediate, and spectacular ; in another it was gradual, for it was the climax or the sum of a series of developments, none of them peculiar to England, some of them later in time in England than elsewhere. Any definition of this new society would make it clear that it could not have been called into being by any single set of forces. Its men and women, in Mr. Hardy's phrase, serve smoke and fire rather than frost and sun ; they produce for commerce and not merely for subsistence ; they use in their daily lives the products of different countries for which they make payment by an elaborate system of exchanges ; they live by an economy in which occupations and processes are sharply specialized ; they rely for most of their production on the help of machines ; the mass of persons taking part in this production have no property in the land, the capital, or the instruments on which it depends. It could not be said of a society so complex as this, that it was created by Watt, by Arkwright, by Crompton or by Stephenson. All that can be said is that the inventions by which those names are known throughout the world were decisive events in its history : decisive, because mass production depends on those inventions, and mass production is an integral part of the new system. Those inventions were essential, but among the causes that made the English people what they became, other events were not less significant.

In one sense the French Revolution created modern France, but modern France is the creation also of Louis XI, of Henry IV, of Richelieu, of the men and the forces that made France a great State before that Revolution made her a new type of society. So with England. Watt invented in an England that had accepted and adapted the Reformation, established an oligarchy in power, achieved a unity of law and government, created a constitution more flexible and liberal than those of its contemporaries, acquired an empire in distant seas. If the French Revolution had come in a different France, or the Industrial Revolution had come in a different England, each would have followed a different path, obeyed different forces, and created a different society. Any attempt then to describe the Revolution, however brief, will demand a sketch, however slight, of the general conditions that determined its time and place, its fortunes and its character. It is the object of these introductory pages not to attempt a summary or an interpretation of history, but to glance at certain salient passages that help to explain why eighteenth-century England was the agent, or the victim, of this revolution: the hero or the villain of this sensational piece.

A society whose habits depend so intimately on foreign exchange as those of modern England, cannot come to life in a world in which overseas commerce is mainly an exchange of luxuries. Before the discovery of the Atlantic routes Europe was such a world. The importance of the industrial expansion of the eighteenth and nineteenth centuries will become clearer, if we glance at the economy of that world as illustrated in two epochs of its history: first the epoch in which Rome, and then that in which Venice held the chief door between Europe and the East. In both of those epochs there was a well-organized and highly developed commerce, and industrial production assumed many of its modern features. It is worth while to survey, however briefly, the character of that commerce and that production, in order to see what was old and what was new in the system round which the life of mankind began to revolve in the eighteenth century.

Roman history presents of course a number of obvious resemblances to our modern economy. Capitalist organization is used to develop agriculture, mines, and forests, and overseas commerce. The story of Italian agriculture in the days of the Roman republic has pointed many a moral in modern controversies, and people who have never read a line that Pliny wrote, know his famous judgment, *latifundia perdidere Italiam.* Large scale production superseded the old peasant economy, and where this production was directed to the most profitable forms, such as growing vines and olives, the purchase of salt fish and clothing for the slaves was organized, as it might be organized in a modern compound ; when this slave system broke down with the gradual failure in the supply of slave labour, it was followed by a system of serf farming, with mean whites attached to the soil ; the loss of the old peasant farmer was lamented by poets and critics like Seneca and Virgil ; statesmen like the Gracchi, Augustus, Tiberius, Trajan, Hadrian, Nerva and Alexander Severus, tried in vain to resettle him on the soil of Italy. There is a familiar ring about this story.

Large capital found even greater openings in commerce. Dr. Johnson thought the English merchant was a new type of gentleman, but eighteen centuries earlier Cicero, discussing the careers that might be held suitable to a gentleman, *liberales habendi*, included trading, if it was wholesale and on a large scale.[1] Successful commerce took a Roman as it takes an Englishman into the ranks of a proud and powerful aristocracy.

Another feature of our modern industrial society is specialization : the distribution of functions and services in production and exchange among classes, districts, peoples,

[1] *De Officiis* I, 42.

climates. But specialization begins early. Damascus or Babylon were as celebrated for a special product thirty centuries ago, as Bolton, or Sheffield, or Kidderminster are to-day. And as first Greece and then Rome brought to Europe the arts of the East, the growing of flax, olives, vines, artificial grasses, and the culture of this or that product, different places in Europe came to be associated with different industries. Under the rule of Rome, Italian and Gallic towns made their mark in one trade or another : Arezzo became famous for pottery, Aquileia for bricks : there were districts in Gaul that could vie with Asia in producing dyes : Varro says that the curing of bacon for the Roman market was a Gallic industry, and that merchants in the valley of the Po sent their wines across the Adriatic to the barbarians on the Danube.

The overseas commerce of this world has been the subject of two famous descriptions, one by Juvenal, the other by Gibbon.[1] Ostia was crowded with merchant fleets. Ships brought corn from Africa or Sicily ; but they brought also luxuries from all parts of the known world : furs from Scythia, amber from the Baltic, carpets from Babylon, silks, precious stones and spices from Arabia and India. Every year a fleet sailed from Myos Hormos, a port in Egypt, to the coast of Malabar, or the island of Ceylon, where merchants awaited them from all parts of Asia. The fleet returned in the winter, and its cargo, unloaded on the Red Sea, was carried on the backs of camels to the Nile, to be taken to Alexandria and Rome. A holiday-maker, indulging his fancy, as he loitered beside the ships

[1] "Aspice portus
Et plenum magnis trabibus mare : plus hominum est jam
In pelago ; veniet classis quæcunque vocarit
Spes lucri, nec Carpathium Gaetulaque tantum
Aequora transiliet, sed longe Calpe relicta
Audiet Hercules stridentem gurgite solem."

Sat. XIV, 275.

See the second chapter of Gibbon's *Decline and Fall*.

at Ostia, might feel, no less than the man who loitered along the docks of Bristol in the seventeenth or of Liverpool in the eighteenth century, that he was in touch with the fables and riches of the East.

How were these luxuries paid for ? In the modern world a country that received from its neighbours all that Rome was receiving would be developing its resources to pay for the luxuries it consumed. Rome was not in this position. In the Mediterranean world there was exchange of products over a wide area, but the States most active in that trade, Egypt, Carthage, Syracuse, were conquered by a power that based its economic prosperity on the plunder of its neighbours. In this sense almost all that was brought up the Tiber was tribute rather than commerce. The great economy on which Rome depended for her lavish life and her power in Europe was not an economy of production,[1] but an economy of pillage. She had at her mercy a number of Sovereigns and States that were rich and weak, and she swept all the treasure they had accumulated, largely, of course, by extortion from their own subjects, into her capital. In the second century B.C. Paulus, who conquered Macedon, brought nearly two millions into the Treasury, and enabled Rome to dispense with a property tax. In the last century of the Republic, the East and the Mediterranean were rifled more systematically : every general or politician in difficulties turned to Asia or Egypt ; Julius Cæsar was meditating an expedition to Parthia at the moment of his death. A modern historian has thus summed up the dealings of Rome with the East : Rome seized the treasures of the East ; then with outward peace and order commerce and industry began to recover, so that the East could buy back its precious metals. Rome would then seize these treasures again. This process was repeated till the East was exhausted.[2]

[1] " Perhaps there has never been a great city so unproductive as ancient Rome." *Companion to Latin Studies*, p. 413.
[2] Ferrero, *The Greatness and Decline of Rome*, Vol. V, p. 23.

It was with this treasure that Rome paid for her imports.[1] Peace was not less profitable than war in this relationship, for the system of farming the taxes gave to a needy nobleman or a contractor with nimble fingers endless opportunities of extortion. The sharp business man from Rome could make money in Syria or Africa in the closing days of the Republic, as quickly as the Englishman or Scotsman in India in the time of Clive.

Augustus arrested this drift into lawless rapacity. Under his system the worst abuses were checked: the provinces received good administration, and with the peace and order of the Empire a brilliant municipal civilization spread throughout Gaul, Spain and North Africa. It might have been expected that great industrial expansion would have followed this improved and methodical government, and that the Empire which was renouncing pillage would find its support in production. For this the Romans had many advantages: organizing genius, wide experience, tolerant politics, tolerant religion, an admirable service of posts and roads that brought the provinces into touch with the capital. Of their baths, amphitheatres, aqueducts and bridges, their use of brick and concrete, their handling of vault and arch, a modern scholar has said that they were the first people with a great secular architecture.[2] The Empire had

---

[1] Of the wealth that came to the State from these sources we get a vivid picture in Pompey's great triumph in 61 B.C. after his rapid victories in the East. One of the features of the procession was a placard announcing that Pompey's successes had brought $2\frac{1}{2}$ millions into the Treasury, besides raising the annual revenue from two millions to over three. This was one episode in a long series. All the vast treasure that had been hoarded in palaces and temples in Syria, Palestine, Pontus, Sicily, and the rich countries of the East, tumbled into the lap of Rome. Besides the bullion she received from these conquests, Rome acquired the mines of Spain, the territory of Carthage in Africa, the Crown Lands of the King of Macedon; she drew tithes from Sicily, tribute from her other provinces. Ferrero, op. cit., Vol. I, p. 309, and Plutarch, *Life of Pompey*, 45.

[2] *The Legacy of Rome*, p. 397.

rulers who sought its material development, and understood the conditions of its success. Augustus brought peace, cheap and safe communications, good coinage, and good government; Nero startled his advisers by proposing something like internal free trade for the Empire;[1] Trajan imitated the vigour of Augustus, draining marshes, constructing harbours, and purifying the coinage. Under these conditions there was a considerable industrial development in the first two centuries of the Empire, though it is to be found mainly in Gaul, which had escaped the fatigue and the impoverishment of the Mediterranean. There was, as it has been put, a movement of industry westwards; for in these two centuries the West was imitating the East. Gallic weavers were sending fabrics to Rome that resembled, and at one time rivalled, the famous products of Syria and Palestine;[2] glass making was introduced from Syria, and factories set up in the Rhine Valley and in Normandy; pottery was exported from Southern Gaul to Britain, Spain and North Africa.[3] The valley of the Po was developed. Verona became famous for blankets, Comum for iron.

The commercial expansion of these two centuries has been compared by a modern scholar to that of the early nineteenth century.[4] The comparison suggests a contrast.

---

[1] M. P. Charlesworth, *Trade Routes of the Roman Empire*, p. 232.

[2] Ferrero, op. cit., Vol. I, p. 345. Rostovtzeff, *Social and Economic History of the Roman Empire*, p. 163.

[3] Charlesworth, op. cit., pp. 199 and 200.

[4] Charlesworth, op. cit., pp. 224, 225, 239. "Within the Empire itself long voyages and journeys were made; without, men penetrated to far distant lands, and the Roman name became known far and wide. The agents of the Roman business man had reached Ireland and touched the margin of the Baltic Sea, knew the Scythians of the Tauric Chersonese, and had met the Chinese traders beside the lonely Stone Tower in Taskurgan, had bought and sold in the marts of India, and bartered goods with the Æthiopians. The purity and good standard of the Roman coinage, the prowess of the Roman armies, the fair-dealing of the Roman merchants everywhere commanded respect."

For this commerce had a strictly limited character; Ostia might look like Liverpool, but Italy never came in the most active days of this commerce to look like Lancashire. One striking fact brings out the vital difference. The Roman people, whose genius could turn African deserts into populous and smiling towns, made scarcely any mechanical improvement in agriculture and industry.[1] In this respect invention stood still. It is characteristic of the Roman Empire that Vespasian, eager as he was for public economy, when offered a machine that would make it easier and cheaper to carry out his public works, rewarded the man, and destroyed his model.[2]

There were several reasons for this stagnation. In the first place, the tradition of the Greek world which put a stigma on industry, had turned the face of science away from the mechanical arts in the great days of discovery. While Rome was wrestling with Carthage for the mastery of the Mediterranean, the University of Alexandria was winning immortal fame by the bold flights of her thinkers. But the great minds of the three centuries that preceded the Roman Empire: Euclid (300 B.C.), Archimedes

---

[1] "But in the world under the Roman supremacy centuries went by with hardly any modification of the mechanical equipment. A small exception may perhaps be found in a sort of rudimentary reaping-machine. It was briefly referred to by the elder Pliny in the first century of our era, and described by Palladius in the fourth. The device was in use on the large estates in the lowlands of Gaul, and was perhaps a Gaulish invention. It is said to have been a labour-saving appliance. From the description it seems to have been clumsy; and, since it cut off the ears and left the straw standing, it was only suited to farms on which no special use was made of the straw. Its structure (for it was driven by an ox from behind) must have made it unworkable on sloping ground. That we hear nothing of its general adoption may be due to these or other defects. But I believe there is no record of attempts to improve the original design." Heitland, *Agricola*, p. 398.

"Save for some new devices in the glass industry, we are unable to detect any new invention in industrial technique after the first century." Rostovtzeff, op. cit., p. 166.

[2] Suetonius, *Lives of the Cæsars*, Book VIII, 18.

FROM THE LEVANT TO THE ATLANTIC 11

(b. 287 B.C.), Aratus (270 B.C.), Ctesibius (120 B.C.), Hero (100 B.C.), all pursued their researches and achieved their triumphs in a world where industry was under a cloud.

"The arts that men call vulgar" (wrote Xenophon) "are commonly decried, and are held in disesteem by the judgment of States, with good reason. They utterly ruin the bodies of workers and managers alike, compelling men as they do to lead sedentary lives, and huddle indoors, or in some cases to spend the day before a fire. Then as men's bodies become enervated, so their souls grow sicklier. And these vulgar crafts involve complete absence of leisure, and hinder men from social and civic life; consequently men such as these are bad friends and indifferent defenders of their country." [1]

Archimedes under the influence of this tradition held that it was degrading to science to put it to practical use; from friendship for Hiero and his native city he gave to war what he would not give to industry, and his military engines kept the Romans out of his hard pressed Syracuse for three years.[2] This aloofness of science from industry helps to explain why the ancient world came so near to economic

---

[1] Xenophon, *Œconomicus*, trans. J. Laistner, *Greek Economics*, p. 39. Mr. P. N. Ure, in his book *The Origin of Tyranny*, offers an interesting explanation of the Greek contempt for industry. He holds that the key to the rise of the tyrants in the seventh and sixth centuries B.C. is to be found in the invention of metal coinage. The Greek tyrants were the first men who grasped the political opportunities created by this invention: they gained financial power and used it to bring great bodies of free labour under their political control. Manual labour at that time enjoyed an honourable position. The tyrant gave the labourer employment. After the overthrow of these tyrannies the governments that succeeded gave employment to these labourers as soldiers or officials (e.g. the jurymen in Athens) and gave them public amusement. In this way the free artisan became dependent on official employment and manual labour became the business of slaves. For a full discussion of the Greek attitude, qualifying the generally accepted view, the student should consult the chapter on "Craftsmen and Workmen" in Zimmern's *Greek Commonwealth*.

[2] Plutarch *Life of Marcellus*, xiv ff. "Regarding the work of an engineer and every art that ministers to the needs of life as ignoble and vulgar, he devoted his earnest efforts only to those studies the subtlety and charm of which are not affected by the claims of necessity."

revolution, and then stood still. Had conditions been different, the steam engine might have been in use eighteen centuries before the time of Watt, for the motive power of steam was discovered by Hero about 100 B.C.[1]

Thus manufactures did not draw science into their service; there were good reasons in the state of Roman society why they were at a disadvantage in the competition for capital. A man who had money at his disposal found more attractive openings. If he wished to cut a figure in politics or society (a knight, for example, who had stepped into the Senate), he would spend his money on giving shows, keeping a great retinue of clients or adorning his city with buildings and parks. If, on the other hand, he wished to make more money, usury, commerce and the development of mines were more profitable than manufactures. In a world where wealth came and went with a turn in the fortunes of politics or war, where men were rich one day and destitute the next, money-lending was singularly remunerative. Cicero's keen business friend Atticus, whose outlook on life was perhaps expressed in his sentiment : " If the republic is lost, at any rate save our property," found ample scope for his large investments in this way. At that time the rates of interest were extraordinarily high : Marcus Brutus lent money to the town of Salamis in Cyprus at 48 per cent. Atticus lived in a time of violent strife, but even under the Empire money did not remain long in the same hands. It was said that in the time of Trajan there was no great fortune that had been made in the time of Augustus.[2] Interest was still high, even in Italy, where it was lower than in the provinces, 12 per cent. was common. We are told of the great Antoninus Pius that he was a benefactor because he lent money at 4 per cent., two-thirds below the current rate.

[1] See Wells, *Outline of History*, chapter xxv., on Science and Religion at Alexandria, for a very interesting account of the process by which the use of books changed into the worship of books.

[2] Salvioli, *Le Capitalisme dans le Monde Antique*, p. 247.

FROM THE LEVANT TO THE ATLANTIC

The crowding of Rome made housebuilding very profitable, and capitalists put up great tenements (*insulæ*) for the poor. Commerce in the luxuries consumed in the capital, and all the business connected with it, were much more attractive than manufactures and agriculture, which were hampered by the great difficulty of land transport. This difficulty encouraged the decentralization of industry, of which M. Rostovtzeff has said that it stopped the growth of industrial capitalism in Italy and then stunted it in the provinces.[1] Thus it may be said that the social conditions were adverse to mechanical invention, and that the lack of mechanical invention made it impossible to escape from the social conditions. The two acted and reacted on each other.

The failure to develop production involved, in the long run, the ruin of the Empire, for Roman civilization was not a light or an easy burden. The social life of Rome was pitched on a plane that demanded an exhausting expenditure. Every one knows the pictures of extravagance painted by the violent rage of Juvenal and the cold contempt of Tacitus. Lucullus, who first showed Rome what easy and defenceless prizes lay in the East, is forgotten as a general and remembered only as the prince of spendthrifts. Pliny's statement that Rome paid nearly a million a year in specie for the Eastern luxuries needed by great ladies has often been cited. The debauching of the populace has filled the imagination of all later ages; corn is distributed first at a low price, then free; wine is added, then oil.[2] Public games begin when the Republic has its first taste of plunder; rival politicians vie with each other in their display; the animals brought to be slaughtered come from a wider and wider area; presents are flung to

---

[1] Rostovtzeff, op. cit., p. 165.
[2] Augustus fixed the number of persons entitled to share in the corn and food gratuities at 200,000. At one time the number of recipients had been as great as 320,000. Salvioli, op cit., p. 172.

the spectators; an ambitious general or politician makes his gladiators fight with silver swords.[1] The achievements and habits of the Republic left to the Empire, that emerged from a long spell of exhausting civil war, the fatal legacy of this mass of extravagance.[2] The Empire had to maintain a capital that was devouring its resources and municipal towns that copied the capital in their taste for rich display.

In such conditions the Empire depended on peace and its early rulers made serious efforts to avoid war. When Trajan let himself be drawn into a policy of expansion the cost brought the Empire to the brink of catastrophe: in the century of disorder that followed the death of Marcus Aurelius, institutions that had proved too heavy a burden suffered blows from which they never recovered. Civil wars and mutinies exhausted the strength of the Empire and the exactions of the State exhausted industry and agriculture. The early Empire checked private extortion: the later Empire had to live by public extortion. Men were deterred from effort or expenditure from which they

[1] Augustus says in the *Monumentum Ancyranum* that 3,500 beasts from Africa were killed at his shows; at Trajan's second Dacian triumph in A.D. 107 11,000 animals, tame and wild, were slaughtered. See Stuart Jones, *Companion to Roman History*, p. 369.

Readers of Claudian's poems on Stilicho will recollect his description of the ship with its perilous cargo of African lions, and of the astonishment of Neptune, who has to admit, as he compares them with his own leviathans, that the sea cannot match the prodigies of the land. *De Consulatu Stilichonis*, III, 356.

It was said of Nero that a ship which should have brought corn to Rome in a time of famine, had been loaded with sand for his court wrestlers. Suetonius, *Lives of the Cæsars*, Book VI, cap. 45.

"The number of days which were annually given up to games and spectacles at Rome rose from 66 in the reign of Augustus, to 135 in the reign of Marcus Aurelius, and to 175, or more, in the fourth century."—Dill, *Roman Society from Nero to Marcus Aurelius*, p. 234.

Cf. Heitland, *Agricola*, p. 381.

FROM THE LEVANT TO THE ATLANTIC

could reap so little benefit.[1] And as the population of the Empire grew poorer, the task of making both ends meet became more difficult; after Diocletian's reforms the payment of tribute and salaries in kind became common;[2] desperate expedients were adopted, first as exceptional, then as normal methods of taxation; and a Government that could not develop industry was obliged in its effort to maintain this vast civilization with its armies of soldiers and officials, to squeeze what industry there was to death.

An industrial nation of the nineteenth century, with so large a part of the world under its rule, would have found in such an empire a market for its products. The British Empire in India is an illustration. In that century England profited in a material sense in three ways from the control of India. For India provided careers for her youth as Civil Servants, doctors, traders, and lawyers, investments for her capital, and, most of all, a vast market for her goods.[3] The Roman Empire drew tribute from the provinces, part of which was spent on luxury in Rome, part in the administration and defence of the Empire, but the possession of the Empire did not stimulate continuous industrial enterprise. For Italy lost her economic supremacy in the first century, and after the failure of Trajan's efforts to restore it Hadrian turned to the provinces, hoping to revive the economic prosperity of the Empire by means

---

[1] "To make the agriculture of a district more prosperous was to attract the attention of greedy officials. To resist their illicit extortions was to attract the attention of the central government, whose growing needs were ever tempting it to squeeze more and more out of its subjects."—Heitland, *Agricola*, p. 399.

Malaria was an adverse influence in parts of Italy. Varro, writing in 37 B.C., advised the use of free labourers in malarious districts because slaves were too valuable. Heitland, op. cit., p. 180. See *Malaria, a Neglected Factor in the History of Greece and Rome*, by W. H. S. Jones.

[2] Heitland, *Agricola*, p. 388.
[3] England ceased to draw tribute from India in 1773.

of their development, which is much as if an English statesman like Peel had concentrated his efforts on fostering production in India to compensate for its decline in England.[1]

Thus though we find in the Roman world the use of capital for production, some degree of industrial specialization, and an active overseas trade, there is a broad distinction between the life of that world and the life of a society that has passed through the Industrial Revolution. The whole life of such a society is governed by world-wide commerce, but in the Roman Empire the basis of civilization was still the self-supporting district, producing for use or for local exchange, with or without the help of slaves, and with the help of few or many slaves according to circumstances.[2] The noise and bustle that impressed the eye and ear at Ostia bore little relation to the occupations of the mass of the people.

When we turn to the second epoch, the period between the Crusades and the discovery of America, we find that capitalism, specialization, and overseas commerce have all made further progress. Men like Crassus and Atticus have their successors in Cosimo dei Medici, or the family of Marco Polo, or the powerful Jacques Cœur of Bourges who came to so tragic an end.[3] Capitalist organization, if it is still much more frequent in commerce, is not confined to commerce. When silk production was acclimatized in Europe, capitalists collected silk workers in mills in Genoa, just as they were collected in mills at Antioch or Tyre. Europe's own indigenous textile industry fell more and more under capitalist direction, with the changes that came over the

[1] See Rostovtzeff, op. cit., p. 318.
[2] E.g. Justinian set up silk factories in Constantinople to supply his own Court and palaces.
[3] Jacques Cœur possessed seven galleys in the port of Montpellier, and employed 300 agents who visited the chief ports, taking French cloth and bringing back silks and spices. A "hard-faced" business man, he restored to the Sultan of Egypt a runaway Christian slave who had hidden himself in one of his galleys. W. Heyd, *Histoire du Commerce du Levant au Moyen-Age*, Vol. II, p. 483 f.

FROM THE LEVANT TO THE ATLANTIC

guilds in Western Europe.[1] There was as fierce a social war in Flanders or Germany in the fourteenth or fifteenth century,[2] as in England in the early nineteenth century. In the guilds there was a competition from early times between commercial and industrial capital.[3]

Moreover, industrial specialization was carried much further than it had been carried in the Roman Empire. The woollen industry was brought to remarkable perfection at different times in the towns of Italy, France, Flanders and England. By 1420 Florence was sending as many as 16,000 pieces of cloth to the Venetian galleys for export to the East. The cloth of Chalons and Douai went to Genoa for export; other towns sent to Montpellier, Narbonne and Barcelona.[4] As early as the thirteenth century, English towns like York, Beverley, Lincoln and Colchester sent cloth to Spain; Stamford sent cloth to Venice.[5] Cairo had a special market for Western cloth, and the linen of Rheims was highly prized

---

[1] In this way capital is used much more widely than under the Roman Empire; it is becoming a force in industrial production as it had long been in the organization and development of commerce. We get from the time of Henry VII industrial capitalists of the modern type, like Cuthbert of Kendal and John of Newbury, who set up factories. M. Mantoux calls this " *cette ébauche précoce du capitalisme industriel.*"

[2] "Whatever the cause, it remains a fact that the conflict of organized bodies of masters and journeymen was one of the main features of German industrial life in the fifteenth century. The cities were drawn together into groups, and opposing federations, representing the masters in a single trade on the one side, and the journeymen employed by them on the other, fought over the labour question in all its aspects, with results that varied widely in the different trades, and from one period to another."—Unwin, *Industrial Organization in the Sixteenth and Seventeenth Centuries*, p. 49.

[3] "The process by which commercial capital was displaced in relative importance by industrial capital was a very gradual one lasting over many centuries, and the several stages of it can be distinctly traced in the successive phases of organization represented by the various London companies."—Unwin, op. cit., p. 79.

[4] W. Heyd, op. cit., Vol. II, p. 707.

[5] Lipson, *English Woollen and Worsted Industries*, p. 9.

by Egyptian women. But in some respects the most remarkable industrial development was the success with which Europe, learning perhaps from the Syrian weavers in the commercial colonies, perhaps from the Saracens in Sicily, copied the silk manufacture of the East. In the thirteenth century Lucca's skilled artisans could match the best wares of Damascus, and those of her citizens who fled or were expelled in the political strife of the early years of the fourteenth century found ready pupils in Genoa, Venice and Florence. The industry travelled from Italy to France, where Louis XI encouraged it, inviting Italian and Greek workmen to settle at Tours.[1] By the fifteenth century Europe was sending silk to Asia, and when the Portuguese arrived in Calcutta in the early sixteenth century, they found Lucca silk in the bazaars.[2] Thus Europe had learnt the industrial arts, as she had previously learnt the agricultural arts of Asia. Moreover, Europe was learning something Asia had not learnt. There were metallic carders in use in Florence under the guilds,[3] and water power was employed to work spinning mills in Bologna and paper mills in Nuremberg.[4]

When trade between East and West began to revive after the Dark Ages, the Italian City States took the place Rome had occupied in the earlier economy. The Crusades, which gave a powerful stimulus to this trade, led to a complete organization of commerce in the hands of the citizens of the stronger of those states. For the fighting crusaders were supported by fleets from the chief towns, carrying provisions and munitions, and their services were rewarded by the grant of quarters and privileges in Syria and Palestine. Venice, Pisa and Genoa acquired commercial colonies in this way in such towns as Jerusalem, Antioch and Tyre. For the next three centuries there was a sharp rivalry between

[1] Heyd, op. cit., Vol. II, p. 709.
[2] Heyd, op. cit., Vol. II, p. 710.
[3] Renard, *Guilds in the Middle Ages*, p. 71.
[4] Hobson, *Evolution of Modern Capitalism* p. 20.

these commercial States in the East, not unlike the rivalry of English, Dutch and French in the seventeenth and eighteenth centuries. Venice gained the chief share in the earlier, for much the same reason that England gained the chief share in the later competition. Her naval power and her situation enabled her to help and to injure the Eastern Empire more effectually than her rivals. She came to the aid of the Empire in the struggle with the Normans, and received in return free access to the markets of the Empire, a commercial advantage of the greatest value, for the Empire connected the East and its treasures with the West and its wants. Venice gained by her services, and kept by her threats, the grant of complete commercial freedom over this great and rich area. She had a trade connexion that stretched from the Black Sea to China, while on the other side she sent every year a large fleet, protected by archers, to the Flemish ports and to Sandwich, Southampton and London, carrying spices, silks, wine of Candia, raisins from Corinth, and taking back, at first hides, tin and wool, and later, manufactured cloth. This service did not cease till 1587, when the last Venetian fleet perished in a storm off the Needles.

Venice was not a great conquering power like Rome, drawing the wealth of the world into her lap; she was a great merchant State. Her citizens reaped their immense profits by the relatively easy process of passing the products of the East to the West, and the products of the West to the East. These products did not differ greatly from the products that were carried to and fro in the days of the Roman Empire. Venice imported pepper from Sumatra and Ceylon; ginger from Arabia, India and China; nutmegs, cloves and allspice from the Spice Islands of the Malay Archipelago; precious stones from Persia; indigo and sandalwood from India; glass, silk, rugs, tapestries and porcelain from one or other of the countries of the artistic East. In exchange Europe sent woollen cloth, arsenic, antimony, quicksilver, tin, copper, lead, coral and species.[1] Although only the rich could buy pepper, Venice sold over 400,000 lb. a year.[2] There were few vegetables for the table; food and drink were monotonous; the rich were eager for condiments to add variety and flavour to rather tasteless dishes. In spite of the progress of industrial production, the chief trade was still in luxuries: silks and jewels for churches and monasteries,[3] fine clothes for the persons, and spices for the tables of the rich.

Thus the elaborate commerce of this age differed as the commerce of the Roman world differed from the commerce of modern times. If anybody had travelled in the days of the Roman Empire from Carthage or Egypt to Rome, he might have travelled with corn for the populace, or wild beasts for the amphitheatre, but the merchandise on his ship would have been carpets, silks, and precious stones. If he had travelled with the Arab or Syrian merchant, making his perilous way from Constantinople to Novgorod in the ninth century, he would have found in the caravan spices or silks for the Russian Court or the Russian noble; if he had travelled with the enterprising Jews who went all the way from France to China,[4] he would have seen in their caravans, as they went East, slaves and furs for the use of Courts and rich men, and, as they returned, musk, aloes, camphor and cinnamon, needed by the rich for their enjoyment or their health. If he had travelled on a Venetian or Genoese merchant ship, coming from Syria in the fourteenth century, he would have admired the brocades that were to decorate a palace in Italy, or a cathedral in France or Spain; and if he had accompanied the Italian merchant

[1] Carlton Hayes, *Political and Social History of Modern Europe*, Vol. I, p. 45.

[2] It is interesting to note that pepper was one of the delicacies carried by the Roman ambassadors to Attila in A.D. 445. Bury, *History of the Later Roman Empire*, Vol. I, p. 279.

[3] Religious display was an important motive in mediæval commerce, for monarchs and nobles vied with each other in lavish gifts to favourite monasteries and churches.

[4] Heyd, op. cit., Vol. I, p. 127.

overland, to Augsburg or Bruges, or any of the towns of the great Hanseatic League, he would have supposed that nothing was so urgently demanded in the West as pepper or cloves. Such a traveller would rarely have travelled with merchandise that was to satisfy the wants of the mass of mankind.

The discovery of the Atlantic routes marked or caused a revolution in this respect; a revolution that took some centuries to produce its full effect. Commerce began to assume not merely a new scale, but a new character; it did not merely employ larger vessels and greater capital, it shipped popular cargoes. When the Dutch and the English first competed in the East, the Spice Islands were counted the chief prize; by the end of the eighteenth century the Spice Islands and India had changed places, and it was doubted whether the cost of keeping those islands was repaid by their profits.[1] For commerce had begun to provide for the many; to depend on popular consumption; to enter into the daily life of the ordinary man. India and America sent new delicacies to England, and in the course of a century, owing to a number of causes—the growth of commercial capital, the development of the arts and machinery of trade, the improvement of transport, changes of habits and manner of life—those delicacies were brought within reach of the poorer classes and passed into general consumption. Tea, sugar and tobacco took the place of pepper, spices and cloves, as the chief articles of commerce.

Tea, when first imported by the East India Company, was a highly priced luxury, but by the middle of the eighteenth century it was a popular drink. A writer complained as early as 1742 that "the meanest families" in the Lowlands of Scotland had given up beer for tea.[2] Cobbett and

[1] Botsford, *English Society in the Eighteenth Century*, p. 76, quoting Macpherson, *Annals of Commerce*, IV, 371-372.
[2] Lecky, *History of England in the Eighteenth Century*, Vol. II, p. 318*n*.

Hanway, the philanthropist, agreed that tea drinking was robbing the English people both of their health and their beauty. "Your very chambermaids," wrote Hanway, "have lost their bloom by sipping Tea."[1] By 1828 the yearly consumption of tea in these islands had reached 36,000,000 lb. Sugar grew rapidly in favour. In the Middle Ages the Englishman sweetened his food with honey. Until the seventeenth century sugar was a rich man's luxury; at the beginning of the eighteenth century England imported 20,000,000 lb., and by 1782 160,000,000 lb. Rice was another novelty brought from America. In a cookery book printed in 1734 there is not a single recipe for the preparation of rice; in another printed at the end of the century there are twenty-two.

Thus ships were now sailing across the Atlantic, or rounding the Cape of Good Hope, bringing cargoes destined, not for palace or cathedral, but for the alley and the cottage. Capitalist commerce was providing for the wants of the peasant and the workman, as well as for the taste of noble or cardinal, rich merchant or prosperous lawyer. Owing to new resources, new products, new materials, new habits, the expansion of wealth and the development of finance, commerce increased rapidly in volume and scale, and this change in degree was accompanied or followed by a change in kind. The day when more profit was to be made by carrying tea for the poor from India, than by carrying pepper for the rich from Java, marked an important stage in the progress of the world to the modern system.

The commercial revolution of the fifteenth and sixteenth centuries was an essential preliminary to the industrial revolution of the eighteenth and nineteenth centuries. For capitalist manufacture on the modern scale was only possible when capital could be applied to the production of goods that were consumed by the mass of the people, and it was the use of capital for this purpose that

[1] Botsford, op. cit., p. 68, quoting Hanway's *Essay on Tea*, pp. 222–223.

gave the Industrial Revolution its sweeping character. Commerce and production take the same course. As pepper gives way to tea, so silk gives way to cotton. The relations of Europe and the world outside are reversed : Europe that had drawn on Asia for manufactures takes the lead in production. The conditions arise that make possible so strange a spectacle as that of a Lancashire town using a raw material, not grown on English soil, to produce goods that are exported for popular consumption to India or China. England has learnt how to make greater fortunes from clothing the poor in the simple fabrics of Manchester, than had ever been made from clothing the rich in the gorgeous fantasies of Babylon or Damascus.

The change from peasant to industrial civilization may be described in another sequence. The wants of the ordinary man were supplied in the early Middle Ages, as in the days of Greece and Rome, either by himself and his family, or by his neighbours ; in the next stage these wants were supplied by special persons plying a craft, in a village or small town, organized sometimes in guilds ; in the third stage the provision of those needs became the business of individual or group production and large scale merchanting ; in the fourth it became the business of large scale production. At that point the world passes to the industrial age : to an age in which commerce and finance are no longer aspects, growing in importance, yet still aspects of its life, but the basis on which a society depends. The English people were the first to develop this system, to enjoy its wealth, to suffer its evils, to struggle with its problems, and to build on this foundation an imposing place and power in the world.

CHAPTER II

ENGLAND AS AN ATLANTIC POWER

THE discovery of America and of the Cape route to the East gave to the peoples who look out on the Atlantic the advantages that had fallen to Genoa and Venice. So long as it was the main task of commerce to bring the silks and spices of Asia to Europe by the caravan routes, or the sea routes of the Levant, those States that could exploit the resources of Syria, Palestine and Egypt were the most active trading powers. Their prosperity was spoilt by the capture of Constantinople (1453), which closed the northern route to the East, and by the fall, half a century later, of Cairo and Alexandria; for the Turks, who now controlled the trade routes, taxed this commerce almost to death. It vanished when the mariners of Spain and Portugal had made the Atlantic more important than the Ægean. From that time the Empire that Spain and Portugal had found was of greater consequence than the Empire the Greeks had lost. For the old world in which merchants in Venice and Genoa sent goods to the merchants of the Hanse Towns, to be sold in Augsburg or Bruges, or some other market town of Flanders or Germany, over roads infested by robbers and interrupted by tolls, there was gradually substituted a new world in which the chief commerce was maritime, and the most successful traders the nations living by the Atlantic.

Of these nations the one most favoured by the new conditions was the one that had suffered the greatest disadvantages under the old. The chief trade of mediæval Europe was the exchange of the wares of the Mediterranean and the East for the raw materials of the Baltic. Venice controlled the first, the Hanseatic League the second. Bruges was their meeting-place. England's share in this commerce had been slight and unenterprising. Her part in the Crusades had not been rewarded by the commercial prizes that had fallen to Venice, Genoa and Pisa; for though there was a *Vicus Anglorum* in Acre in the thirteenth century, there were no important British commercial settlements in the East. In the early Middle Ages England received the spices of the East from German merchants, who received them in their turn from merchants in Venice and Genoa. There is a statute of the time of Ethelred, which stipulates that the German merchants shall make payments in grey cloth, brown cloth, gloves, pepper and vinegar, for the favour of admission to the London market.[1] At a later time the Eastern spices were brought by the regular Venetian service to Sandwich, Southampton and London. England's trade was largely passive; nor is this surprising, for her position when the Mediterranean was the most important of the seas of the world, was as unfavourable as any in Europe.

The change in the map of the world gave England a place in the new complex of economic forces as commanding as Venice had enjoyed in the old. But Venice had used her opportunities to become a rich trading state; England used hers to become a great industrial as well as a great commercial people. This was due partly to the nature of her resources, partly to the spirit of her politics, partly to the time and circumstances of her expansion. Accident and design, character and events, combined to make a nation which ranked after Spain, France, and the Low Countries in prestige, industry and finance, at the time when America was discovered, the leader of the revolution that increased with such rapid and perplexing strokes the power and the difficulties of mankind.

Between the fifteenth and the nineteenth centuries, five

[1] Heyd, op. cit., Vol. I, p. 87.

several peoples had a considerable share in the plunder or the development of the world on which Columbus had stumbled in his search for the Indies. The first in time were Spain and Portugal, between whose splendid shadows the Borgia Pope had drawn his famous dividing line [1]; in the seventeenth century the chief part falls to the Dutch; in the eighteenth to the French and the English.[2] The history of America, with its diversities of religion, politics and culture, illustrates the different kinds of civilization that these several European Powers brought to her shores; the history of Europe illustrates the reactions upon those Powers of their contact with that world.

This chapter is occupied with the influence that America exercised on England's industrial development, and it is worth while, in order to see what that influence was, to contrast the experience and the fortunes of England and Spain. Both nations had acquired large overseas possessions in the New World, but those possessions in the one case helped, and in the other case injured the industrial life of the nation to whom they had fallen, or by whom they had been seized. The contrast is the more interesting, because it was only by an accident that the first nation to reap the first, and, as it proved, fatal results of Columbus's discovery, was Spain and not England. Columbus, disgusted with the treatment he received in Portugal, sent his brother

---

[1] Carlton Hayes, op. cit., Vol. I, p. 55. Alexander VI's famous Bull (May 4, 1493) drew a line from pole to pole, 100 leagues west of the Azores; a year later the line was redrawn. "Portugal had the eastern half of modern Brazil, Africa, and all other heathen lands in that hemisphere; the rest comprised the share of Spain."

[2] A convenient summary is given by Ramsay Muir (*Expansion of Europe*, p. 24), who puts it that the Iberian monopoly came to an end in 1588; that there followed the rivalry of the three nations who broke the Spanish power. From 1588 to 1660 is a period of experiment, when the Dutch are in the ascendant; from 1660 to 1713 there is a systematic colonial policy and rivalry between the French and the British; from 1713 to 1763 intense rivalry between French and British, ending in complete ascendancy of the British.

Bartholomew to England, with an offer to Henry VII. Bartholomew was taken by pirates, and when at last he reached Spain with the news that the English King had accepted the offer, Columbus had already set sail for the West, with the blessing of Ferdinand and Isabella and promises that were afterwards flagrantly broken.[1]

The discovery of the Atlantic routes brought within the reach of Europe a world with richer treasures than the treasure of Macedon and Pontus, and rulers still less able to defend their property. The first nation to finger this dazzling prize was almost certain to treat it as Rome had treated the wealth of the East. This is what Spain did. After a number of discoveries that seemed merely a succession of disappointments (Columbus was called the Admiral of the Mosquitoes because he found neither spices nor silk), Spain was made by Pizarro and Cortes mistress of the great mineral treasure of Peru and Mexico. When Philip II conquered Portugal in 1580, Spain, adding Portugal's acquisitions to her own, commanded the gold mines of America, the spices of Asia, and the rich and industrious provinces of the Netherlands. Over a vast theatre, in the imagination of Charles V no less a theatre than the whole of Europe,[2] she sought to play a part not unlike the part Rome had played, using for that purpose, as Rome had done, the treasure that had fallen into her hands.[3]

Adam Smith has an amusing passage comparing the early Spaniards, who measured wealth solely by the precious

---

[1] Walter Raleigh, *The English Voyages of the Sixteenth Century*, p. 8. A different account, however, is given in Markham's *Life of Christopher Columbus*, p. 52. It is there stated, on the authority of Oviedo, that Henry VII rejected Columbus's proposal.

[2] Martin Hume, *The Spanish People*, p. 341.

[3] Bacon, in his Essay on the true Greatness of Kingdoms, argued that Spain was the only nation in Christian Europe at that time that imitated the Roman devotion to arms.

Portugal was involved in this adventure. From 1580–1641 her policy was directed by Spain, and this contributed to the fall of her Indian Empire. Morland, *From Akbar to Aurangzeb*, p. 11.

metals, with the Tartars who measured it solely by cattle.[1] The Spanish Governments followed in the steps of the Spanish settler, for though they took measures to encourage industry in their new possessions, they spent their strength on the effort to wring the last peso out of this wealth for the use of the Crown. At first the Crown took two-thirds of the spoil, but enterprise was so sadly discouraged that it was found necessary to reduce this share first to a half, then to a third, and finally to a fifth.[2] The vast stores of bullion that crossed the seas to Spain came in great fleets, sailing at regular times, resembling the corn fleets that had once served Rome, and the merchant fleets that had once served Venice. As these fleets were the natural target of corsairs—English, Dutch, and French, who treated with equal respect the moral authority of the Pope [3] and the naval power of Spain—it was necessary to give them armed protection, and

[1] " For some time after the discovery of America, the first inquiry of the Spaniards, when they arrived upon any unknown coast, used to be, if there was any gold or silver to be found in the neighbourhood ? By the information which they received, they judged whether it was worth while to make a settlement there, or if the country was worth the conquering. Plano Carpino, a monk sent as ambassador from the king of France to one of the sons of the famous Gengis Khan, says, that the Tartars used frequently to ask him, if there was plenty of sheep and oxen in the kingdom of France ? Their inquiry had the same object with that of the Spaniards. They wanted to know if the country was rich enough to be worth the conquering. Among the Tartars, as among all other nations of shepherds, who are generally ignorant of the use of money, cattle are the instruments of commerce and the measures of value. Wealth, therefore, according to them, consisted in cattle, as, according to the Spaniards, it consisted in gold and silver. Of the two, the Tartar notion, perhaps, was the nearest to the truth."—Book IV, cap. I.

The Spaniards, for whom Bacon had such admiration, neglected one of his warnings. " But moil not too much under Ground, for the Hope of Mines is very uncertain, and useth to make the Planters lazy in other Things."—Essay on Plantations.

[2] Haring, *Trade and Navigation between Spain and the Indies*, p. 156.

[3] Catholic France treated the Pope's award with the same levity as Protestant nations.

the cost was defrayed by a tax on all merchandise, known as the *averia*.[1]

This treasure, while aiding the economic development of Europe, arrested that of Spain. The Spanish kings used it for their political designs:[2] for their zeal and ambition in the religious wars: for their effort to maintain an empire threatened by rivals and by rebels. Their extravagant politics soon brought them into difficulties, and they behaved like spendthrifts who allow their expenditure to anticipate their income. They had to resort to foreign bankers, like the famous house of the Fuggers, and to mortgage their share of the bullion on the sea. Kings and bankers, spenders and lenders began to look as anxiously for the treasure fleet, as the rulers of Rome had sometimes looked for the corn fleet that was to feed a hungry and turbulent capital.[3] In time they were driven to desperate measures, for when specially hard pressed they would seize the whole cargo, instead of taking only their lawful share.[4] Treasure so guarded and so treated is apt to slip through the fingers. Much of the bullion was lost by capture, much by fraud among officials and seamen, and much of it passed

[1] Haring, op. cit., p. 72.

[2] "By the abundant treasure of that country," wrote Sir Walter Raleigh, "the Spanish King vexeth all the Princes of Europe and is become in a few years from a poor King of Castile the greatest monarch of this part of the world."—Raleigh, *English Voyages of the Sixteenth Century*, p. 82.

[3] "The fleet from Spanish India, praise be to God, arrived upon the 13th day of this month without mishap. It carries a shipment of about fifteen millions. It is said that they unloaded and left a million in Havanna, because the ships were too heavily laden. This is a pretty penny, which will give new life to commerce."— From Madrid, September, 1583. *The Fugger News-Letters*, 1568–1605, p. 75.

[4] "King Philip of Spain intends to confiscate and keep for his own use and purpose the share of gold and silver belonging to different persons, which the fleet has just brought home. This comes to nearly ten millions, as shown below, and its confiscation will be detrimental to many."—From Lyons, September, 1596. *Fugger News-Letters*, p. 199.

to the bankers from their royal debtors. In this way it reached capitalists, French, Dutch, English and German, who could apply it to the purposes of industry and commerce. Spain brought all this treasure to Europe, as Rome had once brought the treasure of the East, but, so far as Spain was concerned, the wealth went to kings who spent it on war and politics, and to merchants who did not spend it on industry.

For the Spanish kings gave the regulation of their colonial trade to a few merchant houses in Seville, and the whole traffic fell into the control of a group of merchants there, and a group of importing houses at Lima and Mexico City, whose object was to secure, not the maximum production in old and new Spain, but the maximum profit for these particular interests. From these perverse methods it resulted that whereas Rome abolished her property tax on gaining the wealth of Macedon, the taxation of agriculture and industry positively increased in the Spain that was taking all these pains to import treasure.[1] Spain used her wealth to show that

[1] The *averia* or tax for the Armada, originally $2\frac{1}{2}$ per cent., was 12 per cent. in 1633. Haring, op. cit., p. 79.

Those readers who wish to study Spain's economic history at this time will find a full discussion in Haring, *Trade and Navigation between Spain and the Indies*, 1918. Among the most important incidents are the power of the *Mesta*, a corporation of large sheep farmers, which was strong enough to prevent the expansion of tillage in Spain, when the demand for corn was growing ; the outcry against foreigners which led to the expulsion of the capitalists who had brought French and Italian workmen to Toledo and Cordova and started industries there ; the unlucky measures taken by the Spanish Governments in the efforts to keep down the rise of prices which followed the influx of the precious metals, and the influence of the monopolies of the favoured merchants. For an account of the relations of this economic failure to the large political designs of Charles V and Philip II, see Martin Hume, *The Spanish People*, chapters ix. and x. ; see also Carlton Hayes, op. cit., Vol. I, p. 57, on Spanish industries in the sixteenth century.

Las Casas described Peru as a hell " which, with its multitude of quintals of gold, has impoverished and destroyed Spain."—Helps, *Life of Las Casas*, p. 47.

ENGLAND AS AN ATLANTIC POWER

if you gained control of the new world, you could live as a crusader, or a marauder, or a gentleman (the terms were sometimes synonymous), but not to show that you could develop great industries to supply a new and expanding market. Other countries turned to an economic use the treasure Spanish ships carried across the Atlantic, but Spain herself, according to Adam Smith, had more industries before than after the acquisition of her Empire. She was like a man who comes into a fortune, lives idly and wildly on it, runs through it, and then learns that he has forgotten how to keep himself.

Great Britain also found and lost an empire in America, but the first event helped and the second did not hinder her industrial development. This was partly because her settlements on the continent of North America were, in this respect, more fortunate both in place and time. Her colonists did not find themselves on soil full of tempting treasure, but on soil that yielded its prizes to hard and steady toil. Thus England possessed from the first, besides the dangerous riches that came to her from the Indies, East and West, a number of colonies that were not a source of rapid and easy wealth, but an expanding world with wants that she could supply, and resources that she could use.[1] While Spain was bringing home at great cost vast quantities of gold and silver, to be wasted by the soldiers and the nobles of Spain, or to be used by the merchants and capitalists of other countries, England was receiving raw materials like the iron of Virginia,[2] that were of use to her

[1] England had the same experience in Asia. The Spice Islands were the lure; England, too late to oust the Dutch from these islands, turned to India.

[2] The early colonies were valued chiefly as a source of raw material. "The possibility of utilizing the apparently limitless forests of America to relieve the strain on the woods of the mother country had been one of the prime motives in the colonization of Virginia."—Ashton, *Iron and Steel in the Industrial Revolution*, p. 105.

Compare Bacon, *Essay on Plantations*. "If there be Iron Ure, and Streams whereupon to set the Mills, Iron is a brave Commodity where Wood aboundeth."

industries, and sending out colonists who were to provide a stable and growing market. Moreover, by the time they came upon the scene the English already possessed a considerable indigenous industry, so that they had every inducement to use their opportunities, not merely as the people of Venice had used theirs, and the Dutch in the main had used theirs, to develop a great carrying trade, but to find a market for their manufactures.

When a new world is discovered, the old world benefits by using and developing its resources, and satisfying its wants. This general truth was put in a famous speech by Chatham : " I state to you the importance of America ; it is a double market : a market of consumption and a market of supply." Chatham and his age made many mistakes in their effort to act upon this truth. They misconceived the relative value of the Sugar Islands in the West Indies and the colonies settled on the mainland. They could not foresee that before the end of the century the continent of America would grow most of the raw cotton of the world ; for, at the time of the quarrel with America, the Sugar Islands sent more cotton than the continent. An issue arose on which the Sugar Islands had one interest, and the continental colonies another ; for the colonies desired to trade with the French and Spanish West Indies, and the Sugar Islands wanted the French and Spanish West Indies to be compelled to send for their supplies to distant Europe. The Sugar Islands were more powerfully represented in the City than the colonists, and their will prevailed. These restrictions were among the chief grievances of the thirteen colonies.

Moreover England, like France, and even more than France, held that a possession ought not to be allowed to become a rival to the mother country or to share its trade with foreigners. So passionate a friend to the Americans as Chatham declared that he would not allow a nail to be made in America without the leave of the British Parliament. Parliament passed a number of restrictive

Acts, in order to suppress any rising industry that could compete with the home market. Thus England admitted American pig and bar iron duty free in 1750, because the continental supply was uncertain and precarious, but forbade the colonists to set up rolling or slitting mills or to make steel.[1] These prohibitions were called by Adam Smith "impertinent badges of slavery."

"It was the system of a monopoly" (said Burke). "No trade was let loose from that constraint, but merely to enable the colonists to dispose of what in the course of your trade you could not take; or to enable them to dispose of such articles as we forced upon them, and for which, without some degree of liberty, they could not pay."[2]

This error was disastrous; it was a cause of war, and in the end cost England her thirteen colonies; but it did not prevent the development either of British industry or of the wealth of the colonies. For the colonies received the benefits, with the disadvantages, of the spirit of British policy. "In everything, except their foreign trade," said Adam Smith, "the liberty of the English colonists to manage their own affairs in their own way is complete."[3] "The whole state of commercial servitude and civil liberty, taken together, is certainly not perfect freedom," said Burke, "but comparing it with the ordinary circumstances of human nature it is an happy and liberal condition." The English at home had cared little about the look of authority, until that authority was challenged, for, unlike France and Spain, they had no desire to govern the lives or the habits or the religion of their colonists. The feudal and ecclesiastical institutions that were a burden on the Latin colonies were unknown in British America. The exclusions

[1] Ashton, *Iron and Steel in the Industrial Revolution*, p. 124.
[2] Speech on American Taxation, House of Commons, April 19, 1774. Burke's Works, Vol. II, p. 380 (ed. of 1826).
[3] Adam Smith pointed out that one consequence was that the natives were worse treated in British than in French America. Lecky says that the Indians fought for the French against the British in the Seven Years' War, and for the Government against the colonists in the War of American Independence.

and restrictions that checked the emigration of Spaniard and Frenchman were never practised by a country which sent Puritan and Catholic to settle in neighbouring colonies, and could pass an Act like the Quebec Act (1775), recognizing the Catholic religion in Canada at a time when severe penalties were still imposed by law on that religion at home. Colbert drilled the colonist as he drilled the manufacturer and workman in France, and stringent laws and customs shackled French companies competing with English rivals who had a free hand. Hence it is not surprising that the British colonies grew and prospered more than those of other countries. At the time of the Revolution of 1688 the French settlers in North America were about 11,000 or a twentieth part of the population of the British colonies, though the population of France was nearly four times that of Britain. At the time of the American Revolution the British colonists numbered 2,000,000, and the population of Great Britain was still under 10,000,000.[1] It is easy to see what a valuable market this population, with the tastes and the wants of Englishmen, would provide for British industries.[2]

The British manufacturers believed that they owed this flourishing trade to the commercial restrictions imposed on the colonies. It is significant that, in the opening stages of the great quarrel, the manufacturing interests supported the repeal of the Stamp Act, which asserted England's right to tax America, but held strongly to the right to regulate American commerce in the interest of the mother country. Turgot, on the other hand, when consulted by Louis XV

---

[1] For these figures see Lecky, *History of England in the Eighteenth Century*, Vol. II, p. 235, and Vol. IV, p. 1; and Knowles, *Industrial and Commercial Revolutions*, p. 3.

[2] "The tendency to rely too much on the American trade was clearly bad, but during the years of dependence it brought much wealth to England, creating the prosperity of Manchester and Liverpool, Kendal, Lancaster and Bristol, of the leather industry of Glasgow, and the export trade in stuffs from the West Riding."
—G. B. Hurst, *The Old Colonial System*, p. 65.

in 1776, predicted that a free America would import freely, and that Europe would learn that the principle of monopoly, by which all European nations had guided their colonial policy, was a complete delusion. The truth of one half of Turgot's prediction was soon demonstrated to the English by the course of their trade, after the thirteen colonies had become the United States. The separation, instead of ruining British trade, was followed by an actual improvement in the trade between the two countries. As it was the towns and farms of America that had suffered in the conflict, the war left much more bitterness among the colonists who had gained their purpose than among the people of England who had been baffled; but though the separation had taken place under the worst conditions, America needed English goods and bought English goods. It was clear that the nation that could produce and could transport its products could command a market in the new world, when that world was free; for in this case we were conducting a larger trade than the French with a part of the world that was actually hostile in sentiment.[1]

This truth becomes more evident when the other half of Turgot's prophecy was falsified. Our trade with America improved after the loss of the colonies, but America did not, as he expected, take the goods of Europe free. After the war of 1812 the United States turned to Protection.[2] But

[1] Two facts have to be remembered in this connexion: (1) The American States had great difficulty in acting together and agreeing on a common policy; (2) The French did not propose any liberal arrangements.

[2] In 1816 duties of 25 per cent. were laid on cottons and woollens, and duties of 20 per cent. on other articles. In 1818 the textile tariff was prolonged till 1826; the duty on all forms of unmanufactured iron was considerably increased. In 1824 a new tariff was introduced "for the purpose of affording additional protection," said President Monroe, "to those articles which we are prepared to manufacture, or which are more immediately connected with the defence and independence of the country." The duties on cotton were not much increased, but the duty on raw wool was increased to 30 per cent.; and the average duties rose from 35 per

with the immense increase in the purchasing power of the world that followed the development of the resources of the Americas, there was ample scope for the expansion of British industry, whatever the obstacles that were offered in a particular market; for events were steadily increasing the opportunities of the nation with industries, ships and capital. Europe was losing her political grasp of America, and in the course of the first thirty years of the nineteenth century, one after another, the several dominions that made up the great Spanish and Portuguese Empires broke away.[1] Thus there were new openings for the capital and the commerce of the nation that could take advantage of them, and England was in the most favourable position for this purpose. Her merchants had traded with South America since the seventeenth century, and with the disappearance of Spain's control there disappeared the regulations that had hampered their enterprise. In the case of Brazil the course of European politics helped her. In 1807 the Portuguese Court, with a great following of nobles and officials, set sail from Lisbon to escape the French army under Junot, and took up its residence in Rio de Janeiro, where it remained for fourteen years. Until that time Brazil had been kept as a close preserve for Portuguese trade, but the Regent now introduced a number of reforms into his greatest colony, and threw open its trade to all friendly nations. It is obvious that England gained more by this

cent. to $40\frac{1}{2}$ per cent. This tariff did not effect all that was expected, because the English Government at this time gave help to its woollen manufactures by removing the 6d. duty on foreign wool, and in 1828 the tariff was made still more severe; all duties on all materials of manufacture, pig iron, hammered bar iron, hemp, flax, wool, were considerably increased.

See Smart, *Economic Annals of the Nineteenth Century*, 1801–1820, p. 495; 1821–1830, pp. 263 and 461.

[1] Paraguay, 1811; Argentine, 1816; Chili, 1817; Colombia, 1819; Mexico, 1821; Peru, 1824; Brazil, 1825.

Florida Blanca, who directed Spanish politics during the negotiations of 1782, dreaded the independence of America as a precedent perilous to all colonial Powers. Lecky, op. cit., Vol. V, p. 198.

concession than any other power, partly because she was the chief trader with America, partly because she was Portugal's most important friend. It was indeed at her prompting that the step was taken.

Thus circumstances conspired to encourage English economic development on a scale out of proportion to her share in the politics of the world. As the Napoleonic wars were drawing to their close, a number of States were embarking on a new and independent political life. They had a powerful neighbour in the United States, but that neighbour could not supply all the capital or manufactures that they needed, or find a use for all their raw materials. Of other nations one was much better able than any others to satisfy their demands and to share in their development: the nation that had emerged from those wars rich in shipping,[1] equipped with industries, with more capital at the service of its trade than any of the peoples who had suffered on their own soil the ravages of that exhausting struggle. Thus England, the first European power to lose colonies by revolt, was the chief gainer by the general collapse of the European empire in America; for her merchants, her financiers, her shippers and her producers found at their door a new world with an expanding economy, whose needs they could serve better and more cheaply than anyone else.

[1] "Great Britain emerged in 1815 without a rival, as the one power able to carry on the shipping of the world in spite of the fact that she had lost about forty per cent. of her ships during the years 1803-1814." Knowles, op. cit., p. 296. At this time British tonnage was double that of the United States, the second shipping Power. See Kirkcaldy, *British Shipping*, p. 25.

CHAPTER III

THE EFFECT OF THE WARS OF EUROPE

THE course of events in Europe, as well as the course of events elsewhere, had helped to put British industry into this special position. If the new world had been colonized and developed without war or violence, the commercial benefits which it offered to Europe would have been shared more equally. This would have been the most fortunate issue both for the English people and for the rest of Europe ; industrial expansion may be too rapid, as it may be too slow, for the health of a nation. But the discovery of the Atlantic routes was followed by a struggle, lasting for two centuries, in which war, brigandage, and commerce are not easily distinguished from one another, and it happened that England, doubly served by the sea which connected her with America and detached her from the Continent of Europe, was better suited than any of her neighbours both to succeed in that struggle and to survive its strain.

The wars of economic nationalism, which succeeded to the wars of religion of the sixteenth century, have to be considered in two aspects. In the first place they determined which of the states of Europe should be the predominant power in parts of the world which had great economic importance : they decided between England, France and Holland as competitors for ascendancy in India and North America. In the second place the strain of these wars told more severely on industry and commerce in some countries than in others, and thus affected their relative material progress. In both these respects England gained at the expense of her neighbours. Her influence at the end of

THE EFFECT OF THE WARS OF EUROPE 39

the struggle was supreme in the new world ; her losses at home, so long as material strength alone is taken into account, were not so heavy as those of the peoples of the Continent of Europe, on whose towns, territory and population the brunt had fallen. No war, for example, in which England was engaged injured her economic life so directly and seriously as the thirty years' war had injured that of Germany in the first half of the seventeenth century, or the war with Louis XIV injured that of Holland in the second.

The wars of economic nationalism begin with the war between England and Holland in 1652. The Dutch, after breaking away from their Spanish masters in the sixteenth century, made themselves, by their skill and enterprise in trade, finance and seamanship, one of the leading States of Europe, By the middle of the seventeenth century they had pushed the Portuguese out of their settlements in India, Africa and the Spice Islands, established themselves in America, and drawn upon their commerce and their fleets the envious eyes of all Europe. Holland lost her naval ascendancy to a nation, far less experienced and versatile in commerce and finance,[1] but enjoying the advantage that an island possesses over a continental State, overlooked by powerful neighbours. England set to work to construct a navy in order to wrest from Holland the carrying trade of the Atlantic.[2] This was the meaning of the Navigation Act of 1651. An English Parliament had passed a Navigation Act in the fourteenth century, but English ships were then so few that the Act was a dead letter. The Tudors were zealous ship builders, and by the time of Cromwell England was in a position to make these Acts effective. The Act of 1651 forbade import or export

[1] On the greater efficiency of the Dutch in Asia, see Morland, *From Akbar to Aurangzeb*, pp. 104, 105.

[2] Sir Walter Raleigh, writing at the beginning of the century, had complained that England had let the Dutch become the great distributing centre of Europe, whereas " the situation of England lieth far better for a storehouse to serve the South-West and North-East Kingdoms than theirs do."—Kirkcaldy, *British Shipping*, p. 14.

of goods between Asia, Africa, America and England except in British ships, manned by British crews. Adam Smith analysed the effects of this Act in a famous passage. He argued that it had not increased England's trade but had changed its course, by increasing distant trade at the expense of trade nearer home ; on the other hand, it had served its purpose of weakening the Dutch. This naval competition told severely on Holland's industrial power, for her taxation (Adam Smith said her taxes doubled the price of bread) was a heavy burden on her linen industry. Her power by sea was embarrassed by the efforts she had to make on land. As Spain had exhausted herself in the religious wars of the sixteenth century, so Holland suffered from her gallant struggle with the ambitions of Louis XIV, and it was due to this strain on her resources that by the time of the Treaty of Utrecht (1713) England had overtaken her as a naval Power. In the war with Louis XIV Holland was England's junior partner. The Dutch remained of course a highly prosperous commercial people, but they lost many of their foreign settlements.

An island's advantages counted still more in the long struggle with France : with France who, when the eighteenth century opened, excelled England in population,[1] wealth, industrial skill, foreign trade and possessions overseas. France, like England, tried to imitate the Dutch and to make commerce and industry the basis of national power. But England could pursue commercial success with a single mind, whereas France, with her long land frontier, always had half her mind entangled in the political problems and temptations of the Continent. The age of Louis XIV is a good illustration of this double interest. Famous in its later phases for war and conquest, the reign produced in its earlier years a Minister who was as intent on industry and commerce as Walpole or Pitt. Colbert's

[1] France's estimated population in 1700 was 20,000,000 ; that of Holland, 3,000,000 ; of Spain, 7,000,000, and of England, 5,500,000. Knowles, op. cit., p. 3.

ascendancy, which lasted from 1661 to 1672, was a striking episode in the history of economic reconstruction. Energy, cold resolution, clear, if limited sight, all these faculties were put at the service of France for her material development. In some of his reforms Colbert followed Sully ; in others he anticipated Turgot. He brought relief to the public burdens by introducing honesty and order into the confusion of French finance, and by removing some of the abuses to which it was due that the wealth wrung from the nation exceeded so grossly the wealth received by the State. He sought to improve the quality of French industry by inviting foreign workmen to settle in France, by organizing trade instruction, by establishing special companies, and by imposing standards and methods of production on the guilds. Some of his proposals were wise and helpful, but his policeman's mind led him into devices that tended rather to stifle industry than to develop it. His schemes for commercial unity were opposed by the great Provinces that had been assimilated to France since the fifteenth century, but he succeeded in establishing a district in the centre of France in which goods could pass freely.[1] Had he kept his hold on the king's mind, France might have escaped the decline of the next hundred years and the fierce catastrophe in which it ended. But he was drawn by protectionist illusions, man of peace as he was, into a business war with Holland, which helped to undermine his own influence, and set a fatal example in Europe. Thus it was partly his own fault that he was displaced in the king's esteem by Louvois, whose heart was as much engaged in military adventure as Colbert's in colonial and commercial enterprise. Under the influence of his new adviser Louis turned from the colder pursuits of trade and internal improvement to the fatal delights of war and conquest.

The consequence of France's dual allegiance, which allowed the pursuit of power to impede her pursuit of commerce, were seen most clearly in the course of her struggle

[1] Tilley, *Modern France*, p. 256.

with England for the new world, west and east. The Treaty of Utrecht (1713), which closed the last and the most disastrous of the wars of Louis XIV, gave England advantages of the first importance in that struggle : territory in the West Indies and round Hudson Bay, and commercial privileges in South America. In the conflicts of the eighteenth century, both in India and America, France was served by brilliant agents and soldiers, and there were moments when the issue was doubtful, but Dupleix, Montcalm and De Suffren missed the steady support that they would have received from a Government which put that conflict first among its cares. England had, it is true, the benefit of a more successful enterprise, for the East India Company prospered, while the French India Company passed from crisis to crisis, but she had also the benefit of a Government that held to a single purpose.

Napoleon sought to recover for France what she had lost in this struggle, and he tried to make his control of Europe as powerful a weapon as England had found in the command of the sea. His attempt on Egypt was part of a scheme for establishing a new Middle Europe and wresting from England her supremacy in the East.[1] The effect of his defeat was to consolidate and increase English influence overseas, and the Peace of 1815 left England secure in the advantages she had won in the wars of the last century and a half.

These wars affected the economic development of the different States of Europe in another way. War is inevitably a violent interruption of the life of a people. When it assumes the scale of the struggle that began in 1792 and ended in 1815, ranging over an entire continent, disturbing the government, politics, business and industry, not of two or three combatants, but of every people in Europe,

[1] In 1672 Leibnitz had proposed to Louis XIV in his treatise *Consilium Ægyptiacum* that he should occupy Egypt instead of attacking Holland directly in India. "Hollandia in Ægypto debellabitur." *Cambridge Modern History*, Vol. V, p. 696.

making and remaking frontiers and States, the economic consequences are as sweeping as those that follow an earthquake or a plague. To understand why England emerged from this struggle with so decisive a superiority in commerce, industry and finance it is necessary to glance at these consequences.

The question to be answered, it is important to remember, is not whether the war did more injury to England or to France, but whether it did more injury to English commerce or to French. The distinction is important. It would perhaps be true to say that if we look at politics, the war did more harm to England; if we look at commerce, more harm to France. It inflicted on the English people damage that was irreparable, because it aggravated the social confusion and hardship involved in an industrial development fatally rapid and headlong. Historians differ in estimating how far the war was responsible for the evils of the Industrial Revolution, but there can be no question that the English people was handicapped in its struggle with the chaos of that revolution by the conditions imposed on it by the war. Great and perpetual burdens were thrown on the nation; wealth changed hands with the fluctuations of prices and the vicissitudes of agriculture; the new financiers who managed the subsidies and loans were bad masters for a State; politics degenerated in the hatred and suspicion bred by the scare of revolution; reform was arrested and reaction assumed a savage and bitter complexion. All these are evils that cannot be measured, and in one sense England has never recovered from them.

Moreover the war caused at times great economic distress. When Napoleon sought by the Berlin Decrees to exclude England from trade with the Continent, British Governments replied by the Orders in Council, which declared France and all countries under French control in a state of blockade. This retaliation was disastrous at the time to our industries (Whitbread said in the House of Commons that thirty-two cotton mills were put out of employment in Manchester), for it involved us at once in difficulties with America which led later to the war of 1812. This was a specially inconvenient quarrel, for by this time we depended on the United States for a great part of our supplies of raw cotton.[1] It is not surprising that the manufacturing world hated the Orders, and hated their author, since industry was gravely disorganized for a time. The misery that followed the Peace, when armies were disbanded, and the orders for munitions and clothing came to a sudden end in a society that had no experience in managing this kind of problem, is of course familiar to all students of the dark years made memorable by Peterloo.

But the war which inflicted all these evils did not arrest industrial expansion. England had more cotton mills, more furnaces, more coal mines, more banks, after 1815 than before 1793; the English people were producing more, lending more, trading on a larger scale. The French war had not exhausted her population or dealt a disabling blow to her commerce and industry. On the contrary, industry and commerce were so active that they enabled the nation to bear a burden of taxation that must have overwhelmed any other people.

In France the conditions were just the reverse of these. The French armies had lived largely on their victims, and taxation was light.[2] But France was exhausted; her losses in men were of course immensely greater than England's, and her industry and trade had been paralysed by a war that had interrupted her foreign commerce. When the war ended, French trade was very much less

---

[1] See for details of imports, Daniels, *The Cotton Trade at the Close of the Napoleonic War*, pp. 5 and 6. In 1814 Georgia cotton was actually cheaper at Leipsic than in London (Hecksher, *The Continental System*, p. 275).

[2] Lord Binning, speaking in the House of Commons, Feb. 22, 1815, said that the people of France paid in taxes less than £1 a head, and the people of England £5 a head. *Parliamentary Debates*, XXIX, p. 982.

THE EFFECT OF THE WARS OF EUROPE 45

valuable than English, whereas before the war it had been greater.[1]

The progress made by France before the war is apt to escape us. We are so accustomed to connect industrial civilization with coal that it is easy to forget that the first textile machinery was worked by water power, and that the importance of coal begins with the introduction of steam. France, though poor in coal, had a very promising textile industry in the eighteenth century. Holker, a Lancashire man, had installed improved cotton looms at Rouen; Vaucanson of Grenoble invented a weaving loom, and a silk-throwing mill; Jacquard invented the loom that is still known by his name. Calonne introduced the mule in 1787,[2] and the spinning jenny and Arkwright's water-frame crossed the Channel before the end of the century.[3] The French Revolution had been preceded by a great deal of industrial development in other directions. Alcock, an English engineer, established hardware factories at Roanne and Charité sur Loire; Wilkinson built a factory on the Loire where he cast heavy cannon. The abundant water supply of the Dauphiné had been used for a great revival of silk and paper making, and for the introduction of metal industries. France had a population of 26,000,000 against Great Britain's 9,000,000, with a vast colonial trade, and a large and increasing export of manufactures. Her exports and imports were £40,000,000, whereas Great Britain's were £32,000,000.[4] Her foreign trade had increased by 500 per cent. between 1715 and 1787.

[1] M. Sagnac gives in *Modern France* the following figures for France's general trade:

1792	1,732 million francs
1813	605 ,, ,,
1814	585 ,, ,,

[2] Ure, *Cotton Manufacture of Great Britain*, Vol. I, p. xxvii.

[3] By 1800 the jenny was well established in the department of the North. Clapham, *Economic Development of France and Germany*, p. 64.

[4] See *Modern France*, p. 269, and Knowles, *Industrial and Commercial Revolutions*, p. 26.

The first effects of the Revolution were favourable. For the Revolution gave France what Turgot had tried to give her, and what England had possessed for over a century: internal free trade. And Revolutionary Governments did not merely remove obstacles: they reformed weights and measures, organized exhibitions of arts and crafts, encouraged schools of Civil Engineering and Mining, and, under pressure of the British blockade, tried all kinds of chemical and industrial experiments. There were more British inventions than French, but French Governments showed more active curiosity than British about the resources of science.

When Napoleon came to power he pursued these aims with the energy of a Colbert. He set up a model weaving shed at Passy, made his prefects encourage the use of machinery, and gave Jacquard, whom he invited to Paris to perfect his loom for weaving figured fabrics at the Conservatoire des Arts et Métiers, more help than any British Government gave to Kay or Crompton or Hargreaves. Moreover he made canals and roads which were useful for commerce as well as for war.[1] But Napoleon was also a Louvois, and in his character, as at the Court of Louis XIV, the Louvois was stronger than the Colbert. If he could have kept his ambitions at rest after the Peace of Amiens, France would have been in a very favourable position for industrial development, since that Peace left her with the coal of Belgium inside her frontiers.

Belgium was the one country in Europe where the process of industrialization was as rapid at the beginning of the nineteenth century as in England. This was due to several causes. The Flemish cloth-workers had been famous from early times, and, in spite of the efforts of the British Parliament, Belgium assimilated British inventions and acquired

[1] "From this point of view the Napoleonic age was a time of restoration and advance for all countries that at any time formed part of the Empire, of arrested development for those that did not."—*Cambridge Modern History*, Vol. X, p. 744.

British machinery. Her skilled metal workers picked up the arts of engineering very quickly from an immigrant Lancashire mechanic, and her great abundance of coal encouraged all the new industries that used or produced iron. Then again she had been helped as an industrial people by the turn in the wars and politics of Europe that had made her for eighteen years part of France ; for revolutionary France abolished in Belgium, as she had abolished at home, a number of traditional regulations that hampered industrial enterprise ; she opened the Schelt to Belgian trade, and she provided, of course, a large market for Belgian coal and Belgian productions. Belgium had in fact, for a time, all the advantages in an industrial sense of belonging to a large political unit where trade was not interrupted by economic barriers. Yet Belgium was more essential to France than France to Belgium, for without Belgium France was relatively poor in coal. In 1807, when France included Belgium, her output of coal was 5,000,000 metric tons : after the Peace of Vienna and the loss of Belgium it was less than 1,000,000.[1]

The war would in any case have thrown an immense burden on industrial production in Europe, but the form that Napoleon gave to it made that burden still heavier. For it became a great industrial and commercial duel with England. In the Continental blockade which provoked the Orders in Council he actually laid heavy duties on imported cotton in 1805–6 and 1810. He cherished at one time the idea of making the Continent an economic unit, equipped for the new industrial production, and he set up cotton mills in Italy ; but this was a *tour de force*, and its failure left Europe impoverished and almost disabled from end to end by the ravages of a long and unsparing contest. Thus when peace came France was far behind England in industrial power and commercial activity. Her exports were now less than half those of England.[2] Alsace,

[1] Clapham, *Economic Development of France and Germany*, p. 57.
[2] Gibbins, *Industrial History of England*, p. 213.

which was the Lancashire of France, began then to develop rapidly, and by 1828 there were 500,000 spindles round Mulhausen : two years later there were 2,000 power looms.[1] But the figures of the Chamber of Commerce of Mulhausen in 1835, which put English cotton manufacture at 150,000,000 kilogrammes and French at 40,000,000,[2] show how far France, whose textile industry had rivalled England's in 1789, had fallen behind. From this time the want of coal was a serious drawback.[3]

The war thus affected the Continent and England in different ways. On the Continent it gave a serious check, in England an unwholesome stimulus, to industrial development. As a collection of producing and trading peoples, Europe was thrown back ; England, emerging with a vast superiority in merchant ships and in industrial plant, was better able to take advantage of the expanding markets of the new world.

In another respect the war hastened the conversion of England to the modern economy. London became the

[1] The power loom was adopted there perhaps more quickly than anywhere else in Europe, not excluding Lancashire. Experiments began with it about 1823. By 1830 there were some 2,000 in use ; by 1846, 10,000. Clapham, op. cit., p. 65.

[2] Ure, op. cit., Vol. I, p. lxxiv. Dr. Clapham mentions that the average number of persons in the twenty-two spinning mills of Lille in 1820 were 60–70, of forty-three Manchester mills in 1816, 300. He also points out that only two towns grew rapidly in France in consequence of industrial development in the first half of the nineteenth century : Roubaix (8,000 to 34,000) and St. Etienne (16,000 to 56,000), whereas between 1821 and 1831 six English towns grew by more than 40 per cent. (op. cit. pp. 54 and 65).

In 1789 the general trade of France had surpassed a milliard of francs ; in 1813 and 1814 it fell to 605 and 585 million. *Modern France*, p. 282. It was not till 1825 that it regained the figure of 1789. See Porter, *Progress of the Nation*, p. 400.

[3] Chaptal, Napoleon's Minister, who gave this reason, gave as another the cheapness of labour in France. France's output of coal was 1¾ million tons in 1828 ; 5 millions in 1847 ; England's, 10 millions in 1800 and over 34 millions in 1845. See Clapham, op. cit., p. 57 ; and Redmayne, *British Coal-mining Industry during the War*, p. 4.

THE EFFECT OF THE WARS OF EUROPE 49

centre of a great organization of financial houses.[1] Amsterdam, formerly so important a rival, never recovered from the shock of the French occupation and the temporary loss of the Dutch colonies.[2] The invader who descended on the shores of England, as it has been well said, was not the French soldier but the foreign capitalist, not a Ney but a Rothschild. For England, offering the richest profits to the men who knew how to handle loans and subsidies, to exploit excited markets, and to manage the rapidly developing arts of banking and investment, presented conditions that make a nation poor and individuals rich. The rich were very rich, and they were for the most part men who valued money as the means to more money.[3] The war, a malign and misdirecting force on the industrial life of the nation, setting too quick a pace and intensifying all the evils that belonged to the new system, hastened also in this way the concentration of wealth, giving England new and dangerous masters. Thus the English people were flung into the modern system, while war tended to keep the Continent in the habits and methods of the past.

[1] "Down to and after 1848, the London financiers and the great international Jewish houses that were half domiciled in London, ruled the loan market."—Dr. Clapham in *Cambridge Modern History*, Vol. X, p. 743.

[2] Holland, as a commercial community with a long coast line facing the continental ports of England, was of course in a special sense the victim of the Berlin Decrees. Napoleon's brother, Louis, the King of Holland, was in a painful position. "Nothing short of the complete abrogation of the Continental System could save Holland, and nothing less than its most rigorous enforcement could satisfy Napoleon."—Simpson, *The Rise of Louis Napoleon*, p. 23.

[3] We get some idea of the way in which wealth escaped its share of taxation from the case of the first Sir Robert Peel. He died in 1830, leaving £900,000. His estate paid in death duties £25,000. To-day it would pay more than ten times that sum. Smart, *Economic Annals*, 1821–1830, p. 569.

CHAPTER IV

THE NEW PRESTIGE OF COMMERCE

IF the wars of the seventeenth and eighteenth centuries helped to determine the time, place, and course of the Industrial Revolution, they were themselves effects, rather than the cause, of the changes that came over Western Europe between the discovery of the new world and the establishment of a series of independent American States. In their character and result they illustrated the new direction taken by the desires and disputes of rulers and peoples: the new orbit in which the common mind was moving. It was not an accident that the nations most successful in those wars were those in whose allegiance commercial prosperity had challenged most confidently other and older ideals; that Holland and England beat Spain, that England beat France, and that the chief profits of the colonial empires went to the State that cared more to exploit their markets than to control their development. A new power had arisen in Europe, represented first by the fortunes of the Fuggers, then by the genius of the Bank of Amsterdam, and later by the tenacity of England's commerce: a power that was a rival to the Holy See and the Holy Roman Empire, to the King of Spain and to the King of France. The world was learning to pay to wealth the homage it had paid to magic, to religion, to courage, to authority, or to the blood of heroes and kings.[1]

[1] It is interesting to see from a footnote in Gibbon, what kind of arguments were used at the time of the Council of Constance (1414) to prove that you were entitled to a voice in the affairs of Europe. For this Council thirty deputies were chosen by the five

When we think of the Middle Ages as a civilization, we think of that civilization in two aspects: as a spiritual unity of faith and custom, and as a social world in which different orders, with different and complementary duties, recognize mutual obligations under a system of government and defence. The great mass of human life and effort is devoted to agriculture, overshadowed by a feudal lord, consoled and admonished by the Church. In the towns, where the feudal lord's power shrinks to little more than a shadow, citizens govern themselves under a charter granted by the Crown or other superior, and practise crafts under arrangements laid down by the Guilds. Luxuries from the East,

great nations of Christendom : the Italian, the German, the French, the Spanish and the English. The French disputed the title of the English, contending that England was one of the lesser kingdoms like Denmark and Portugal. "The English asserted that the British Islands, of which they were the head, should be considered as a fifth and co-ordinate nation, with an equal vote ; and every argument of truth or fable was introduced to exalt the dignity of their country. Including England, Scotland, Wales, the four kingdoms of Ireland, and the Orknies, the British Islands are decorated with eight royal crowns, and discriminated by four or five languages, English, Welsh, Cornish, Scotch, Irish, etc. The greater island from north to south measures 800 miles, or forty days' journey ; and England alone contains thirty-two counties, and 52,000 parish churches (a bold account !) besides cathedrals, colleges, priories, and hospitals. They celebrate the mission of St. Joseph of Arimathea, the birth of Constantine, and the legantine powers of the two primates, without forgetting the testimony of Bartholomy de Glanville (A.D. 1360), who reckons only four Christian kingdoms: 1. of Rome, 2. of Constantinople, 3. of Ireland, which had been transferred to the English monarchs, and, 4. of Spain. Our countrymen prevailed in the council, but the victories of Henry V. added much weight to their arguments."—Gibbon, *Decline and Fall*, cap. 70, p. 377.

Compare with this Burke's description of the importance of England in the eighteenth century : "When I first devoted myself to the public service, I considered how I should render myself fit for it ; and this I did by endeavouring to discover what it was that gave this country the rank it holds in the world. I found that our prosperity and our dignity were principally if not solely from two sources : our constitution and commerce."—*Works*, Vol. III, p. 7 (Edition of 1826).

the wares of the industrial towns, the products of the Baltic, pass from one part of Europe to another by a commerce in which merchants, such as those of the City States of Italy, or the Hanse towns, Guilds of all kinds, and money-lenders, at first Jews, later Germans and Italians, have their share in greater or less degree. War is frequent and savage, manners are coarse and cruel, but the trader, or the pilgrim, or the story teller who travels from York to Rheims, from Chartres to Florence, from Ghent to Rome, is reminded by noble buildings speaking a sublime language, of the hope and fear that give to Europe a common culture.

This culture, if it kept about the peoples of Europe a common atmosphere, was, it is well known, no check on strife or ambition in their relations with each other. The Hundred Years' War between England and France in the fourteenth and fifteenth centuries was as wanton as any war in later history. The sack of Cesena by Robert of Geneva, afterwards Pope Clement VII, was not less barbarous than the sack of Drogheda by Cromwell. When we say that Europe had a common civilization, we mean that all that part of Europe which had been under the Roman power had similar institutions and a similar background, just as Greece had similar institutions and a similar background in the fifth century B.C., though the Greeks were incapable of creating from this common basis a single State, or even a world of peaceful and tolerant neighbours.

This civilization does not disappear all at once. Over a great part of Europe manners are not perhaps very different in the thirteenth and the eighteenth centuries. But from the fifteenth century there is a movement towards a new society, acquisitive rather than feudal in character, in which individual liberty succeeds mutual obligation as a guiding principle and the attraction of adventure is stronger than the spell of custom. In some countries men move fast to this new civilization; in others slowly, in others not at all.

THE NEW PRESTIGE OF COMMERCE

By the eighteenth century part of Europe belongs to one order, part to another.[1]

This change has been brought about by a number of events : the emancipation of the villeins, the creation of a middle class, the new mobility of labour, the Renaissance, the Reformation, and the commercial revolution caused by the discovery of the Atlantic routes. The precise effect of these revolutions, their relations to each other, what Europe would have been with the Renaissance and without the Reformation, what the Reformation would have been with Erasmus and without Luther, or with Luther and without Calvin ; how, why and where the religious revolution disturbed, destroyed or reformed the old economic ideas, how far it helped to produce the Whig logic of Locke, or the Liberal philosophy of Adam Smith : these are questions on which historians are no more agreed than they are in counting what the world lost and what it gained in the most passionate quarrel of its history. Part of Europe emerges with a changed outlook, in which authority and obligation have new and revolutionary meanings, obedience and faith new and revolutionary masters. And at some point, from some cause, after the substitution here of the State for the Church, there of private judgment for a corporate discipline, the world passed from an atmosphere in which rapid wealth was apt to be blamed as a sign of sin, to one in which it was apt to be praised as a sign of virtue.[2]

---

[1] " Finally the destruction of German economic life was completed by the devastation of the Thirty Years' War (1618–1648), which paralysed Germany's economic development. For the next two centuries and a half Germany remained both politically and economically a mediæval state. At the beginning of the nineteenth century she was an agglomeration of over three hundred states separated from one another by tolls and tariffs, with many different coinages, weights and measures and laws, while communications were hampered by almost impassable roads. She was still a country of serfs and mediæval gilds in 1800."—Knowles, *Industrial and Commercial Revolutions*, p. 4.

[2] The revolution in the general view of usury is a good illustration of the forces that brought about this change. See for a full

If the mind of Europe passed through new experiences, so did the economy of its life. For the discovery of the Atlantic routes, and the acquisition of the gold of the new world inevitably transformed the scale and character of the commerce and finance that had served the Middle Ages. Distant overseas trade demanded operations that were beyond the range of the groups or guilds of merchants who used to trade between Italy and Germany or Flanders. For this new commerce Europe needed larger ships, larger harbours, larger cargoes, larger capital. The organization of credit became an art, its use a science. The merchant made way for the chartered company, the money-lender turned into the banker, and Governments, recognizing that a new world had arisen in which the command of capital was a greater power than the command of men, took a new and directing part in commercial enterprise.[1]

The Chartered Company was a typical product of these new conditions. It was a combination of public and private enterprise, used specially by the Dutch, the French and the English,[2] for promoting trade and sometimes colonization in distant regions. These companies were given a monopoly of trade in a particular area; they often undertook public duties of government, and had the right to make war by sea and by land. Holland had her East India Company in 1602, and her West India Company in 1621. England had such companies for trade with Russia, Morocco, Guiana, Bermuda, the Canaries, Hudson Bay, the Levant, and, of course, the famous institution which governed India down to the great shock of the Mutiny. France had

description, Tawney's *Introduction to Wilson's Discourse on Usury*, and Ashley's *Economic History and Theory*, Vol. I, Part II, chapter vi.

[1] Carlton Hayes gives the following figures for the fortunes of three banking families in the fourteenth, fifteenth and sixteenth centuries respectively: 1300, The Peruzzi, $800,000; 1440, The Medici, $7,500,000; 1546, The Fuggers, $40,000,000. *Political and Social History of Modern Europe*, Vol. I, p. 66.

[2] There were Swedish, Prussian, Scottish and Danish companies as well.

THE NEW PRESTIGE OF COMMERCE

companies for trading with the Levant, the Northern Seas, and the Indies, East and West.[1] These companies took as a rule one of two forms. In the Regulated Company each member traded for himself, observing the rules laid down by the company and bearing his share of such expenses as those of the provision and maintenance of forts.[2] In the Joint Stock Company the trading was carried on by factors, clerks and sailors employed by the Company, whose business was conducted by a Board of Directors, and its profits divided among the members in proportion to the capital they invested.[3] These shares could be bought and sold, and thus the creation of these companies led to the introduction of stockbroking.[4]

The commerce of the East, with its immense profits, legitimate and illegitimate, and its still greater expectations, gave scope and stimulus in England to these new arts. Stockjobbing became a mania, and seventeenth-century England reproduced many of the phenomena of the gambling days of Rome: the South Sea bubble would have made an apt theme for Horace or Juvenal. But these new methods were used, not only for colonization and foreign trade but for industrial enterprise at home. As early as

[1] France came last into the struggle for supremacy in India, Henry IV tried to foster Eastern Companies, but France had not recovered from the wars of religion. The first French company to trade with India was founded in 1674.

[2] These companies were like the Merchant Adventurers of the fourteenth century.

[3] The constitution of the Dutch East India Company was particularly interesting. "The capital of the Company was administered by a court of sixty-five directors, chosen by the different towns of the republic, each of which elected a number proportionate to its shares in the stock of the association; and the amount of these was determined by that of their respective contributions to the general taxes of the State."—Hewins, *English Trade and Finance*, p. 57.

[4] "Even as early as the sixteenth century, shares were sold outside personal acquaintances and without limiting conditions. For instance, a transaction is mentioned below, where Leicester had directed a share should be sold, just as a modern stockholder gives an order to his broker. In the next century adventures in the East

the reign of Elizabeth, the woollen industry, lead, and tin mining were financed with borrowed capital. In Tudor England the draining and enclosing of land, the deepening of old mines, and the sinking of new, the manufacture of glass and alum, were all attracting capital on a large scale. The expansion of the cloth industry in the closing years of the sixteenth century is revealed in the figures of the export trade. The trade was just under £900,000 in 1564; Camden put it a little later at just under £1,150,000; at the end of the first decade of the reign of James I it was estimated at £2,250,000.[1] In the sixteenth and seventeenth centuries there were companies for working pumps, for paper-making, for smelting iron, for coal and copper-mining, for glass-making and for textile manufactures, wool, silk and linen.[2] Industry, like commerce, was discovering its new mechanism.

The development of banking was not less important or revolutionary in its consequences. Money-lending was originally the business of the Jews, for it was forbidden to Christians by canon law. As these restrictions broke down, Italians and Germans took to money-lending, and they became a great power; they have been called the condottieri of the new order.[3] The Italians invented banking or

India Company were sold by auction at the court of sales. It is true that purchasers must become freemen of the company, but in a joint stock company there was no test for admission (as in the regulated companies) and the fine was of moderate and decreasing amount. In the second half of the century references to dealings in shares become more numerous, and the transfer books of the Royal African Company—some of which are in existence—show many changes of ownership. Finally, transactions became so frequent that a stock and share list was printed. . . . In fact, early in the reign of William III put and call options, bear sales, and bull accounts were perfectly well known: so that before the end of the seventeenth century, there was an open and highly organized market at London in stocks and shares of companies."
—Scott, *Joint Stock Companies*, Vol. I, p. 443.

[1] Tawney, *Introduction to Wilson's Discourse on Usury*, p. 43.
[2] See the two volumes of Scott's *Joint Stock Companies*.
[3] Tawney, *Religious Thought on Social and Economic Questions in the Sixteenth and Seventeenth Centuries*.

THE NEW PRESTIGE OF COMMERCE

the system of taking care of other people's money and using it to make a profit for yourself. The Dutch went further and invented bank money, giving to Dutch commerce the advantage of the easiest credit in the world and substituting Amsterdam for Antwerp as the commercial centre of Europe. Thus Europe took a long step from the system under which peasants and small traders borrowed from a neighbour to tide over the difficulty of the hour, and kings borrowed from great money-lenders to pay for their wars, to the modern system, under which economic life depends on the use of credit for capitalist enterprise.

Banking developed later in England than in Italy and in Holland. Merchants took to depositing money with goldsmiths whose receipts were the origin of our banknotes. The goldsmiths began to lend money lying in their cellars to the Government or to business men needing a loan. The depositors, who at first paid rent, then received a small interest. As Governments got more and more into debt, lending to them became a greater risk, and loans earned exorbitant rates of interest. To meet this difficulty the Bank of England was set up in 1694 : a joint stock company, established by charter, whose principal object was to lend a large sum of money to the Government at 8 per cent.[1] A century later London had a Stock Exchange, or a market where stockbrokers and dealers in money did their business, and Liverpool set up a Cotton Exchange on this model.

In this development the lead had been taken by Holland. The part played by England in the Industrial Revolution of the eighteenth century was played by the Dutch in the commercial revolution that preceded it and helped to bring it about. All Europe looked to Holland ; it was not only England that learnt from her, but circumstances enabled the English to learn more rapidly than the French from their Dutch masters. When Sir William Petty, writing in 1699,

[1] Napoleon established the Bank of France in 1800.

sought to explain the success of the Dutch, he described their government as under the control of men in trade, their private life as free from interference, their chief ambition as the accumulation of wealth. By the middle of the eighteenth century Dean Tucker could draw a contrast between England and France, in which he could ascribe to England all the virtues Petty had found as causes of the prosperity of the Dutch. He laid stress on the prestige of commerce, the freedom of industry and the absence of tax farming ; the only drawback he found was the English workman's "turbulent love of pleasure." England, having learnt all that Holland could teach in finance and commerce, could apply the lesson over an area that combined the finance and commerce of Holland with the industries and the coal of Belgium. The progress both of Holland and Belgium towards the new order was rapid, but if the two had formed a single and harmonious State, their progress would have been more rapid still, and it would have made that State a great power in Europe. The Netherlands possessed all the essential conditions for the creation of a strong national State of the new kind, but religious differences, skilfully used by the Duke of Parma when he was sent to pacify the rebellion in 1579, had separated the Northern from the Southern provinces, and left behind a lasting discord. England united the finance of London, the commerce of Liverpool and Bristol, the industries of the textile North, and the coal and iron of the Midlands in a single economic area. Over this area, with its complementary economy, there was internal free trade.[1]

[1] Sir William Ashley points out that before the close of the Middle Ages a step had been taken towards internal free trade by inter-municipal treaties of reciprocity, by which the burgesses of the contracting towns were exempt from tolls when they came to trade. There were such treaties between Winchester and Southampton in the thirteenth century, between Salisbury and Southampton in the fourteenth, and between Nottingham, Coventry and Lincoln in the fifteenth century. Ashley, *Economic History and Theory*, Vol. I, Part II, pp. 44–45.

THE NEW PRESTIGE OF COMMERCE

Adam Smith held this to be one of the chief causes of England's prosperity, and he contrasted the obstacles that hampered internal intercourse elsewhere. France, when he wrote (1776) had three different sets of customs in addition to all her local duties, and the little Duchy of Milan was divided into six provinces with different systems of taxation.[1] Henry IV and Colbert had wanted to remove the internal customs barriers in France, but their plan of establishing privileged manufacturers in the towns frustrated their efforts for internal free trade. Vauban's famous *Projet d'une dîme royale* (1707) included this reform in the admirable programme which might have brought salvation to France but only brought disgrace on its author. Turgot was the first French Minister to try to give to France the benefit that England had enjoyed in this respect for more than a century. For in England there had been sharp struggles between rival interests of trade, class and place under the Tudors and the Stuarts; the Tudors had protected the town capitalist, but they had ended by leaving room for the free development of industry outside the towns: a development " which had already for more than a century been the mainspring of the productive power of England."[2] Thus England and Scotland, from the time of the Union of 1707, composed the largest free trade area in Europe, and the new economy had nowhere in Europe so wide or so convenient a theatre.

The course of politics had helped to produce a State that could exploit this advantage. For there had emerged from the struggles of the seventeenth century a society in which commerce had at once prestige and freedom. In this respect England was very different from France. In France the aristocracy had been destroyed as a rival to the Crown by Richelieu, and an aristocracy that has lost all share in government clings to any privilege that makes rank look as impressive as power. Feudal distinctions consequently kept and even increased their importance in

[1] *Wealth of Nations*, Book V, chapter ii.
[2] Unwin, op. cit., p. 188.

France. The Executive at the same time, having drawn all authority into its own hands, was not easily persuaded to let the merchant or manufacturer manage his business; Colbert laid down the most binding regulations for both. Thus eighteenth-century France was a society in which commerce and industry had to bear the burden of an idle aristocracy which escaped its share of taxation and to submit to the discipline or dictation of a Government that was often unintelligent: the French merchant and the French manufacturer had neither freedom nor prestige.

Conditions in England were the exact converse. Political control was in the hands of the aristocracy, and this aristocracy, unlike the French, had a strong commercial bent. Henry VIII, instead of keeping the confiscated Church lands for the Crown, had used them largely to reward new men from the City or from the ranks of commerce who had helped him. The English landlords, at once an old class and a new class, for riches carried outsiders into its circle, had become in consequence exceedingly powerful. The Whig Revolution effected in the crises of 1688 and 1714 had had two results. It had made the aristocracy the master of the Crown, and it had given the Whigs, the patrons of the commercial classes, complete victory over the Tories, who represented the collective rural and feudal prejudices of the small squires. Consequently England was governed in the eighteenth century by a strong commercial aristocracy; Voltaire remarked with surprise that great gentlemen in England were not ashamed of trade; the chief Ministers of the century, Walpole and the two Pitts, though they differed about the principles of commercial success, agreed in their view of its importance as the sovereign end of government.

This aristocracy moreover had special reason for giving commerce a free hand. The Colbert policy had been tried under the Stuarts,[1] who had established monopolies and

[1] The industrial policy of the Stuarts was in its aims the same as that of Colbert, but pursued with less ability and consistency. Unwin, op. cit. p. 187.

THE NEW PRESTIGE OF COMMERCE 61

privileged companies, with a view partly to the promotion of trade, partly to the advantage of securing revenue. These experiments had failed, and commercial methods of this kind were in consequence discredited. But they were discredited on political grounds as well in the eyes of the Whig aristocracy. For the Whigs looked upon State control, as they looked upon a standing army, as a weapon that might be used by the Crown against their liberties; it belonged to the politics of the defeated enemy. Thus all the political conditions in England favoured the development of the new system. The common law was supreme; there were few of the feudal and guild restrictions that were still in force in France; and the inclination of politicians was to seek the benefit and respect the judgment of the commercial classes.

There was another respect in which politics encouraged English commercial expansion at the expense of French. Rulers who wished their nation to advance in industry had always tried to tempt skilled immigrants to their country: Solon in Greece,[1] Louis XI and Henry IV in France, Edward III and Elizabeth in England are notable examples. The Reformation did for England, in this sense, the sort of service that Sulla's victories did for Rome; Sulla brought from Asia trained slaves who taught the Italians the scientific culture of the vine and the olive; the Reformation sent to England a body of industrial immigrants from a country her superior in skill and knowledge. England, who had learnt a great deal from Flemish immigrants in the simpler textile arts, was enabled by these Huguenot exiles to introduce the finer textile industries.[2] The Revocation of the Edict of Nantes (1685), a piece of intolerance that did France more injury than the good that Colbert had done when

[1] Solon's legislation was so successful that Pericles made the conditions of naturalization harder. Cornford, *Thucydides Mythistoricus*, p. 19. These aliens included Phrygians, Lydians and Syrians as well as Greeks.
[2] Ashley, *Economic History*, Vol. I, Part II, p. 237.

he invited foreign workmen to settle there, sent to England artisans, merchants, leaders of commerce and industry. Vauban gave as one of the reasons for condemning the revocation, " the damage done to our special manufactures, most of which are unknown abroad, which brought to France considerable sums of money from all the countries of Europe." Throughout the civil wars in France England was receiving religious refugees who saw no future in their native country.[1] England was largely indebted to such refugees, and to the Dutchmen who came over with William III, for the remarkable industrial development that followed the collapse of the Stuart monopolies: silk weaving, calico printing, pottery, fine glass and plate glass were some of the industries that made a rapid advance. English manufacturers, who used to send their cloth undyed and undressed to Holland learned to dye as successfully as the Dutch themselves. The religious strife, which cost some of her neighbours so much in vitality and skill, spared English industry these losses, because English exiles and refugees went to English colonies, whereas the Huguenots, forbidden by France to go to French colonies, went to England, or Holland, or Germany; and the Jews expelled by the Spaniards carried their special knowledge and experience of commerce and finance to Holland and Turkey. The language of Salonica is Spanish to this day.

Thus before the great inventions began, England had a Government favourable to commerce, internal free trade, a prosperous and growing textile industry, exporting its products to the Continent, with large commercial connections, joint stock companies, and a banking system. Nature added gifts of great importance: coal, abundant and placed near the ports, a position on the great water route between

---

[1] Chardin (1643-1713), son of a Huguenot jeweller in Paris, made himself, by travels and residence in Persia, the chief authority on the commerce, customs and history of the East. This knowledge he put at the service of England, and represented the East India Company at Amsterdam.

THE NEW PRESTIGE OF COMMERCE

Europe and America, and a climate specially suitable for the spinning of cotton. It was in this England that invention achieved its greatest triumphs.

Before this age inventions had come slowly and at long intervals ; in the eighteenth century inventions were incidents rather than events, and invention not a kind of miracle but almost a habit. In the space of half a century inventions were completed in England and Scotland which changed the character and range of the textile arts as cannon and gunpowder had changed the character and range of the art of war.[1] It is idle to try to account for the incidence of genius, but certain reasons for the time and place of this burst of inventive power will occur to anybody who considers in what respects this eighteenth-century England was like, and in what respects unlike earlier ages of the world's history.

In the first place natural science absorbed the interest and curiosity of the times. The world had not borne this complexion since the sunset of Hellenism. The intellectual daring of the Greeks, " their instinctive and effortless faculty for looking truth in the face," [2] had been succeeded by the natural caution of the Romans, and the deliberate caution of mediæval Christianity. Both these great civilizing forces had made contributions to progress that were essentially conservative in character : in one case a system and habit of law : in the other a system and habit of faith and of conduct. The " unscientific centuries " had played an essential part in the development of Europe, but not a part favourable to adventures of mechanical genius. There is a passage in Pliny describing the invention of sails, that speaks of this discovery not with enthusiasm but with awe : *Audax vita, scelerum plena.* Men who were grateful for the shelter

[1] The chief inventions are connected in the popular mind with half a dozen men, but they were the result of a large number of experiments and discoveries, the man, whose name is known, often merely putting a lucky or a finishing touch to the work of many predecessors. See Hobson, *Evolution of Modern Capitalism*, p. 79.

[2] Toynbee's Introduction to *Greek Historical Thought*, p. xviii.

and unity that civilization had found under the Roman Empire or the mediæval Church looked on intellectual daring as a doubtful virtue.[1] Under these conditions a great deal was learnt about the relations of man to man, of one social unit to another; political experiment was active; the arts that demand and express the range and the passion of sympathy found a noble language, but not much was learnt about the nature of the world.

The Renaissance brought back the bold curiosity of the Greeks; speculation was no longer discouraged; the widest and wildest horizons spread out before the traveller, the scholar, the student of nature. In England after the Restoration all this excitement went into the pursuit of the physical sciences. Bacon's *Novum Organum* had become the bible of the age. In 1662 the Royal Society was founded; six years later Newton invented his telescope. Dryden's *Annus Mirabilis* illustrates the wild hopes that filled men's minds and composed their quarrels.

"Dreams of perfect forms of government made way for dreams of wings with which men were to fly from the Tower to the Abbey, and of double keeled ships which were never to founder in the fiercest storm. All classes were hurried along by the prevailing sentiment. Cavalier and Roundhead, Churchman and Puritan, were for once allied. Divines, jurists, statesmen, nobles, princes, swelled the triumph of the Baconian philosophy."[2]

It is obvious that a world that was full of hydrostatics and chemistry, of air pumps and microscopes, was singularly favourable to mechanical invention.

Now there was an important difference in atmosphere and circumstances between this age and the earlier age of scientific ardour. In the earlier age industry was of little account. In eighteenth-century England, on the other hand, industry seemed the most important thing in the world. All classes put industrial expansion high among

[1] See Canon Streeter's Essay in *The Spirit*, p. 354, for the explanation of the conservatism of the Church.
[2] Macaulay, *History of England*, Vol. I, p. 361 (1905 edition).

THE NEW PRESTIGE OF COMMERCE

the objects of public policy; it was for this and not for glory that England went to war, and made or found an empire.[1] Men of enterprise and talent, against whom politics, national and local alike, had closed their doors, turned to industry for a career. In the life of the time there was no rival incentive or inspiration. Among the Italian cities of the Middle Ages, the power and activity of the Guilds marked the renown of the cloth trade that had been brought to such perfection in Florence, Lucca and other towns; but the citizens of those towns pursued eager and contentious politics. Their town halls, their churches, their pictures, their sculptures tell us as much of this absorbing life, as the guild halls tell us of the life of their industry. In the England of the Industrial Revolution the self-governing town of the past was as dead under a close corporation or a borough manager, as it was dead in Italy in the eighteenth century under a Spanish or a ducal or a Papal tyrant. The new industrial districts had no articulate life; they were ruled by the county justices. In national politics the inflaming conflicts of the preceding century had died down; the seventeenth century was the century of strife and argument; the eighteenth the century of peace and acquiescence. Men differed, but not fiercely, like Arian and Athanasian in the fourth century, or Calvinist and Catholic in the seventeenth. Politics were languid; social life was a spent routine; industrial development, on the other hand, was active, and it put pressing problems and offered tempting prizes to the imagination and energy of the age. It was thus as natural for the disciples of Sir Isaac Newton to turn to industry, as it had been for the disciples of Archimedes to turn away from it.

[1] Compare Burke's saying of the East India Company, that it began in commerce and ended in empire.

PART II

THE ENGLISH INDUSTRIAL REVOLUTION

CHAPTER V

THE REVOLUTION IN TRANSPORT

A LANCASHIRE town to-day receives its raw material from Egypt or the United States: it sells its products as far away as India or China: it lives largely on meat from the Argentine and corn from Canada or Australia: in the windows of its shops there are boots that have been made in America and clothes that contain the products of several countries: the windows of many of its houses may have come from Norway and the rails on which its trams are running from Belgium. Almost everything its inhabitants use has been made by machinery: almost every transaction in which they engage is part of a world-wide system of exchange.

This complicated economic life may be contrasted with the habits that still prevailed in inland Germany a generation after the steam engine had turned the English into an industrial people. "Trade was medieval in its simplicity. Peasant and townsman everywhere dealt directly with each other in the weekly markets. No intermediary came, as a rule, between the working craftsman and the consumer. The man who wanted a new town-house himself bought the materials and directed the workmen. In the country the peasant often built for himself with the aid of his neighbours. Local supplies of food for the most part satisfied all local needs. Even in Berlin the bulk of the flour consumed was ground at the neighbouring mills. Outside the

THE REVOLUTION IN TRANSPORT

greatest towns the pure shopkeeping class hardly existed Pedlars and travelling dealers took its place, from whom both small townsman and peasant bought any implements, utensils, articles of clothing, or luxuries, that could not be made on the spot." [1]

It is clear that a society living as inland Germany was living a century ago cannot turn itself into a town like Bolton or Oldham until and unless certain things have happened to it. In the life of Bolton machinery plays a predominant, in the life of this German society an insignificant part. Now machinery implies invention, and invention is ineffective unless capital is available to set up plant and to maintain that plant until returns come to the owner of the capital in the form of profits. Moreover, machine production implies large scale production, and large scale production demands wide markets. If the mills of Bolton were only clothing the people living within a narrow radius, but a small proportion of those mills would find employment. Therefore the command of a wide market is essential to the organization of large-scale industry. This in its turn demands the provision of good communications. If Bolton depended on a mountain track for its contact with the world, it could not get rid of its products fast enough to employ its mills. Finally men will not invest capital in production unless they are living in conditions of political security. Thus a number of conditions must be fulfilled before a peasant society can become an industrial society. There must be taste and scope for invention, wide markets, ample capital, good transport, organizing power, political stability, and exchange of products over a wide area.

By the beginning of the eighteenth century a number of these conditions had been partly realized in England. The English people had political stability and a constitution that allowed more personal freedom than any of the great monarchies of contemporary Europe. They had begun to

[1] Dr. Clapham in *Cambridge Modern History*, Vol. X, p. 758.

found colonies, to develop overseas trade, to open up distant markets, to accumulate capital from the profits of the woollen trade and of foreign commerce and to organize credit by a system of banking. But they were as yet more like the second kind of society than the first. This is evident if we consider the daily life of the country and the methods by which its wants were supplied and its internal communications conducted.

England had only one town, London, that was in permanent relationship with the whole of the country and one fair, held at Stourbridge, at which the trading interests of the whole nation were represented once a year. This fair, which was compared to the famous fair of Leipsic, lasted from mid-August to mid-September, and it brought together the clothiers of Leeds and Norwich, the linen-drapers of the South of Scotland, the cutlers of Sheffield, the nail-makers of Birmingham, and the merchants of colonial produce from London, Liverpool and Bristol. There were less important general fairs for different parts of the country, Winchester for the West, Boston for the East, Beverley for the North. There were also the local markets for particular industries : the woollen industry had important centres at Leeds, Bradford, Huddersfield, Halifax and Wakefield. The great Piece Halls built at some of these towns later in the century illustrate the volume and value of the business done by the little cloth merchants coming to market with their pack-horses.

Internal commerce was carried on mainly by travelling merchants and by pedlars. The travelling merchants took their wares on the backs of horses or mules to the different towns, where they sold them to the shops. Defoe tells us that the Lancashire and Yorkshire merchants would go

" to all the fairs and Market towns almost all over the Island, not to sell by Retale, but to the shops by wholesale, giving large credit. It was ordinary for one of these men to carry a thousand pounds worth of Cloth with him at a Time : and having sold that, to send his horses back for as much more ; and this very often in a single summer."

THE REVOLUTION IN TRANSPORT 69

Aikin gives an account of the Manchester chapmen, as these travellers were called :

"When the Manchester trade began to extend, the chapmen used to keep gangs of pack-horses, and accompany them to the principal towns with goods in packs, which they opened and sold to shopkeepers, lodging what was unsold in small stores at the inns. The packhorses brought back sheep's wool, which was bought on the journey and sold to the makers of worsted yarn at Manchester, or to the clothiers of Rochdale, Saddleworth, and the West Riding of Yorkshire." [1]

These merchants dealt with the shops in the towns. The villages as a rule had no shops till late in the eighteenth century. They relied on the pedlars, men who carried their goods on their own back or on the back of a single pack-horse. Most of the village wants were supplied by the village itself, with its peasants producing food and clothing, and the wheelwrights and blacksmiths producing wooden and iron implements and vessels. The pedlar would bring handkerchiefs, scissors, fancy leather goods, cheap jewellery. Every pedlar was licensed and the class was regarded with some suspicion as apt to be extortionate and not too honest. The Derbyshire pedlars were said to combine brigandage with commerce, imitating in their humble way the practice of great nations.

Besides merchants and pedlars the traveller would meet near London great droves of cattle, sheep and pigs being driven to the Smithfield markets and perhaps two or three thousand geese and turkeys " waddling slowly and loquaciously along all the roads to London for a hundred miles round . . . feeding on the stubble of the fields through which they passed." [2] Scotch cattle were brought south by the Great North Road : they were shod with iron at the beginning and in the middle of their long journeys and they turned the stretches of grass by the side of the road in the North of England into a morass. [3]

[1] Quoted Daniels, *Early English Cotton Industry*, p. 61.
[2] Trevelyan, *British History in the Nineteenth Century*, p. 11.
[3] J. S. Fletcher, *Making of Modern Yorkshire*, p. 17.

A people that conducted its internal business by these methods needed good roads. The roads, in point of fact, were as bad as they could be. There had been no systematic construction or mending of roads since the Romans left the island, and even the admirable Roman roads could not stand the wear of fourteen centuries without repair. The state of the roads made the use of pack-horses, instead of carts, necessary in the most unsuitable cases. Thus the coal needed by country smiths in the Midlands was brought slung in bags across the backs of horses because the roads were too bad for carts, and for the same reason horses and donkeys in the Potteries carried packs and panniers filled with crates of pottery or bolls of clay. Until the road was made down the Taff Valley in 1767, the coal exported from the Merthyr and Dowlais district was carried on the backs of ponies and donkeys over mountain paths into Herefordshire and down to Cardiff.[1]

During the winter communication between districts was often interrupted for months together. Defoe, writing of a great highway early in the century, says that it

"is not passable but just in the middle of summer, after the coal carriages have beaten the way, for the ground is a stiff clay, so after rain the water stands as in a dish, and the horses sink in it up to their bellies."

The main road of a parish was often "a mere horse track across a miry common, or a watery hollow lane twisting between high banks and overhanging hedges." We can imagine how deep and narrow these lanes were from an incident described by a writer: "The stag, the hounds and the huntsmen have been known to leap over a loaded waggon in a hollow way without any obstruction from the vehicle." An inhabitant of Kensington said that the road to London was impassable and that he was like a person "cast on a rock in the middle of the ocean." It is easy to understand the feelings of a travelling merchant when

[1] H. S. Jevons, *British Coal Trade*, p. 99.

the sound of the bell carried by the first horse in these caravans to warn other travellers of their approach told him that he was about to meet a rival procession. With the roads in this state comparatively short journeys occupied several days. Stage-coaches were infrequent and slow. When Smollett wrote *Roderick Random* there was no regular service between England and Scotland. In 1700 it took a week to get to York from London and a Yorkshireman who had to go to London made his will and bade a solemn farewell to his friends.[1]

In this respect England was behind France. England was free from the hundred and one custom barriers that hampered internal commerce in France, but so far as roads went it was much easier to move about France than about England. The English system left it to the unpaid parish officers to look after the roads. These persons were ordinary ratepayers appointed for a year at a time to act as surveyors of highways or parish constables or overseers of the poor. An Act of Parliament had been passed in the sixteenth century by which the J.P.'s were instructed to see that the surveyors did their part and the surveyors could call on their fellow-parishioners to turn out for six days in the year to work at the roads. The road-menders made a holiday of it and the roads got worse and worse, as traffic increased with the expansion of industry and the growth of wealth.

The nation was rescued from this plight by a plan characteristic of the race and the time. Turnpike Trusts were set up by private Act of Parliament, charged with the duty of constructing and maintaining a definite piece of road. They could raise a loan and pay the interest on it by collecting tolls. This method put private enterprise and public direction in much the same relation as that established by a Chartered Company. Individual interests undertake the

[1] For above description of roads see Webb, *English Local Government: Statutory Authorities*, p. 203; Stocks, *Industrial State*, p. 152; and Fletcher, op. cit., p. 18.

task of construction and development: Parliament merely authorises and lays down certain conditions. An aristocratic government, in which all local power is in the hands of a small governing class, naturally keeps the functions of the central authority within narrow limits, and Parliament tends to become a sanctioning or licensing rather than a legislating body.

The creation of these Trusts raised a number of difficult questions in local government, but Parliament never troubled its head at that time about making administration orderly and methodical. Authorities were multiplied for different needs as those needs became urgent, without adjustment of their mutual relations and their several functions. At first the Turnpike Trusts were subject to the Court of Quarter Sessions, but from the middle of the eighteenth century they began to shake themselves free from any control over their administration and their expenditure.

"They could spend what they pleased, borrow what they pleased, and manage the business as they pleased. They might, at their option, have their own official establishment of collectors and surveyors, or farm out both toll collection and road repair for lump sums." [1]

The first of these bodies was set up in the early years of the century, but it was not until the middle of the century that Turnpike Trusts became common. The inconvenience of the bad roads was brought home to the governing class at the time of the Pretender's Raid in 1745, when troops had to be moved to the North. They were then set up in rapid succession all over the country. The new turnpikes were at first very unpopular. At Selby the town crier called out the townsfolk with axes and crowbars, and in the Harrogate and Wharfedale districts many toll bars were burned or wrecked in an organized attack which ended in some loss of life. For ten years there was intermittent rioting in Somerset, Gloucester and Herefordshire, and as

[1] Webb, op. cit., pp. 164, 169, 170.

THE REVOLUTION IN TRANSPORT

late as 1749 there were very serious riots in Bristol. Parliament made the destruction of turnpike gates a capital offence in 1734.[1]

The opposition came partly from users who found no improvement in the roads for which they were now paying and partly from farmers who were afraid of competition. But from the middle of the century, though there were complaints of the conduct of this or that body of trustees and sharp quarrels between different trusts, opposition of the violent kind went out of fashion. The projectors of new trusts prudently included all the chief local interests among the trustees, farmers and traders as well as country gentlemen and parsons. Moreover, foot passengers paid no toll.

This method of reforming the roads had obvious defects. System and plan were lacking and some districts were left without roads while others had more than they needed. Powerful persons would divert roads for their own purposes: important towns would prevent the establishment of toll bars in their neighbourhood: trusts would protest against the making of roads that would compete with their own, though the new road might be designed for a necessary improvement.[2] The development of our roads, like that of our towns at this period, was left to these haphazard arrangements, and local or personal interests often overruled the needs of the nation.

[1] Fletcher, op. cit., p. 48; and Webb, op. cit., pp. 171 and 174.

[2] "A foreign visitor in 1752, travelling on the Great Western Road, declares that 'after the first 47 miles from London, you never set eye on a turnpike for 220 miles.'"—Webb, op. cit., p. 177.

"Even as late as 1828, when the efficacy of public opinion had enormously increased, we see no less a personage than Sir Robert Peel, the elder, not scrupling to attempt to divert the new turnpike road between London and Liverpool out of its way, in order that it might pass close to his own residence and cotton-mills, to the ruin of the town of Tamworth—an attempt frustrated by counter-petitions from Tamworth and, most potent of all, an able letter to the *Times*."—Webb, op. cit., p. 179.

But though the English people did not secure from these methods a well-planned and economical system of communications, a great deal of energy was applied to the making and the improvement of roads. Reformers had an organ and a journal at their service, for in 1793 Pitt set up a Board of Agriculture with Sir John Sinclair as President and Arthur Young as Secretary.[1] This Board was not like a modern Department of State : it was more like a Royal Society receiving a subsidy from Parliament. It published a periodical, *The Annals of Agriculture*, in which public-spirited landowners and country gentlemen related their experience and aired their ideas. Arthur Young used its pages with great effect to agitate for better roads.

The motives for reform were strong, for landowners wanted to make travelling more comfortable for persons and more economical for goods, and commercial interests of all kinds were pressing for improvement. It happened also that the spirit of invention so characteristic of the age was ready with its help in this as in other departments of life.

The century produced three great road engineers. Metcalfe (1717–1810), known as blind Jack of Knaresborough, was a typical figure of the Industrial Revolution. The child of poor parents, he lost his sight from smallpox at six, but this disability did not prevent him from becoming a great horseman, an expert tree climber, a guide who could take a traveller across the wildest moors round York and Knaresborough, and a successful tradesman and carrier. In 1765 he obtained a contract for repairing a Yorkshire road and from that time he devoted himself to roadmaking with remarkable results. Several of the principal roads in Yorkshire, Lancashire and Cheshire were his work, and, blind though he was, he had no difficulty in designing culverts, bridges and embankments on the worst surface.

Thomas Telford (1757–1834) was, like Metcalfe, a self-made man, son of a shepherd who started life as a stone-

---

[1] It was dissolved in 1822.

mason. In 1787 he was engaged by the Shropshire Justices as Surveyor of Public Works and in that capacity he built forty-two new bridges, besides repairing roads and constructing the great Ellesmere Canal.

The other famous name in the history of our roads is that of J. L. Macadam, who substituted for unbroken flints a packing of angular granite fragments which consolidates into a natural concrete. Macadam's improvements were adopted all over the world. He was a Scotsman of small independent means who, having settled in the neighbourhood of Bristol as Victualling Agent for the Admiralty, became a member of the Turnpike Trust of the Bristol district, the largest single road authority in the Kingdom. Macadam threw himself into the work of reform first as a member and then as an officer of the Trust. He made himself the leading authority on road construction in the country, and by 1819 he was acting, with the help of his son, as salaried surveyor to no less than thirty-four different bodies of commissioners. He worked hard in concert with the Board of Agriculture at improving the administration of the Turnpike system.

The work of the Trusts effected a revolution in transport. Whereas it took a week in 1700 to go from York to London, in 1815 it only took twenty-one hours to go from Leeds to London.[1] In 1784 the first mail-coach left London for Bristol, and the Post Office began to play an active part in pushing road construction, reforming the Trusts and employing Telford to make the road to Holyhead.[2] Stage-coaches supplied a service between all the chief towns as regular as the service of the modern railway. To see what provision was made in this respect for a Lancashire town it is only necessary to look at Baines' *History and Directory of Lancashire*, published in 1824, and note the particulars he gives for the several districts. Bolton, for example, had three coaches a day to Carlisle, Edinburgh

[1] Fletcher, op. cit., p. 49.
[2] Trevelyan, *British History in the Nineteenth Century*, p. 166.

and Glasgow, going through Chorley, Preston, Lancaster and Kendal; a coach every day to Leeds and York, going by Bury, Rochdale, Halifax and Bradford; a coach four days a week to Newcastle-on-Tyne, through Preston, Lancaster, Kirkby Lonsdale, Barnard Castle and Durham; three coaches a day to Liverpool, going through Wigan, St. Helens and Prescot.[1] There were, of course, any number of coaches to Manchester. Manchester had six coaches a day to London and the journey was done in twenty-four hours.[2]

Internal commerce was transformed by these changes. It was no longer necessary for the travelling merchant to carry his wares with a great train of pack-horses. He rode out for orders (the new type was known as a " rider out "), taking patterns only, and when goods were ordered they were sent by wagon. For with the improvement of the roads a wagon service was organized comparable to the service of stage-coaches. A tradesman could send his goods to London from Leeds by one of these wagons in thirty-six hours.[3] The Manchester trade was pushed rapidly by this system.[4]

[1] It is interesting to see that there were two coaches a week to Southport in the bathing season.

[2] Joseph Aston, in his *Picture of Manchester*, published in 1816, has this note on stage coaches (p. 230):

" In the year 1770, there was only one stage coach to London and one to Liverpool, which went from or came into Manchester, and these set out only twice a week. There are now seventy distinct coaches, which run from hence, of which fifty-four set out every day, and sixteen others, three times in the week, to their different places of destination. In the year 1754, a Flying Coach was advertised, and boasted that 'However incredible it may appear, this coach will actually (barring accidents) arrive in London in four days and a half after leaving Manchester!!' The mail coaches now constantly travel that distance in thirty hours; and on several occasions, when Bonaparte was tottering to his ruin, and on the news of the terminating battle of Waterloo, the Traveller, the Defiance, and the Telegraph coaches, came down in eighteen hours!'

[3] Fletcher, op. cit., p. 50.

[4] Daniels, *Early English Cotton Industry*, p. 62.

England passed through a second revolution in transport before the introduction of the railway. In the seventeenth century France had built three great canals ; the canal between the Seine and the Loire was opened in 1640 ; the Canal of the Two Seas from Toulouse to Cette in 1681 : the Orleans Canal in 1692. England had done nothing, perhaps, as it has been suggested, because internal communication seemed to matter less to a country with a number of great estuary ports like London, Hull, Newcastle and Bristol and no town very distant from the sea.[1] Yarranton (1616-1684), after a visit to Holland, had urged the construction of canals, but in vain : all he could do was to deepen the Stour and the Avon, so improving the communication between the midland iron district and the Severn. The Severn was the principal highway of the charcoal iron industry. The laden trows or barges were drawn by men. When the traffic increased merchants petitioned for the construction of a horse towing path from Bewdley to Worcester, but the opposition of local landowners and ironmongers postponed this reform till the beginning of the nineteenth century.[2]

Early in the eighteenth century some of the rivers in the industrial districts had been made fit for navigation : the Aire and Calder were made more serviceable for Leeds and Wakefield, the Trent and Derwent for Derby and Nottingham, the Irwell, the Mersey and the Weaver for Liverpool, Manchester and Northwich. But England had no canal until the middle of the century, at which time the development of the coal fields that followed the substitution of coal for charcoal in iron production made the construction of canals urgently necessary to a powerful class.

Coal was obviously unsuitable for land transport before the age of railways and consequently the only coal that could be obtained in England at any distance from the source was coal brought by sea like that from Newcastle.

[1] Mantoux, *La Révolution Industrielle au XVIIIe Siècle*, p. 108.
[2] Ashton, *Iron and Steel in the Industrial Revolution*, p. 243.

In the middle of the century the large landowners who possessed coalfields were anxious to develop their property and it was essential to find the means of transporting their coal. With this object the rivers near Wigan and St. Helens were improved. One of the largest coal owners was the Duke of Bridgewater who, finding that the cost of taking his coal from Worsley to Manchester on horseback was nine or ten shillings a ton, consulted James Brindley (1716-1772), a genius who could neither read nor write. Brindley built a canal for him between Worsley and Manchester, and the Duke was encouraged by his success to take the considerable risk of financing the construction of a canal between Manchester and Liverpool.[1] These achievements with their immediate results made canal-making in the last half of the eighteenth century what the making of railways was in the nineteenth. The great coal-owning aristocrats, like Lord Anson, were eager to follow Bridgewater's example, and in this case, as in that of the roads, commercial interests were not less eager to second their exertions. Companies sprang up in all the industrial districts: private Acts were hurried through a willing Parliament and before the century closed nearly three thousand miles of canals had been constructed in England.[2] Manchester could send goods to Liverpool every day by the Bridgewater Canal; to Birmingham, London, and the South of England by the Grand Trunk; to Hull by the canals that connected Lancashire and Yorkshire. The opening of the Glamorgan Canal from Merthyr to Cardiff in 1798, and its extension later to Aberdare, gave a great

---

[1] The cost of transporting merchandise and goods from Liverpool to Manchester fell in consequence from twelve to six shillings a ton. Mantoux, op. cit., p. 113.

[2] The opening in 1774 of the stretch of the Leeds and Liverpool canal that connects Bingley and Shipley was celebrated by the ringing of bells in all the neighbouring villages and the spectators watched with amazement the passage of a fleet of boats through locks having a fall of nearly 70 feet in half an hour. Fletcher, op. cit. p. 52.

THE REVOLUTION IN TRANSPORT

stimulus both to coal mining and to iron production in South Wales; the first dock at Cardiff was constructed in 1839.[1] England had solved a problem that had made an industrial revolution impossible in the ancient world, for one of the standing difficulties of that world was the provision of transport for heavy goods otherwise than by the sea.

These were the methods of transport in use during the first phase of the Industrial Revolution, for the textile revolution was in essential respects complete before the introduction of the railway. The Stockton and Darlington Railway was opened in 1825; the Manchester and Liverpool Railway in 1830. By 1830 the cotton industry had been established as a factory industry; hand-spinning had ceased; all the processes previous to weaving were carried on by complicated machinery in factories, while weaving was partly done in factories, by power-looms worked by girls, and partly by hand-loom weavers in their own homes. In 1829 there were nearly 50,000 power-looms in England. The volume and importance of the cotton trade before the age of railways can be seen from a few statistics: the import of cotton wool, which was under 4,000,000 lb. in 1764, was over 300,000,000 lb. in 1833; the declared value of cotton exports in 1830 was over £18,000,000, and the number of persons employed in 1831 was over 800,000. The changes in the woollen and worsted industries came more gradually, and the woollen handloom weaver survived longer than the cotton hand-loom weaver, but by 1830 spinning in both industries was passing into the factory and in other processes machinery was displacing hand labour.

Thus the textile revolution was effected in the age of the canals. The change that was most directly encouraged in England by the railways was the development of engineering or the use of machines to make machines. The railways turned Germany into an industrial people by

[1] Jevons, *The British Coal Trade*, pp. 100 and 107.

solving more effectually than canals the problem of internal transport, but so far as England is concerned they fall into the second chapter of the Industrial Revolution, not the first.

Another important operation of the Industrial Revolution was effected in this stage : the change in the distribution of population. In 1700 the five most populous counties in England are believed to have been Middlesex, Somerset, Gloucester, Wiltshire and Northamptonshire. In 1800 they were Middlesex, Lancashire, the West Riding, Staffordshire, and Warwickshire. The iron industry had gone from Sussex to the coal fields of the Midlands : the worsted industry had grown faster in the West Riding than in Norfolk, the woollen industry faster in the West Riding than in the South-west : the great new textile industry, cotton, was strongest in Lancashire and Cheshire. The introduction of railways thus marks a stage in the Industrial Revolution in England, not as in some countries its beginning. For Stephenson ran his first train in an England that had established its chief factory industry, made Liverpool more important than Bristol, redistributed its population, thrown up a new type of town and dissolved the peasant village.

CHAPTER VI

THE DESTRUCTION OF THE PEASANT VILLAGE

PEASANT life in the Middle Ages had a common character and common foundations throughout a great part of Western Europe. Men and women were grouped in a unit known as the Manor ; a unit of government and cultivation having a lord as its responsible head. Half or more of the tilled land was in the hands of small peasant cultivators. Of these cultivators some were freeholders who owed military service and paid certain fixed dues ; some, the socagers, were freeholders who owed peasant labour and payment in money or in kind ; others, the majority, were villeins, in varying degrees of servitude, who had to render personal services to the lord, to work on his demesne, to make his ditches and walls, to grind their corn at his mill and pen their sheep in his fold. The rest of the arable land was the lord's demesne. Besides the arable land there was waste, used for pasture both by the lord and by the peasants. The life of this community was regulated by a court which prescribed the arrangements for cultivation, for it was a co-operative community ; the men cultivated the land in strips scattered over the common arable field, sowing the crops and observing the sequence ordered by the Court. This Court decided questions that arose between the lord and his tenants and it appointed the officials who looked after the common pasture and the other affairs of the village.

This community had come to life out of the chaos of the Dark Ages. It had established some degree of settled government ; providing some kind of security against violence and want. The villeins, if liable to the caprice of the lord, found some protection in the courts and the custom that ruled their practice. Life was hard; man and beast often shared the same dwelling; and as the village was self-contained, depending on its own resources and exertions for food, shelter and clothing, its horizon was clouded by anxieties unknown to the modern world. Rain and drought were followed by famine, and disease made death a constant image to the mind. In such a world fear was primitive in its simplicity and power: the sense of man's dependence was strong and impressive: the litany that filled the aisles of the village church with its lingering chant brought awe as well as peace to the peasant's mind as he knelt in their solemn shadows.

This peasant village was dissolved in different countries, at different times, by different forces, and under different influences, so that its dissolution left in England a society quite different from that which it left in France, Denmark and most of Germany. This difference possesses a vital importance in the history of the Industrial Revolution. The most significant thing about that revolution was that it gave to capital a much wider control of the life of men and of States. In the peasant village initiative was checked by custom; enterprise by the system of the common fields and the manor courts. So long as agriculture was an art practised by a community for its own maintenance on co-operative conditions, capital could not be used freely in its direction by a rich man thinking and planning on a large scale. In England this freedom was gained by capital earlier and more completely than elsewhere. This was the result of an agrarian revolution, of which the first episodes belong to the sixteenth and seventeenth, the later and more decisive events to the eighteenth century.

Before the sixteenth century some important changes had come over this society in England. Owing to a number of causes, among them the Great Plague and still more the growth of the cloth industry in the towns, villeinage had

DESTRUCTION OF THE PEASANT VILLAGE 83

almost lost its servile character. When the villein could run away and find employment in the town, the basis of serfdom was shaken. When currency was increased and money was wanted for improvements of one kind and another landlords had new needs, and the old restrictions designed to keep the serf at his lord's disposal were commuted into fines. By the time of Elizabeth, the English villein whose forefathers had been liable to be sold, had come to be a man holding so much land and making a fixed money payment.[1]

The other important change was the growth of the leasing system. This system was first applied to the lord's demesne land and afterwards it was extended to the common fields. Under this system the landlord supplied the implements and the stock, the tenant paying part of the produce in return. Thus just as the English villein began to differ from the French villein, the English landlord began to differ from the French landlord; the English landlord becoming a contributing partner, whereas the French became a mere receiver of rent. But these changes did not affect the essentially peasant and co-operative character of the village. The manorial courts continued: the village co-operative methods were still in force; custom was still a power, restraining the strong and preserving the past.

This village was extinguished by a revolution that began in the sixteenth century and acquired between the middle of the eighteenth and the middle of the nineteenth centuries a much more sweeping force and range. The revolution never quite ceased, but its form and scope changed in the eighteenth century. In the sixteenth century the chief motive for enclosure was the stimulus given to farming for

[1] " Henceforward, while the German peasant is driven afield to gather snails and wild strawberries for his lord, is plundered and harried and tortured without hope of redress, his English brother is a member of a society in which there is, nominally at least, one law for all men."—Tawney, *The Agrarian Problem in the Sixteenth Century*, p. 43. Cf. Johnson, *Disappearance of the Small Landowner*, p. 30.

the market by the rise in prices and the expansion of the cloth industry. When commerce increased its profits and the classes engaged in it stepped into a more lavish style of living, the landlord found himself in a world in which he had to make drastic changes if he wished to maintain his social prestige. In feudal times the lord's pomp and state depended on the number and condition of his tenants. As domestic order became more secure, the command of men counted for less and less ; as wealth grew and all classes acquired more expensive habits, the command of money counted for more and more.[1] With a prosperous cloth trade demanding larger supplies of wool, rich profits were to be made by substituting good pasture for poor arable farming in the Midlands. Several landlords seized the opportunity and pushed out tenants who held by custom, in order to graze sheep. These evictions caused disturbances ; they were denounced by popular preachers, and they were checked for a time by Royal Commissions set up by Cardinal Wolsey in 1517 and the Duke of Somerset in 1548. But the enclosing interests, led by Warwick, were too powerful. At the end of that century there was still a serious body of opinion, of which Bacon was the most illustrious representative, that regarded a robust and independent peasant population as a source of steady strength to a nation. Later some ineffectual measures were taken to arrest and modify enclosure ; the last attempt was made in 1656, when Parliament rejected a Bill of this character.[2]

The enclosure movement of the eighteenth century was more general and more vigorous. Over a large part of the country rural society, at the beginning of that century, still kept the foundation of the old peasant economy.

[1] See the remarkable account given by R. H. Tawney of the debts of the old landlords at the end of the sixteenth century. The Earl of Leicester was reported to owe £59,000, the Earl of Essex £23,000, the Earl of Huntingdon £20,000. Lord Vaux of Harrowden had to pawn his Parliamentary robes. Tawney, *Introduction to Wilson's Discourse on Usury*, p. 32.

[2] Tawney, *The Agrarian Problem in the Sixteenth Century*, p. 377.

DESTRUCTION OF THE PEASANT VILLAGE

The common field was still the chief feature, the peasants still cultivated their strips in that field as owners or tenants. These peasants, and also the cottagers who neither owned nor rented strips, had rights of pasture on the common waste. The manor courts survived. There were still pinders who looked after the pound, chimney peepers who looked after the chimneys, viewers and shepherds who looked after the arrangements for the use of the waste. The man who lived partly by working for himself and partly by working for others was still a common figure. The landlords, on the other hand, were more powerful than they had ever been, for the confiscated Church property had been used by Henry VIII to reward his servants and allies, mostly new men from the world of commerce and finance, and not to enrich the State or to strengthen the Crown. Their political power had increased with the Whig Revolution, which had decided that they and not the Crown should be the masters of Parliament. This aristocracy then alone in Europe could do what it pleased with the village, for in every other country the aristocracy either lacked power, as in France, or shared it with a rival, as in Austria or Bavaria or most of the petty States of Germany.

The village with this mediæval pattern was an obstacle to the development of agriculture. Its system of common regulation had helped progress in earlier stages, for it had imposed a discipline on the less industrious peasant and maintained a common standard. But the needs of agriculture demanded reform if the soil was to be made more productive. Reform is difficult in a society that looks to the past more than to the future, and honours custom rather than science, piety rather than enterprise. Agriculture was standing still.

This stagnation was not due to the want of ideas or knowledge or experiment. Two pioneers had shown the way to a revolution in agriculture. One was Jethro Tull (1674–1740), originally a lawyer who was struck when travelling in the South of France by the success of the methods employed in the vineyards. He noticed that the vines were planted in parallel lines and that the land was kept friable by constant ploughing. On his return he tried these methods on a farm of his own with some remarkable results.[1] He was particularly successful with turnips, which at that time were hardly grown in England. It was the custom to kill off large numbers of cattle at the end of the summer because there was insufficient winter food.[2] An ample supply of turnips removed this serious difficulty from the farmer's path. Tull taught and showed the importance of care in the choice of seed, the value of constant tillage and drilling in rows in contrast to the established custom of sowing broadcast thickly and at varying depths. The other great pioneer was Bakewell (1725-1795) who did for stock what Tull had done for crops and roots. By experiments in breeding he effected a remarkable improvement in the quality of horses, cattle and particularly of sheep.

These ideas made a great impression on some of the leading landlords, including George III who contributed to the Annals of Agriculture under the pseudonym of Farmer George. Lord Townshend (1674-1738) earned the nickname of Turnip Townshend, Coke of Norfolk (1752-1842) introduced all the modern improvements and transformed the agriculture of a great part of his county, and the Duke of Bedford was not less enterprising on his large estates. Not all landlords had their passion for progress, but the English landlords were often men of public spirit and men of

[1] "Without fallows or manure, he grew on the same land, by constant tillage, for thirteen years in succession heavier wheat crops, from one-third of the quantity of seed, than his neighbours could produce by following the accepted routine. By this discovery he anticipated one of the most startling results of the Rothamsted experiments."—Prothero (Lord Ernle), *English Farming, Past and Present*, p. 172.

[2] Power, *Mediæval English Nunneries*, p. 110. In the Highlands of Scotland the cattle were so exhausted at the end of a hard winter that they had to be carried out of the cowshed to their pastures.—Grant, *Everyday Life on an Old Highland Farm*, p. 61.

DESTRUCTION OF THE PEASANT VILLAGE

initiative. It seemed to them, therefore, that the way to bring the new light of science into this old world of custom was to get rid of the peasant economy and by means of enclosures to substitute a system under which the landlord had a free hand and men with capital every incentive to apply it to agricultural development.

In this spirit they set to work to destroy under the form of law the mediæval village and the rights it bestowed on the small and ignorant peasant. They proceeded sometimes by agreement, but as a rule by Act of Parliament. A member would bring in a private Bill which would go before a Committee. After examination in the Committee it would become law. Commissioners appointed by the Act would inquire into local rights and make the enclosure award. Throughout this procedure two interests and two alone were assured of protection: the interest of the lord of the manor and that of the owner of the tithes. A large proprietor had no great trouble. In some cases he had influence in Parliament, but if not he could at any rate send a lawyer to put his claim before the Commission. The small farmer or peasant was in a very different case. Often he could not read or write, and he could not afford to get a lawyer to speak for him. About his rights he knew little except that so long as he could remember he had kept a cow, driven geese across the waste, pulled his fuel out of the brushwood and cut his turf from the common and that his father had done all these things before him. Even if he succeeded in making out his claim, he would often receive his compensation in the form of a small plot of land, which he had to sell because he could not afford to fence it. It followed, therefore, that when the mediæval village disappeared in England, the peasant, as a rule, sooner or later, disappeared with it.

This was the result at which the enclosing landlord aimed. He held that production was hampered not merely by the system of common fields and co-operative control, but also by the wide distribution of rights of property and rights of common. He believed that the best work was done by labourers who depended on their wages and had nothing to distract them from their duty to their employer. This relationship he considered the best for production, and production was everything. Public spirit and private interest seemed to draw the landlord to the same conclusion. The population was growing faster than its resources; the Industrial Revolution was throwing up towns where food was consumed and not produced; the French war brought new dangers, and it happened that in the course of the war six harvests were failures and only two were not deficient. The experience and, even more, the anticipation of scarcity sent up prices to astounding figures; in 1800 wheat was 130*s*. the quarter. Between 1810 and 1812 the charge for the transport of foreign corn was 50*s*. a quarter.[1] It is not surprising that during the war nearly 2,000 enclosure Acts were passed. Corn growing was immensely profitable to the landlord and urgently necessary for the State.

In substituting capitalist farming for the old peasant economy the English aristocracy did what the aristocracies elsewhere would have done if they had had the power. Quesnai had told the French that the best thing for agriculture would be the organization of large farms managed by men with capital. But in France the aristocracy was as powerless as the Crown in England, and when the mediæval relationship was dissolved in France it was dissolved not by a body favouring the landlords but by a body favouring the peasant. Consequently French history supplies the exact converse of English. The bulk of the French peasants in the eighteenth century were customary tenants, retaining a number of obligations from the feudal system, some of them harsh and degrading. Subject to these services they held the land they cultivated with some degree of independence, and it was not uncommon for parishes to go to law with their lord. The French Revolution released the peasant

[1] Prothero, *English Farming, Past and Present*, p. 270.

from all dues and services and made him the unqualified owner of his holding. This conversion was accomplished in three stages. In August 1789 the National Assembly abolished degrading services such as servitude and forced labour, as well as the rights of the lords over markets, fairs and courts of law. Most of the important seignorial rights, like ground rents, were declared redeemable. There were agrarian disturbances in different parts of France in the following year, and in 1792 a further concession was made to the peasants. Landlords who claimed seignorial rights were compelled to present their original title deeds. Next year, July 1793, the Revolutionary Government passed to the final act, abolishing all seignorial rights without compensation and ordering that all title deeds should be burnt.[1] Thus when the mediæval village disappeared in France the peasant became an owner, whereas when it disappeared in England he became a labourer. This happened because the relationship between lord and peasant was abolished in France in a revolution that made the peasant more powerful than the lord, whereas in England it was abolished when the lord was supreme.

The case of Denmark differs both from the English and the French. Denmark became an absolute monarchy not long before the revolution that created in England a Parliamentary oligarchy. Whereas in England the aristocratic Government made it easy to get rid of the peasant, in Denmark the Royal Government took great pains to keep him. Enclosure, in the form of consolidation of the strips into larger units and the release of the cultivator from the customary sequence, progressed in Denmark as in England;

[1] *Modern France*, edited by Tilley, p. 273. The tenant, without loosening his purse strings, became full proprietor of the land which he cultivated; all old contracts were broken; it was an immense revolution which was not imitated in the nineteenth century by the various European States, monarchical and feudal, who contented themselves with the redemption of dues in accordance with the methods of the Constituent Assembly. Tilley, op. cit., p. 274.

husbandry was improved and modernized and foreign experience turned to account. But the Royal Government took definite action not only to protect the peasant from the clutches of the landlord (by ordinances of 1682, 1725, 1769, 1791) but also to secure for the cottager who lost his rights of common enough land to keep a cow and pigs.[1] Thus in Denmark the agricultural reforms that led in England to the destruction of this class of cultivator ended in creating a nation of peasant owners. On the other hand, the services due from the mediæval peasant were not abolished as they were in France by a violent act which allowed no compensation to the lord; they were commuted and gradually redeemed.

The disappearance of the mediæval economy was an essential stage in the Industrial Revolution. It came earlier in England than elsewhere: it led to great technical improvement and a rapid increase in production;[2] it took a different course and its ultimate consequences were different. On the Continent the peasant as a rule survived. The commercial motives that gave such encouragement in England to headlong enclosure had less play elsewhere: reasons of State that had once made all Governments wish to keep a peasant population still counted in countries with a land frontier: the enclosing class nowhere else made the laws. Consequently England alone emerged from this revolution as an agrarian society without peasants or the obstacles that a peasant economy presents to an industrial system based on concentration of power and specialization of tasks. In other countries the capitalist system was confined for the most part to industry: in England it began by overspreading the village as well as the town.

[1] For full account see Sir William Ashley's Memorandum, *Final Report of Agricultural Tribunal of Investigation*, 1924.
This course had been urged on the English Parliament by Arthur Young, Cobbett and others.
[2] Between 1789 and 1815, when English agriculture was rapidly changing, there was very little change in French agriculture.— Clapham, *Economic Development of France and Germany*, p. 21.

DESTRUCTION OF THE PEASANT VILLAGE

The transformation of the village brought new problems. The peasant had partly fed and partly clothed himself. His place had now been taken by the labourer who depended on the farmer for wages and the shop for food. By a paradox that roused Cobbett to fury, the village itself went short of food under the system that was maintaining the rapidly growing populations of Manchester and Leeds. The farmers, producing for a larger market, would not take the trouble to supply their labourers with milk and the milk went out of the village, so that the labourer who no longer had a cow could not get milk for love or money. The price of his flour went up because the farmer now sold to the miller, the miller to the mealman and the mealman to the shop. Davies, the parson, a shrewd observer, quoting Nathaniel Kent, said that the labourer's wife paid 10 per cent. more for her flour in consequence.[1] The difficulties of the labourer reached a crisis at the end of the century when two or three bad harvests in succession brought famine prices. He could no longer live on his wages. Some remedy had to be found. A number were discussed.

The first was a proposal for a minimum wage. There were several Acts of Parliament on the Statute Book for the regulation of wages. The most important were an Act of Elizabeth, an Act of James I and an Act of George II. The Act of Elizabeth provided that the magistrates should meet annually to assess wages, and penalties were imposed on all who gave or took a wage in excess of this assessment. The Act of James I imposed a penalty on all who gave a wage below the wage fixed by the magistrates. The Act of George II provided that disputes between masters and men could be referred to the magistrates, although there had been no assessment of wages by the magistrates. This legislation was virtually obsolete and was regarded as a curiosity, but in this crisis some minds turned to it. In October, 1795, Arthur Young sent out to the various

[1] David Davies, *The Case of Labourers in Husbandry*, p. 34.

correspondents of the Board of Agriculture a circular letter containing this question :

"It having been recommended by various Quarter Sessions that the price of labour should be regulated by that of bread corn, have the goodness to state what you conceive to be the advantages or disadvantages of such a system."

Arthur Young was himself in favour of this proposal, and the Suffolk magistrates, at a meeting which he attended, called upon the members for the county to introduce a Bill for this purpose into Parliament. In the country generally most of the correspondents were hostile, but the supporters of the proposal included two parsons who had made a very special study of the general problem. These were Howlett, the Vicar of Dunmow, and Davies, the Rector of Barkham in Berkshire. Howlett wrote an exceedingly interesting pamphlet on the subject recommending that wages should be regulated by the prices of the necessaries of life and not merely of bread corn, and that the magistrates should have the assistance of all the information that Government could secure for them.

The proposal was put before Parliament by Samuel Whitbread, who introduced a Bill next month. The Bill allowed exemptions in the case of the old and the infirm. An employer who broke the law was to be fined, and if he refused to pay the fine he could be committed to jail. The Bill was supported by Fox and Grey, but it was opposed by Pitt, whose influence was supreme. Burke attacked the proposal in a pamphlet, arguing that the farmer, having an interest in keeping his labourers healthy and contented, would never underpay them. Whitbread introduced a second Bill in 1800, but with no better success.

The second remedy that was proposed aimed at enabling the labourer to produce some of his own food. This was the object of the allotment movement. Arthur Young was anxious that all Enclosure Acts should contain provision for allotments for the labourers. A scheme was put before the Whigs by Cobbett in 1806; Davies, Rector of Barkham, had also urged this policy in his well-known book, *The Case of Labourers in Husbandry.*

"Hope is a cordial, of which the poor man has especially much need, to cheer his heart in the toilsome journey through life. And the fatal consequence of that policy, which deprives labouring people of the expectation of possessing any property in the soil, must be the extinction of every generous principle in their minds. . . . No gentleman should be permitted to pull down a cottage, until he had first erected another, upon one of Mr. Kent's plans, either in some convenient part of the waste, or on his own estate with a certain quantity of land annexed."

A few landlords like Lord Winchelsea encouraged this movement, and a few parsons, but there was strong and generally successful opposition from farmers and shopkeepers.

If either of these remedies had been adopted in an effective form, the labourer would have escaped the fate which overtook him. For it was a paradox of the new system that agriculture became very profitable, and yet the mass of the workers in this thriving industry sank into greater poverty.[1] In the recent Great War, the peasant gained at the expense of the townsman throughout Europe, because war had enhanced the value of his products. In England the labourer received a definite share in the increased profits of the industry, in the form of higher wages, secured to him by law. But in the French War all the profits went to the landlord and the farmer, and the same process that made these classes richer turned the labourers into paupers.

[1] See for an illustration the case of the parish of Tysoe described in Ashby's *One Hundred Years of Poor Law Administration in a Warwickshire Village*, pp. 21 and 22. Tysoe was enclosed in 1796. The assessment of 1800 shows that fourteen of the larger landowners had found it possible to redeem their portions of the land tax, by paying a capitalization sum equal to about thirty years purchase. Between 1790 and 1800 the Poor Rates in this parish rose from £565 to £2,912. "The larger landlords could redeem their Land Tax at considerable expense, the larger farmers were increasing their farms and amassing capital, the smaller cultivators became labourers, and the labourers were impoverished and demoralized."

This happened because the enclosures, their full force unqualified by measures such as were taken elsewhere to keep the peasant on his feet, robbed him of the opportunity of producing for this rising market, while no arrangement was made to give him, as a labourer, a legal claim to any share in the high profits of the industry. Remedies that would have secured these results were rejected, and a remedy was adopted which drove him into pauperism in its most degrading forms.

The remedy that was adopted is known in history as the Speenhamland system. The Berkshire magistrates met at the Pelican Inn at Speenhamland in May, 1795, to discuss proposals for regulating wages. The meeting ended by adopting a resolution that where wages were insufficient they should be supplemented from the rates, in accordance with a scale which they fixed. When the gallon loaf of second flour cost a shilling, a man's wages were to be made up out of the rates to such a sum as would give the man three shillings a week for his own support and one and sixpence for the support of his wife and each member of his family. This system spread rapidly, and by 1834, when it was extinguished by the new Poor Law, Northumberland and Durham were almost the only counties which were free from it.

To understand the terrible degradation it produced we have to take into account the arrangements of the Poor Law at the time. The Poor Law was a system of employment as well as a system of relief. Under an Act of 1782 it had been provided that in the parishes incorporated under that Act the guardians were not to send able-bodied poor to the Poorhouse, but to find work for them, or maintain them until work was found. Thus there grew up a variety of systems of public employment, paupers might be employed directly on parish work, or they might be distributed among the farmers under what was known as the Roundsman system. The combination of the Speenhamland system with the Roundsman system produced universal pauperism. A man could not get any help from the rates unless he was destitute, and unless he got help from the rates he could not obtain employment, for a farmer would not pay a man 10s. a week when he could employ the roundsman at half that sum. Free movement from village to village was checked by the settlement laws. Nor were the labourers the only victims; the yeoman and small farmer who spent little on wages had to pay part of the wages bill of their richer neighbours.

The despair and distress of the villages in the south of England broke out into revolt in the winter of 1830 when there were riots in several counties, Wiltshire, Hampshire, Berkshire, Buckinghamshire, Gloucestershire, Essex, Kent, Sussex, Dorset, Norfolk, Oxford, Suffolk and Hunts. Mobs of labourers marched from village to village, demanding a minimum wage of 2s. a day and the reduction of tithes. In many cases they destroyed threshing machines; hand-threshing was still a comparatively well-paid job and a Kent landowner said: " An industrious man who has a barn never requires poor relief. He can earn from 15s. to 20s. per week. He considers it almost as his little freehold and that in effect it certainly is." We can see in the accounts of the mob diplomacy in these riots how bitterly the indignity of the new form of pauperism was resented by its victims. The ruling classes were terrified by these demonstrations, because though they were accustomed to disturbances in the towns they had always counted on the patience of the villages. But a movement of this sort could have but one end, and that end came quickly. For a few weeks labourers were paid a decent wage, but as soon as the movement was crushed the villages relapsed into the old condition. These riots were punished with the most brutal severity. Not a single life was lost except among the rioters, and nobody had even been seriously wounded. More than 450 men and boys were transported to Australia after trial before special commissions.

As his plight grew worse, game laws, vagrancy laws, and settlement laws were drawn more tightly and savagely round the labourer's life and liberty. He became a kind of public serf, at the disposal of the parish overseer, maintaining himself by poaching and stealing when his allowance no longer kept him. Englishmen might boast that the English plough could feed the great towns of the north and enable England to defy Napoleon, but they could not call the new agriculture, in the classical phrase, the mother of men. For the labourers in the Southern counties had lost every vestige of the rights that had given them some degree of independence, and every vestige of the co-operative tradition that had made them a community. In one district it was the custom for the overseer to put up the labourers to auction every Saturday night : they were let generally at from 1*s*. 6*d*. to 2*s*. a week and their provisions, their families being kept by the parish. The villein of the Manor, in the early days of the long struggle from which he gained his rights, was not much poorer in the conditions on which freedom and self-respect depend.

CHAPTER VII

THE DESTRUCTION OF CUSTOM IN INDUSTRY

A TRAVELLER passing from one part of Western Europe to another in the Middle Ages would have seen that the resemblance that marked the agriculture of the several countries extended to the organization of industry. For alike in Norwich and in Florence, in Preston and in Ypres, in York and in Paris, he would come upon an institution known as the Guild, and though its precise form and structure might vary from place to place, its general character would be identical. The origin of the guild is not less controversial than the origin of the manor, but for the purposes of this study it is enough to know that commerce and industry were largely regulated by guilds, either craft guilds or an organization called a guild merchant, which embraced traders as well as manufacturers. The guild merchant was, as a rule, the earlier of these bodies.

The history of industry in the Middle Ages, in Italy, France, and England, is in the main the history of these bodies and their varying relations to the State, to the City, and to one another. The extent of their power and the length of their life depended to some extent on the political arrangements of the society in which they exercised their functions. The Italian Republics were more favourable to their growth and influence than the stronger national Governments that established themselves in France and England. But for some time, and in some form, they were as integral a part of town life as the manor of country life. The early English boroughs were communities that had secured their exemption from the obligations of the manor :

within their walls the guilds helped to control industry and commerce, as outside their walls the manor court helped to control agriculture.

The history of these guilds is not unlike the history of the English town, for in both cases rights that were widely shared at first became in time the privileges of a small minority. In most English boroughs the term burgess or freeman had a wholly different connotation in 1500 and in 1800, because the government of the town had passed into the hands of small oligarchies which kept persons, who should have been freemen, out of their rights, and sold the freedom of the town, for their own purposes, to outsiders who had no claim to it. The perversion began with the Tudors, who set up select corporations, to which they transferred the powers that belonged to the general body of burgesses. The Crown adopted this plan in order to make the boroughs subservient to its influence. These small bodies later introduced the practice of selling their freedom to persons who were ready to vote for the party or the patron who wanted the representation of the borough in Parliament. In 1835 when the Commission on Municipal Corporations issued its report, Ipswich, with 20,000 inhabitants, had 350 resident freemen, and Plymouth, with 75,000 inhabitants, had less than 300 freemen. The freemen often had no connexion with the borough, except that they had paid for the honour or the profit to be derived from that status. Thus an English borough had completely changed its character between the fifteenth and eighteenth centuries; it had become a close body whose organization and constitution were quite different from those of the earlier town.

Something of the same kind befell the craft guilds. They began as a rule as associations of producers, representing the masters, journeymen and apprentices of the several crafts. Certain interests within these guilds proved stronger than others, and the struggles that took place within their organization changed their character. There were struggles between rich and poor, between master and journeyman,

DESTRUCTION OF CUSTOM IN INDUSTRY 99

between commercial and industrial interests, between this and that craft or branch of a craft.[1] The most important struggle was that between the small masters and the commercial capitalists, which began in the later Middle Ages. The small masters tried to keep the guilds in a form favourable to their independence ; the commercial capitalists often evaded the control of the guilds by setting up outside the incorporated towns, in places where it was difficult to enforce guild regulations.[2] But there was another method open to them : they could capture the guilds themselves, and turn their machinery to their own purposes. This internal struggle reached its climax under the Tudors.

During the fifteenth century it became more and more difficult for the small master to keep a status in the guild, or for the apprentice to attain it. Entrance fees were raised, new conditions enforced, and devices of all kinds were adopted to limit influence and effective membership to the richer craftsman. The need of the small man for credit helped of course to undermine his independence, and to weaken him in his struggle with the power on which he was compelled more and more to rely.[3] Finally the craft guild disappears into such bodies as the London Livery Companies, which had about as much connexion with the original craft guild as the body of freemen in an English borough in 1800 with the freemen of that borough three centuries earlier. Some companies of this kind took definite form in the fifteenth century, but it was in the two succeeding centuries that most of them came into existence, and that they assumed their modern character. They had legal incorporation, with the power of holding land, and they

---

[1] "As a result of these combined causes, there grew up in every industrial centre of Western Europe from the middle of the fourteenth century onward, a body of workmen in every craft who had no prospect before them but that of remaining journeymen all their lives."—Unwin, *Industrial Organization in the Sixteenth and Seventeenth Centuries*, p. 48.

[2] See R. H. Gretton, *The English Middle Class*, p. 100.

[3] Tawney, *Introduction to Wilson's Discourse on Usury*, p. 21.

were governed by a select body, called the Court of Assistants. A man reached this office by a long series of promotions, involving great delay and expense, so that all but the wealthiest members were permanently excluded from office.[1] Thus the history of the English guild is the history of the defeat and loss of the working classes in a social struggle.[2]

The change in the character of the guilds was accompanied and encouraged by a change in the character of industry and commerce. The guilds in their original form were adapted to the needs of a strictly local commerce. When commerce expanded and the range and scale of trade increased, merchanting became much more elaborate and this organization was no longer adequate. For commercial development involved specialization, and the craft guild had represented interests and functions that were combined in the fourteenth century, but were quite separate in the seventeenth. Professor Unwin's analysis of the mediæval craftsmen illuminates this aspect of industrial development. The mediæval craftsman, as he showed, was at once a workman, a foreman superintending his journeyman and apprentice, an employer undertaking responsibilities and supplying capital for materials, food and wages, a merchant buying something, and a shopkeeper selling something. As specialization follows the development of trade these functions are no longer concentrated in a single figure, they are distributed. By the end of the seventeenth century the mediæval craftsman has split up into no less than six different persons: the large merchant, the shopkeeper, large or small, the merchant employer, the large master, the small master and the journeyman.

The place of the guilds, as they lost their efficiency and power, was taken in part by the national government. The

[1] Unwin, op. cit., p. 42
[2] Gretton (op. cit., p. 65) gives an interesting illustration. In the fifteenth century the Gild Merchant of Newcastle "excluded from membership any one who had 'blue nails' (these being a proof that the person worked with his own hands at dyeing)."

first instinct of the Government was to reform the guilds and adapt them to new needs. In this category must be put the Acts of 1531 and 1536, which tried to protect apprentices from the disqualifying practices that had been introduced, and forbade guild officers to require an oath from journeymen that they would not set up for themselves.[1] Similar measures were taken in France. When Colbert set about his plans for French industry, he combined the use of the guilds with the use of State authority. He issued edicts and regulations through the guilds, dictating methods of manufacture, and the size, colour, and quality of manufactured goods.[2]

In the time of Elizabeth English statesmen chose another course. Instead of trying to reform the guilds, they tried to set the State to do for industry what the guilds had done when they were effective organs. The most notable illustration is the great code of industrial regulations passed in the early years of Elizabeth; the Statute of Artificers (1563) included among its aims that of securing a fair standard of skilled labour both in towns and villages, by extending outside cities the regulations relating to apprenticeship that had been enforced by the craft guilds within their walls. Other legislation gave to new companies, or to existing companies, such as the London Livery Companies, rights that had been exercised by guilds; it conferred, that is, on associations of persons having a financial interest in the trade, who paid for their patents or charters, the power formerly belonging to the guilds, to supervise wares and

---

[1] See Unwin, op. cit., p. 56.
[2] "A famous edict of 1671 on the weaving and dyeing of cloth will show to what lengths he was ready to go. If bad cloth is produced specimens of it are to be exposed on a stake with a ticket attached giving the name of the delinquent. If the same fault is committed again, the master or the workman who is at fault shall be censured in the meeting of the guild. In the event of a third offence, the guilty person shall himself be tied to the post for two hours with a specimen of the faulty product tied to him."—Professor A. J. Grant in *Cambridge Modern History*, Vol. V, p. 11.

control certain trades. The London Upholsterers, who included only six men of substance, paid £100 for such a grant. All men working at leather crafts within three miles of London were under the superintendence of the Wardens of the Companies connected with those trades : the Companies of the Curriers, the Saddlers, and the Shoemakers. Thus, whereas industry had formerly been regulated by guilds of producers receiving their authority from the City, it was now regulated by the Crown or by Parliament, which passed Statutes for that purpose, and bestowed privileges or patents on bodies or companies, that differed from the earlier guilds, since they represented only particular interests in a trade. At a later stage these companies turned into privileged bodies without any interest in the trade, except the rights given to them by their charters.

At one time it looked as if English industry might be put under the same system of police as the French, for under the Stuarts England made an experiment in regulation that went far beyond the legislation of Elizabeth. Charles I anticipated Colbert's method of setting up privileged and monopolist companies for the purpose of fostering English manufactures, and forcing them on foreign markets. His motives were, partly regard for the interests of the workmen who asked for protection against the capitalist merchant, partly mercantilist theory, partly the desire for revenue and authority outside the reach of Parliament. A number of joint stock companies were launched on this plan ; among them companies of pinmakers, felt makers, cloth-workers, and playing-card makers. Charles I actually gave his sanction to a proposal to set up a clothing corporation, with officers nominated by the magistrates in every city and county where the new draperies were carried on.[1] These plans miscarried, and as they were identified with the general traditions of Stuart despotism, political sentiment in eighteenth century England was strongly hostile.

[1] Unwin, op. cit., p. 147 *n.*

DESTRUCTION OF CUSTOM IN INDUSTRY

In the case of the boroughs, the Whig Governments that succeeded the Stuarts preferred to enjoy rather than remove the abuses introduced by the Tudors and aggravated by the Stuarts. In the case of industry, the Stuart policy was reversed, partly because the Whigs represented commercial interests that suffered under that policy, and partly because they were afraid of any scheme that might be used for the profit of the Crown. The experiment in regulation was thus followed by a strong reaction against State authority over industry.

Thus down to the time when the great inventions come into use the history of industry bears a certain resemblance to the history of agriculture. Both agriculture and industry had been regulated originally, in greater or less degree, by associations of producers. These associations differed in power, character, history and length of life, in different industries and different places; nor did they exist everywhere and in all industries; for guilds did not cover all industrial life, just as the common field communities did not cover the whole of agriculture. Roughly speaking, this type of rural and industrial life loses first the substance, and then the look of power, as the range of commerce develops, the relations of the persons engaged change, and agriculture and industry become richer and more ambitious.

What obstacles then still remained to the free play of enterprise and the power of capital in either field? The only obstacle in the case of agriculture was the system of common farming, which had been set aside already in the tracts that had been swept by the enclosure movement in the sixteenth century. To remove this obstacle all that was needed was a series of private Acts of Parliament, and though tithe owners here, or powerful proprietors there, might put difficulties in the way, still the landlords controlled Parliament, and Parliament made the laws. Thus the landlords could dispossess the groups of producers who still had any rights in the soil.

In the case of industry there were no bodies surviving

resembling the commoners who met in the Manorial Courts, for the privileged Companies, though they might be able to embarrass one industry in the interests of another, did not give to any group of producers the power to resist the capitalist. But though the Guilds had disappeared, there were still Acts on the Statute Book for controlling industry: Acts already mentioned, that had been passed as the Guild system crumbled away, when Parliament sought to provide by law, and by the administration of the magistrate, for some of the needs that had been served by the Guilds. Of these Acts, some restrained the liberty of the workmen, and the employers had no quarrel with them.[1] But others restrained the liberty of the employer, and the capitalists set to work to get rid of those Acts, just as the landlord set to work to get rid of the system of common rights over the Manor.

Thus the struggle between commoners and enclosing landlords in the villages in the eighteenth and nineteenth centuries has its counterpart in industry, in the struggle of the workmen for the maintenance or the revival of customs and laws, from which the employers wish to be free. The employers are for unchecked enterprise; the employed, and in some cases the smaller masters, are for restoring or putting into practice regulations that had been imposed first by the Guilds and then by the State.

This is the significance of the episodes generally known as the Luddite Riots of 1811–1812. They occurred in three counties, Lancashire, Yorkshire and Nottingham. They were the resort to violence on the part of workers who had failed to persuade Parliament to protect their interests by enforcing the law. Different industries were concerned in the three counties: the woollen industry in Yorkshire, the hosiery or framework-knitting in Nottingham, and the cotton industry in Lancashire. To understand the several risings it is necessary to recall the controversies that had preceded them.

[1] E.g. The Worsted Acts.

The woollen industry, as an ancient industry, was regulated by many laws. Some of them aimed at protecting the interests of the towns, others at protecting the interests of a branch or craft, others at promoting the good conduct of the industry. Among them there were laws prohibiting a machine known as the "gig mill," for raising the fibres in the cloth, in order to form a nap on the surface; laws imposing an apprenticeship of seven years for weavers; a law, passed in the interests of the towns, forbidding any clothier outside a corporate town to have more than one loom, and any weaver outside a corporate town to have more than two, and a law providing for the fixing of wages by the magistrates. During the last half of the eighteenth century there was a constant struggle between masters and men over these laws. The law about fixing wages was applied in Gloucestershire in 1728, but the employers refused to obey the magistrates' order. Parliament passed a stronger measure in 1756 in consequence of an agitation among the weavers, but a new difficulty arose, for it was now the turn of the magistrates to refuse to act. At length the Gloucestershire Justices were induced by a series of riots in the county to fix a wage, but the masters again held out, and applied to Parliament with such success that the Act was repealed. There was a longer struggle over the other Acts, and the men were constantly prosecuting, or threatening to prosecute masters for infringing them. In the case of the law against gig mills, there was some doubt whether the gig mill in use in the eighteenth century was the machine that Parliament had forbidden in the sixteenth. For several years in succession Parliament passed Acts suspending these laws, but finally the masters gained the day, and in 1809 Parliament repealed them.

It was after this series of disappointments that the shearmen, or croppers, as they were called in Yorkshire, tried to intimidate the masters who were introducing a new machine by which the shears handled by the cropper, a highly paid workman, could be worked by mechanical power. Readers of Charlotte Brontë's *Shirley* will remember the vivid description of the attack on Horsfall's mill, where these hated machines had been installed.

The Nottingham Luddites were bands of framework knitters, who went about the country destroying frames of a particular kind. There had been for some time two kinds of frames in use in the industry : the ordinary stocking frame which was narrow, and a wide frame that turned out pantaloons and fancy stockings called "twills." The demand for pantaloons and fancy stockings had ceased, and some of the masters used these frames to turn out pieces which could be cut up into gloves, socks, sandals and stockings, of an inferior kind. The market was soon flooded with these articles, and the makers of the properly finished stockings were faced with a ruinous competition. The new method which produced a clumsier article was cheaper. The masters who used the regular stocking frame disliked the innovation as much as the men, and many of them co-operated with the men in their efforts to put an end to it. The men appealed to Parliament for a minimum wage, which was one way of meeting this illegitimate competition, but they were recommended instead to apply to the old London Company. By the Charter granted to that Company by Charles II framework knitters were authorized to destroy all engines and frames that fabricated articles in a deceitful manner. The Company was defunct, but many of the workmen paid £1 13*s*. 4*d*. to become freemen of it. Unfortunately, when they took action against an employer who had broken bye-laws regulating the number of apprentices, the jury only awarded 1*s*. damages, and employers using this frame were naturally not deterred by this penalty. In the riots the Luddites tried to do by force what they had failed to do by agitation, although in that agitation they had had the support of many employers. Parliament replied by making machine breaking a capital felony (1812), and the debate on that Bill has been made memorable by the scathing attack delivered by Byron in his maiden speech in the Lords.

The Luddite riots in Lancashire were connected partly with high prices, and partly with the distress of the cotton weavers. The cotton industry differed from the woollen and hosiery industries, because it was a new industry and, as such, had escaped the regulations to which they were subject. The chief cause of distress in the cotton industry was the steady decline in the wages of the hand-loom weaver. Hand-loom weaving was not a difficult or arduous art, and as it was open to anyone to practise it, labourers who had lost their work in their own occupation, and the Irish immigrants who poured into Lancashire, turned to it as their easiest refuge. This overcrowding sent down wages. The degradation of the hand-loom weaver from this cause was hastened by the introduction of the power-loom. From the beginning of the nineteenth century the great mass of the pauper population of Lancashire was largely made up from this class.

The workmen sought a remedy in the application to the cotton industry of the principle of the regulation of wages, which had been adopted in the case of the Spitalfields silk industry in 1773. They had some measure of success, for though Pitt refused their demand for a minimum wage, he passed an Arbitration Act in 1800 by which each party in a dispute on wages or hours was to name an arbitrator. If the arbitrators could not agree, either of them could submit the dispute to a magistrate. But the masters refused to carry out the Act, and no steps were taken to compel them. The agitation for a minimum wage continued, and from time to time it received support from sympathetic employers, just as the framework knitters received help and encouragement from employers in their resistance to the use of the frame for the production of inferior articles. The famous John Fielden was an active leader of this movement. But a Parliament that was anxious to get rid of any restrictions on free enterprise that remained on the Statute Book, was not likely to welcome the idea of such legislation, and the weavers were left to their fate. The Luddite riots in

Lancashire, attacks on mills where the power-loom was in use, were an expression of the misery and despair of this class.

The workman and the peasant alike would have refused to admit that they were merely defending obstructive survivals from the past. They saw the political rulers defending property in land and capital with great zeal, and they felt that their own property was equally entitled to the protection of the law. "Parliament may be tender of property," said the peasant in the case put to Arthur Young, " all I know is that I had a cow and an Act of Parliament has taken it from me." [1]

"The Weaver's Qualifications" (said the Cotton Weavers in a petition manifesto in 1823) "may be considered as his property and support. It is as real property to him as Buildings and Lands are to others. Like them his Qualification cost time, application and Money. There is no point of view (except visible and tangible) wherein they differ." [2]

The analogy looked false to the statesmen of the time, who showed equal enthusiasm for putting Corn Laws on, and taking Minimum Wage Laws off the Statute Book. The upper classes divided their world into capital and labour, and they held that the struggle was between custom and initiative, between the prejudices of the poor which hampered industry, and the spirit of acquisition and adventure in the rich which encouraged it. In the case of industry, as in the case of agriculture, the victory of capital was complete. In 1809 Parliament repealed the Acts regulating the woollen industry; in 1813 the Acts authorizing magistrates to fix wages; in 1814 the apprenticeship sections of the Statute of Artificers; in 1815 the Act establishing the Assize of Bread in London. The repeal, in each case, registered a decision taken and applied much earlier. Sidmouth, in asking Parliament to pass the repealing Act of 1813, said that most of his hearers were, no doubt, as much

[1] Hammond, *Village Labourer* (1920 ed.), p. 59.
[2] Hammond, *Town Labourer*, p. 300.

DESTRUCTION OF CUSTOM IN INDUSTRY

surprised as he had been to find that the Acts now to be repealed were still on the Statute Book. Thus by the defeat of the workman and small master, first in the politics of the Guild, then in the politics of Parliament, industry, like agriculture, escaped sooner in England than on the Continent of Europe from the restraints that the institutions and the temper of the Middle Ages had placed upon it.

CHAPTER VIII

THE STEAM ENGINE

ONE Sunday afternoon in the spring of 1765 whilst James Watt, mechanical instrument maker, aged twenty-nine, was taking a walk on Glasgow Green, and meditating, in spite of his Covenanting ancestors, about the same subjects that occupied his thoughts on weekdays, there flashed across his mind the solution of a problem that had long troubled him: how could the cylinder of a steam-engine be both hot and cold at the same time? His solution, known as the device of the separate condenser, made it possible to employ steam as the motive power for industry. Watt's first patent applying his Sunday inspiration was taken out in 1769; his first successful engine was finished in 1776; by 1800, when the patent expired, his engine, improved in several respects, was in use in mines and foundries, in textile and paper mills, and great columns of smoke from innumerable chimneys spoiling the light and colour of the skies declared the triumph of industry and the glory of man.

The motive power of steam was no new discovery of the eighteenth century. Hero of Alexandria, who lived in the first century B.C., left writings which show that he understood the force of steam and the uses of "cylinder and piston, three-way cock, slide valves and valve clacks." He described methods for employing this force, not for industrial purposes, but for such magical devices as changing water into wine, opening temple doors, or pouring out libations without apparent human agency. Hero's book, when rediscovered at the Renaissance, ran into eight editions in different languages, and set a succession of ingenious minds to work at plans for using the force whose power is apparent to the simplest observer as he watches the lid of a kettle of boiling water. One of the most interesting figures among these pioneers was the romantic cavalier, the second Marquis of Worcester (1601-67), who divided his fortunes between the cause of the King and the cause of science. Worcester invented a " water commanding engine for raising water by steam," was taken by his age for a crank and, like many of his successors, died in want, the secret of his invention dying with him. On the Continent the credit for the invention of the steam-engine is often given to Dr. Dionysius Papin (1647-1712), a French Protestant doctor, compelled by his religious opinions to leave France, who made several experiments and some discoveries in the management of steam, first in England and later in Germany, where he became a Professor in the University of Marburg. Experiment had shown that if steam is cooled and so condensed in a vessel, a vacuum is produced into which the air presses from outside. Papin saw that not only the direct expansive force of steam but also the suction set up by a vacuum might be used for producing mechanical power by the aid of a piston working up and down in a cylinder. A theorist and not a practical mechanic, he helped others to harness steam for the use of industry and failed in his own designs. His last project was to build a mechanically propelled boat, to perfect which he gave up fifteen years of his life. But the boatmen at Münden destroyed the boat when on its way to be tested in the port of London, and as he was unable to raise funds to build another, and died two years later, a disappointed man, it will never be known how his boat worked, or indeed whether it worked at all.

It was Thomas Savery (1650-1715), a Devonshire gentleman, trained as a military engineer, a contemporary of Papin's, who invented the first steam-engine actually employed in industry. It was called " The Miners' Friend or an engine to raise water by fire." Savery patented it in

1698, and, unlike his predecessors, made no mystery about it. His engine dispensed with Papin's piston; it was a mechanism by which the water to be drained off was sucked up directly into a vacuum and then forced out by steam.[1] The engine worked satisfactorily for pumping water from ordinary wells, and it was used for several mines in Cornwall, but when tried for a coal-mine in Staffordshire it proved a failure. The truth was that the boilers and vessels of that time were not strong enough to stand the pressure of steam required for dealing with a large volume of water, and were in consequence often "torn to pieces." Hence Savery's engine was more suited to "the pumping of water for fountains and the supply of gentlemen's houses" than to deep mine work, and it was superseded by an improved engine, invented by Thomas Newcomen (1663-1729), a blacksmith and ironmonger of Dartmouth, and a neighbour of Savery's. In Newcomen's engine the water was not sucked up directly into a condensing vessel, but was pumped up by an ordinary pump which was itself worked by the engine.

The pump was connected with the engine by a lever beam to which were attached on one side the pumping gear, on the other a piston which moved up and down in a cylinder, communicating its motion to the pump. The piston went up because it was pulled by a weight fixed to the other side of the lever-beam; it went down because

[1] The apparatus consisted of a condensing vessel connected by pipes with the boiler on one side, with the well on the other side. Steam was first forced into the condensing vessel from the boiler; next, the condensing vessel was cooled by an application of cold water outside it; this cooling caused the steam inside to condense and so created a vacuum in the vessel which was now shut off by a valve from the boiler. Into this vacuum the water from the well was sucked up; a valve prevented it from running down again. The connexion with the boiler was then reopened; steam was forced into the condenser and by its direct action expelled the water through a pipe that discharged into the open air. The working depended, as has been seen, on a system of valves. In Savery's actual engines there were two condensing vessels acting alternately, so that the water was sucked up in a continuous stream.

THE STEAM ENGINE

it was sucked into a vacuum in the cylinder. This vacuum had been created by two processes: first the injection of a dose of steam, second the injection of a dose of cold water, which by cooling the steam and causing it to condense produced the required vacuum. The alternate doses of steam and water were managed at first by turning cocks by hand, but later a labour-saving device was invented, connected with the legendary story of an idle boy, Humphrey Potter, which joined the cocks by strings to the ever beam so that they opened and shut automatically.

It was this engine, often called the "atmospheric" engine, because it utilized the direct pressure of the atmosphere on a vacuum, of which Watt was thinking on his Sunday walk. It was employed for draining water out of mines in all the mining districts in England,[1] but was costly to work because it consumed large quantities of fuel. Most of the fuel was used in reheating the cylinder after it had been thoroughly chilled by the cold water injection; in fact it was calculated that four-fifths of the steam produced was spent in bringing the cylinder up to a temperature in which the remaining fifth could do its work. Hence arose the question that was puzzling Watt: How could you keep the cylinder hot, and at the same time produce conditions in which the steam could condense?

The answer that flashed into his mind was "By means of a separate condenser." In his engine built on this plan the steam, instead of being cooled and condensed in the cylinder itself, rushed into another vessel to fill a vacuum and was condensed there without lowering the temperature of the cylinder itself. Thus the cylinder was kept hot, and at the same time a vacuum was created by the exit of the steam. Whilst experimenting with a model of a separate condenser, Watt, whose object was to keep the cylinder as hot as possible, invented other supplementary devices for this purpose: he put an air-tight cover on

[1] By 1769 there were nearly 100 steam-engines in the Northern Collieries. See R. L. Galloway, *History of Coal Mining*, p. 105.

the cylinder and pushed the piston down by the pressure of steam instead of the pressure of air: finally he encased the whole cylinder in a bigger vessel, filling the intervening space with steam.

It now remained to be seen whether these devices, which worked satisfactorily enough on a toy model, could be successfully embodied in a large engine. To construct a large engine would cost several thousand pounds, and Watt was a poor man. His father, a "housewright, shipwright, carpenter, and undertaker as well as a builder and contractor," a merchant, a holder of shares in ships, and baillie of Greenock into the bargain, did not acquire riches from any of his callings. James Watt the younger (born 1736) was a delicate child, the only survivor of a family of five,[1] cursed with sick headaches till old age and prosperity brought relief. At the age of eighteen he was sent to Glasgow to learn the trade of mathematical instrument maker, but failing to find there any competent mechanic to teach him he took the advice of a Glasgow professor and went to London to learn his trade (1755). But in London too there were difficulties, for Watt had no mind to serve an apprenticeship of seven years as the rules of the trade required. Ultimately he came upon a mathematical instrument maker in Cornhill who agreed to take him into his shop for a year, for the sum of twenty guineas. In this irregular position Watt was in great danger from the press gangs, which were numerous and active on the outbreak of the Seven Years' War (1756). Victims taken within the City precincts were carried before the Lord Mayor, who released apprentices and "creditable tradesmen." But Watt was neither: he was not technically an apprentice and he was breaking the laws of the City by working within its liberties without being a freeman. So he was obliged to stay indoors, and as he had to rely for fresh air on the draught from the workshop door, he suffered severely

[1] Two brothers and a sister died in infancy. A third brother was drowned at sea.

in health and spirits. He returned home in 1756 meaning to start business in Glasgow ; there was no mathematical instrument maker living there and he had thus a promising opening. But Glasgow was a chartered town, and the guild of hammermen objected that Watt was not the son of a burgess and had not served an apprenticeship within the borough. The Corporation accordingly refused to allow him to set up business. Fortunately the university authorities came to his rescue and gave him an asylum within their precincts which were outside the borough's jurisdiction.

Watt had previously repaired some instruments for the Professor of Natural Philosophy, and he was now able to work for the University and to sell his instruments to the outside public. The demand for quadrants and other mathematical instruments was slight, so to make a living he did odd jobs, turning his hand, though he had no ear for a tune, to musical instruments : flutes, fiddles, even an organ. Though his shop did not bring him riches it became the resort of students and professors, and so provided him with the stimulus of congenial society. In 1759 he found a partner, with the help of whose capital he set up a shop outside the University precincts, the Corporation apparently having dropped their opposition.[1] By the end of 1764 as many as sixteen hands were employed by Watt and his partner, but the profits were modest and Watt's salary was only £35 a year. He used his spare hours to educate himself, making experiments with steam and studying a model of the Newcomen engine that was in the possession of the University. It was when he was brooding over the defects of this engine that his inspiration came to him.

Watt, who had married the year before, could not provide the money for constructing a larger engine out of a salary

[1] The fixed capital of mechanical tools at the entry into partnership was valued at £91 19s., which, with the cash in hand of £108, made a total capital of £200.—J. P. Muirhead, *Life of James Watt*, p. 44.

of £35 a year, and the prospects of outside help in Glasgow were poor. From the Act of Union to the American War Glasgow was the chief market for the tobacco trade, and the tobacco lords who were Glasgow's rich men were not keenly interested in projects for using steam in industry. Watt's scientific friends, like the men of science of all ages, had not much money at their command, but one of them, Dr. Black, the celebrated Professor of Chemistry, whose doctrine of "latent heat" had contributed to the invention of the separate condenser, lent him money to help in the construction of models, models over which Watt was soon spending a good deal more than his spare time. Black did him an even greater service in introducing him to Dr. Roebuck, an enterprising English doctor from Birmingham, who was developing the famous Carron Iron Works in Scotland. To secure coal for his furnaces Roebuck had leased a number of mines, and he was finding the Newcomen engines unequal to the task of keeping his pits clear of water. He was naturally much interested in Watt's plans, and entered into correspondence with him, urging him to visit the Carron works, and pressing him to proceed with his invention "whether he pursued it as a philosopher or as a man of business." The appeal was not happily phrased, and Watt's reluctance to visit Roebuck was perhaps due to a premonition of the troubles he was to endure when he was no longer handling impersonal forces as a philosopher, but handling forces of a very different kind as a partner in industrial enterprises. At any rate he was always ready with excuses: his foot did not let him walk: it was too far to ride: a journey disabled him for work for several days. It was not till 1768 that he accepted the invitation and paid Roebuck a visit.

By this time his partner had died, his business had declined, and he was making his living as a land surveyor. He still tried experiments with his model, and had kept up a correspondence with Roebuck, who made an arrangement in 1767 by which he was to pay the debts (over £1,000) incurred by Watt for his experiments, to finance further experiments, and to pay the cost of the patent in return for two-thirds of the property in the invention. Watt prepared specifications for a patent which he took out early in 1769; but his progress was too slow for Roebuck with his water-logged mines: " You are now letting the most active part of your life insensibly glide away. A day, a moment, ought not to be lost." A trial engine constructed in accordance with the patent was at last erected with great secrecy in an outhouse by a glen behind Kinneil House where Roebuck lived. It was finished in September, 1769, but proved a failure. The workmanship of the mechanics at Watt's disposal, even the skilled mechanics imported from England to the Carron Works, was clumsy and defective; the cylinder was badly cast, the piston not air-tight: the mechanism did not work.

Meanwhile Roebuck's financial difficulties, like the water in his pits, increased every day; so far from being able to finance further experiments, he could not even provide the money for the patent. Watt was forced to borrow again from Dr. Black. " Of all things in life," wrote the despondent inventor, " there is nothing more foolish than inventing." To earn his living he was obliged to devote himself again to surveying, and took up the uncongenial task of directing the construction of the Monkland Canal. To prepare plans for a canal was pleasant enough, but to manage rough navvies was a hard business for a man who would rather " face a loaded cannon than settle an account or make a bargain." But the work was comparatively well paid, £200 a year, and " I cannot afford," he wrote, " to trifle away my whole life, which—God knows—may not be long. Not that I think myself a proper hand for keeping men to their duty." Life dragged on in this way till the commercial panic of 1772 brought bankruptcy to Roebuck, whose drowned mines had swallowed up his own fortune, his wife's fortune, much of the money of his friends and relatives, as well as the profits of his refining works at Birmingham and his prosperous vitriol works at Prestonpans.

The prospect for Watt looked desperate, but his invention was saved by Matthew Boulton, a hardware manufacturer of Birmingham. Boulton (born 1728) was the typical business genius. As a boy he had shown the powers of initiative and organization that marked his career as a man. The son of a prosperous manufacturer, he invented, before the age of seventeen, an inlaid steel buckle that caught the fancy of the fashionable world and brought large profits to the firm. France had then, as always, an unchallenged ascendancy in graceful production, and Boulton exported his buckles to France in order to bring them back to England as luxuries from Paris. His adventurous disposition was balanced by solid qualities which inspired confidence in his most hazardous undertakings, and made him a complete contrast to the mercurial and despondent Watt.

"His temperament" (wrote an admirer) "was sanguine, with that slight mixture of the phlegmatic which gives calmness and dignity . . . with a social heart he had a grandiose manner, like that arising from position, wealth and habitual command."

In 1762 Boulton had moved his works out from Snow Hill in Birmingham to larger premises at Soho, two miles north of Birmingham, just inside the borders of Staffordshire. Here he employed about a thousand men, women and children, making anything in hardware goods the elegant world might fancy, from a statuette of Hercules and the Hydra, copied from the antique, down to an ornamented toothpick: buttons, buckles, clasps, snuff-boxes, watch-chains, clocks, brackets, ormolu goods, plated goods, and, in a special department, even copies of pictures so cunningly wrought that it was said that even the best connoisseurs were deceived and took them for originals.[1] His works became a fashionable spectacle, and no tour in England was complete without a visit to Soho. "I

[1] See *Annual Register*, 1801, p. 404.

had lords and ladies to wait on yesterday," wrote Boulton, "I have French and Spaniards to-day; and to-morrow I shall have Germans, Russians and Norwegians." Catherine of Russia bought his goods and visited Soho. Queen Charlotte replaced the china ornaments on her mantelpiece by Boulton's vases from the antique. The gross returns of the firm had risen from £7,000 in 1763 to £30,000 in 1767. Boulton's partner, Fothergill, managed the foreign departments of the business, Boulton the home markets and the business itself.

Boulton was an adept in scientific management. Direct contact between employer and worker was of course impossible in a business on the scale of Soho, and Boulton trained managers and foremen to act as his lieutenants, whilst he sat in his office, like a general at headquarters, directing operations.

"While sitting in the midst of his factory" (so runs the well-known description), "surrounded by the clang of hammers and the noise of engines, he could usually detect when any stoppage occurred, or when the machinery was going too fast or too slow, and issue his orders accordingly."

The supply of power had always been the chief difficulty at Soho. The grinding mill was driven by a waterwheel, but as the water often ran dry in the summer months, Boulton was reduced to using horses to turn the wheel, an expensive and unsatisfactory form of power. He had long played with the idea of using a fire engine to pump back the water when it had already done its work once. He had a correspondence on the subject with Benjamin Franklin, to whom he had sent a model of the Newcomen engine. Franklin gave him advice which, had it been taken by the age, would have saved the world many of the calamities that followed Watt's invention. He recommended Boulton to save fuel by consuming the smoke, for smoke was fuel, and the sooty crust formed underneath the boiler delayed the process of heating it. "All that is necessary is to make the smoke of fresh coals pass descending through those that are already thoroughly ignited."[1]

Boulton was a friend of Roebuck, and in this way he had become acquainted with Watt and his project. He had already considered and discussed some plan for a partnership with them. Roebuck's bankruptcy brought matters to a head. He owed money to Boulton, who agreed to take instead two-thirds share in the engine patent, an arrangement with which the other creditors, thinking the patent worthless, were well satisfied. Boulton was to pay £1,000 from the profits of the patent, if it succeeded. Watt at the same time agreed to discharge Roebuck from the obligations he had incurred in 1767.

Boulton was in difficulties himself at the moment, but at no time in his life did financial straits discourage him from undertaking fresh liabilities. "The thing," he wrote to Watt of his engine, "is now a shadow; 'tis merely ideal and will cost time and money to realize it." Long before this he had foreseen that to make a success it would be necessary

"to settle a manufactory near my own, by the side of our canal, where I would erect all the conveniences necessary for the completion of engines, and from which manufactory we would serve the world with engines of all sizes."

The trial engine, in the outhouse at Kinneil, that had made so many hearts sick, was taken to bits, packed up and sent to the Soho works in 1773. Next year it was followed by its author. Watt, who, to add to his other misfortunes, had lost his wife in 1773, shook off the dust of his native land without regret, intending, unless his engine proved an unexpected success, to find work in England as a surveyor or engineer. No definite arrangement had yet been made between him and Boulton, for the first thing

[1] Smiles, *Lives of Boulton and Watt*, p. 184. Watt himself apparently took out a patent for consuming smoke in 1785, but unfortunately for mankind the steam engine was pushed on and his plans for the consumption of smoke never got beyond the specifications of a patent. J. P. Muirhead, op. cit., p. 304 f.

THE STEAM ENGINE

was to give the engine a fresh test. The fresh test, thanks to the superior skill of the Soho workmen who put the parts together, proved promising. But as the original patent was for fourteen years, of which nearly six had elapsed, Boulton was unwilling to sink capital in an invention which might only begin to be profitable by the time the patent expired. Accordingly Watt made a journey to London early in 1775 to see what could be done. The result was the introduction into Parliament of a Bill to extend the patent.[1]

The Bill provoked considerable opposition in Parliament from the enemies of monopoly, reinforced by mining interests naturally anxious to use any new pumping devices as cheaply as possible. Burke was one of the chief opponents of the extension of the patent rights. But the Bill became law; the Act passed in June 1775 prolonged the patent rights for twenty-four years, and Boulton was now free to prosecute his schemes. Whilst the Bill was passing through Parliament Watt had been offered a post under the Russian Government at a salary of £1,000 a year; princely pay compared with anything that he had ever earned before or seemed ever likely to earn. The offer came through his friend Dr. Robison, at that time Mathematical Professor at Cronstadt. After some hesitation Watt refused.

The trial engine at Soho had been improved during Watt's absence in London : a cast-iron cylinder made by the famous ironmaster, John Wilkinson, was substituted for the old tin cylinder that had served at Kinneil.[2] A partnership arrangement between Boulton and Watt was now concluded, Fothergill, Boulton's partner, refusing to be associated with the project. Boulton agreed to pay

[1] An Act cost £110, a new patent £130.
[2] For the relations between Wilkinson and Boulton and Watt, and Wilkinson's claim to have invented the steam engine, see the authoritative account in Mr. Ashton's book, *Iron and Steel in the Industrial Revolution.*

all the expenses connected with the scheme, and to keep Watt till the business brought in profits. The salary Watt received was £330, and in August, 1775, he moved his home to Birmingham to devote himself to the steam engine. One of the first engines sent out from Soho was, suitably enough, used for blowing the bellows of John Wilkinson's blast furnaces at Broseley. Another was sent to the Bloomfield Colliery in Staffordshire to pump water. Both began to work early in 1776, and both answered. In the Midland counties the fame of the engine brought enquiries and orders; London, on the other hand, was sceptical. The Society of Engineers in Holborn, of which Smeaton was the leading light, considered that the machine was too complicated to work satisfactorily. It was therefore most important, for the sake of the reputation of the firm, and for future orders in the South, to finish an engine already bespoken for pumping water at the Bow distillery in London. This work, delayed by Watt's absence in Glasgow to arrange about his second marriage, was finished by the autumn, and the engine sent off in parts with a skilled mechanic in charge, but Watt himself had to go to London in November to deal with defects in its working. This engine proved a success, except for a relapse in the spring of 1777, after a visit from Smeaton, who had been over-generous in obeying the injunction (written up over a famous Newcomen engine):

> "Whoever wants to see the engine here
> Must give the engine-man a drop of beer.

On this occasion the engine, stimulated to excess, ran so wildly that the valves had to be replaced.

Watt was in constant difficulties over his workmen. His own complaints that they drank, that they were inefficient, that no Scotsman could be turned into a good mechanic, must be received with caution, for Watt was no more able to judge his workmen than to train them. Impatient, irritable, exacting, and yet reluctant to delegate a task to

THE STEAM ENGINE

anybody else, his character made him as unfit to be a good master as the habits with which he taxed his men made them unfit to be good mechanics. That he suffered at their hands, and that they often disobeyed their instructions, displaying apparently not too little but too much initiative, and thinking they could improve on the directions given them, is very evident. The supply of skill did not keep pace with the supply of engines, and yet Watt wanted to dismiss any workman who made a mistake. "If possible," he wrote to Boulton, "have the whole brood of these engine-men displaced, if any others can be procured; for nothing but slovenliness, if not malice, is to be expected of them." Boulton was wiser, for he knew that they had to make the best of the men as they were.[1]

Boulton and Watt had also to combat the efforts of foreigners to tempt their best men abroad. Till 1824 it was illegal for a skilled mechanic to accept work abroad, but industry had as active a secret service in that age of industrial expansion as diplomacy, and there were French, German and Russian agents in England, ready to offer large bribes to workmen who would run the risk.[2] Watt had considered very seriously the suggestion that he should take himself and his inventions to Russia, but it was a different matter when two fitters sent to London to set up the Bow engine received a similar invitation from a Russian agent. They were summoned back to Soho, and arrangements made for their apprehension in the event of their attempting to leave the country.

The engines set up in the Midlands and London had proved

[1] The ablest of their workmen, William Murdock, himself a considerable inventor, asked for his wages to be raised from one pound a week to two; Boulton replied by giving him £20, half of it provided by a mining company.

[2] There were similar agents in Paris. The first Act, 1719 (5 Geo. I, cap. 27), "to prevent the Inconveniences arising from seducing Artificers in the Manufactures of Great Britain into foreign Parts," had originally been prompted by Peter the Great's efforts to introduce the iron industry into Russia.

a success, but it was in Cornwall that Boulton and Watt found most of their custom. The Newcomen engines had long been in use in the tin and copper mines, but they worked badly in the deeper mines that were now being exploited, and many owners had to choose between closing down their mines or finding better methods of pumping. The improvements in the steam engines had all been inspired by this motive. Spinning or weaving could be done by hand, though less rapidly than by machinery, but no hands in the world could keep pace with the flooding of the deeper mines.

The parts for the first two engines for Cornwall, for the Wheal Busy and Tingtang mines, were shipped in 1777. By 1780 as many as forty engines had been sold to Cornwall, and twenty of them were already at work. Watt spent all his time there, and Boulton, unable to supply engines fast enough, thought at one time of moving from Soho. Yet Boulton and Watt were in great financial embarrassment, and Roebuck's fate stared them in the face.

The method of payment for the engines was largely responsible for this perverse result. The principal parts of the engine, such as the cylinder, were not made at Soho but elsewhere, usually at John Wilkinson's works, and the customers paid Wilkinson, or the other firm, for them at the time. Boulton and Watt supplied certain parts from Soho, and also undertook to put the different parts together and erect the engine. For these services Boulton and Watt were paid at cost price. Their profit was to come from a complicated system of royalties: each customer was to pay annually one-third of the saving he had effected in fuel by substituting Watt's engine for its predecessor. Watt devised an accurate but complicated method of estimating this saving, but disputes were perpetual and bitter. Watt, who had always had a sharp eye for the less amiable qualities of his neighbours, assigned to his new customers a distinguished pre-eminence as having " the most ungracious manners of any people I have ever yet been amongst." The Cornishmen on their side felt that they had already paid for their engine and resented the recurrent outlay. There were mines, too, that could not bear this cost, and Boulton and Watt had in such cases to choose between receiving less than was due to them or receiving nothing at all. In other cases they were offered a share in the mines, but to accept payment in this form was to sink deeper into the morass of financial obligations in which they were already floundering. In addition to all these losses, they were put, like all inventors, to incessant expense and trouble by pirates who infringed their patents.

Boulton had further cause for discouragement, because his Soho works were doing badly; during the eighteen years from 1762 to 1780 it was estimated that the loss on a capital of £20,000 was upwards of £11,000. Fothergill would have liked to wind up the business, but Boulton saw that this might damage the prospects of the engine business, to which he looked for the repair of his fortunes. There was nothing for it, so he decided, but to go on raising money. Watt's only idea was to curtail commitments by lessening business: Boulton's plan was to increase receipts by expanding business. Watt was robbed of sleep and peace of mind by the thought of the debts already incurred, whilst Boulton undertook further risks with fresh money borrowed from friends. In 1778 Boulton had obtained an advance of £14,000 from the bankers, Lowe, Vere and Williams, and a loan of £7,000 from a merchant, Mr. Wiss, both on the security of royalties from engines. In 1780 the question of repayment of these loans became acute. Personal bonds for repayment within a certain time were required by the bank. Watt was recalcitrant. His nerves were in disorder; he was a martyr to dyspepsia ("I am quite eat up with the mulligrubs," he wrote), he could not work for thinking of the load of debt already incurred, and to enter into a personal bond seemed the final calamity. "What signifies it to a man though he gain the whole world, if he lose his health and his life?" "Without I can spare time this next summer to go to some more healthy climate to procure a little health, if climate will do, I must give up business and the world too." " There is no pitch of low spirits that I have not a perfect notion of, from hanging melancholy to peevish melancholy." Boulton had indeed undertaken to finance the business, but on the other hand the bank was dissatisfied with security from one partner only, and Roebuck's fate was a warning of what might happen if Watt insisted on the letter of the law. Watt, like most men of his temper, was unable to look at things from any point of view but his own : he " would brood for days together on the accumulation of misery and anxiety which his great invention had brought upon him."

Watt said that this load of care and fear had destroyed his power of work, but it was in this atmosphere of gloom, with body sick as well as mind, that he achieved the most important of his triumphs. The machinery in use in spinning mills was worked by water-power, and consequently it was necessary to build factories on streams. The substitution of steam-power for water would make it possible to set up factories wherever the general conditions were most advantageous. Watt's adaptation of his engine to rotary motion achieved this revolution with all its momentous consequences. Boulton saw at once what success with such an experiment would mean. He was all for haste, for " the people in London, Manchester and Birmingham are steam-mill mad." Watt was less enthusiastic ; first he said he was at the end of his inventive power ; then that such an invention would be useless. These protestations were in his regular manner ; in the event he produced the necessary specifications for the patent he had secured in October, 1781. He was debarred from using a crank, the most obvious method to employ, because a Birmingham button-maker had already patented this device, stealing it, according to Watt, from one of his garrulous workmen. He arranged instead a system of wheels rotating round an axis, finally adopting a plan suggested by William Murdock, called the sun and planet motion. Smeaton, the famous engineer, consulted about this time by the Navy Board on the possibility of using steam-power to grind flour at Deptford, gave a damping reply. " I apprehend that no motion communicated from the reciprocating lever of a fire engine can ever produce a perfect circular motion like the regular efflux of water in turning a water-wheel." Watt himself did not foresee the full consequences of the revolution that would follow when the power, derived at the time from streams, could be created and applied here and there at the will of man.

"If you come home by way of Manchester " (he wrote to Boulton) " please not to seek orders for cotton-mill engines, because I hear there are so many mills erecting on powerful streams in the North of England, that the trade must soon be overdone, and consequently our labour may be lost." [1]

Boulton, with his belief that " they present a field that is boundless," was nearer the truth.

Watt's inventive faculty was still active, in spite of financial anxiety and continual friction with Cornish clients. In 1782 he invented a reciprocating expansive engine [2]: in 1784 a method for applying the steam-engine to tilt hammers in iron and steel forges, and for " parallel motion." He declared that he was more proud of this last invention than of any other. The governor, a device for regulating the speed of engines automatically, was another of several inventions to improve existing machinery. By 1786 orders for rotary engines were pouring in. The charge for these engines was made on the basis of their horse-power (£5 a year per horse), and no engine was made under four horse-power. Though Watt remarked that if the patent lasted

[1] The first cotton mill to use a steam-engine was a mill at Papplewick in 1785.

[2] To use the expansive force of steam was an early idea of Watt's, but experience showed him that in practice it was impossible to employ it " until the illiterate and obstinate people who are intrusted with the care of engines become more intelligent and better acquainted with the machine."

long enough " the power of a horse would grow to that of an elephant," and though he considered them at first an unremunerative form of business as compared with pumping machinery, there were fewer opportunities for disputes about payment, and the engine business now definitely turned the corner and became productive. By 1785 Watt no longer needed his salary of £330 from the Soho business; in 1787 £4,000 was placed to his private account, and another £2,000 was to be paid in a month's time. In 1788, a year of commercial crisis, it was Boulton and not Watt who needed help from his partner. Boulton had put his profits from the engine into fresh undertakings, many of them unremunerative, like the Albion Mills, a large establishment for grinding flour: a good advertisement for the rotary engines,[1] but not otherwise profitable. He was now in straits for ready money, and turned to Watt; but Watt " had got together his share of gains with too much difficulty to part with them easily: and he was unwilling to let them float away in what he regarded as an unknown sea of speculation." Boulton, who felt that he had treated Watt generously, for he had agreed to give him half of the profits from the engine instead of the stipulated third, took this refusal hardly, and an attack of stone, a disease from which he was to suffer for the rest of his life, reduced him to the despondency from which Watt was just beginning to emerge at the age of fifty-two. Fortunately he survived the crisis without the help of Watt, and he interested himself in the use of the steam engine for coining. In 1788, misled by an interview with the Privy Council, and underrating the opposition of the Mint Officials, he set up prematurely six presses; at last, in 1797, he received employment from the Government.

With prosperity Watt came to the end both of his will and his skill as an inventor in connection with steam, and he left it to others to find new uses for steam power. In

[1] Cast iron was first used by Rennie for the wheels and other parts of the machinery at the Albion Mills.

his patent of 1784 he had included a plan for driving wheel carriages by steam, but he never gave his mind to it, and William Murdock, who startled the parson at Redruth by driving a noisy hissing engine down the Vicarage lane, received no encouragement from his employer. " I wish William could be brought to do as we do," wrote Watt, " to mind the business in hand, and let such as Symington and Sadler throw away their time and money in hunting shadows." He was equally cold about the prospects of steam navigation which was exercising many minds. Henry Bell consulted him in 1801 on this subject. " How many noblemen, gentlemen, and engineers," was the answer, " have puzzled their brains, and spent their thousands of pounds, and none of these, nor yourself, have been able to bring the power of steam in navigation to a successful issue." But Bell was not daunted, and eleven years later he launched a successful steamer on the Clyde.

In 1800, when Watt's patent expired, he and Boulton dissolved their original partnership, and their sons carried on the business.[1] The old age of the two men was as great a contrast as their active life had been. Boulton, who cared for nothing outside his business, " tottered down the hill to see what was going forward at Soho." Watt, released from care and headache, began to enjoy his life, toyed with the idea of becoming a country gentleman,[2] read novels

[1] Between 1775 and 1800 Boulton and Watt erected 289 steam engines in England; of these 55 were in Lancashire, 41 in Middlesex, 31 in Staffordshire, 25 in Shropshire, 21 in Cornwall. Eighty-four were for cotton mills, 9 for wool and worsted mills, 30 for collieries, 28 for foundries and forges, 22 for copper mines, 18 for canals and 17 for breweries. See tables in J. Lord, *Capital and Steam-Power*, pp. 174 and 175, a book in which the reader will find new and important information.

[2] Watt was a Tory in politics, and his biographer is anxious to make it clear that his refusal of a baronetcy was not due to Radical sympathies. His son, on the other hand, went to Paris in 1792 to congratulate the Jacobin Club on behalf of the Constitutional Society of Manchester, and was denounced by Burke in Parliament. He settled down to business later and enjoyed the litigation over his father's patents, which was incessant.

and settled down to a life of happy leisure in a new house near Birmingham. Here he had a garret upstairs as his sanctum, for his wife, a stern disciplinarian, found it easier to teach her pugs to wipe their feet than to teach her husband to wash his hands. Boulton died in 1809 ; Watt died ten years later.

The first revolution, the revolution in the textile industries, was immensely accelerated but not caused by Watt's invention. Until that invention mills had to be placed by the side of streams, and most of the machinery was made of wood with metal fittings. Watt made it possible to set up mills anywhere, and, as engineering developed from his discovery of rotary motion, it was easy to provide metal machinery. Such machinery came into general use between 1825 and 1840.[1] Moreover, the application of steam power to spinning and weaving was followed of course by an immense expansion of the textile industries. The second revolution, that of transport, and the third, the use of machines for making machines, depended entirely on his invention. If one man in the history of the world is to be taken as the author of modern civilization, it is this melancholy mechanic, in whose outlook on life the superstitious might perhaps discern a warning of its ambiguous blessings.[2]

[1] Clapham, *Economic Development of France and Germany*, p. 21.
[2] This chapter is based mainly on the *Lives of Boulton and Watt* by Samuel Smiles, and *The Life of James Watt* by J. P. Muirhead. Since it was written a good short life of Watt has been published— *James Watt*, by T. H. Marshall.

CHAPTER IX

THE REVOLUTION IN IRON

In one sense the character of the Industrial Revolution is stamped most definitely on the textile industries, because in those industries inventions took the worker from his home to the factory; in another sense on the iron and steel industries, because the introduction of new processes in these industries had a direct and revolutionary effect on a number of others. The substitution of coal for charcoal in iron production led to a great development of coal-mining; the increase of iron production led to a great development of all those industries that used iron as a raw material. If the textile revolution made the new Lancashire, the iron revolution made the Black Country, and the industrial districts of South Wales and Scotland, described by an enthusiastic witness of the change as " country which Nature seemed to have damned to perpetual sterility," now " covered by the fruits of human industry and gladdened by the face of man."[1]

Iron is iron-ore or ironstone that has been exposed to heat in such a way that the metal is separated from the ore. The better the ore, the less the heat that is needed. Consequently primitive man, crude as were his methods of heating, often produced excellent iron, because he was using ironstone of high quality. Steel is a form of iron that has been submitted to complicated heating processes, and contains a certain proportion of carbon.

[1] Wilberforce, House of Commons, May 9, 1806. See *Parliamentary Register.*

At the beginning of the eighteenth century the production of iron in England was declining, while the subsidiary industries that used iron were expanding. These trades imported some two-thirds of the iron bars they needed, and their fortunes consequently depended on political contingencies. The decline of the domestic iron industry was due to the scarcity of fuel. Blacksmiths and nailworkers could use coal as their fuel, but the production of iron itself needed charcoal, and, in spite of the efforts of Parliament, the woods that supplied the charcoal had been shrinking fast. The most important effect of the Industrial Revolution in the eighteenth century was to release the iron industry from its dependence on charcoal. The importance of this revolution is clear if we glance at the methods and circumstances of the industry at the time.

Iron production fell into two main divisions. Iron was smelted in a blast furnace at the foundry, and "fined" at the forge. The foundry turned out pig-iron or else cast-iron objects; the forge converted pig-iron into bar-iron, suitable as raw material for the smith. At the foundry the iron-ore was first heated, broken up into small pieces and mixed with lime to fit it for the furnace. This was done in the open by means of fires of charcoal, wood, or coal. It was then placed in a furnace already heated with charcoal: for each basket of ore a basket of charcoal was added. Bellows were then applied, worked as a rule by water-power, and after intense heat had been kept up for fourteen days the iron was liquid enough to run out into sand furrows placed by the mouth of the furnace. There was a main furrow known as the "sow," and from this furrow some twenty-three smaller furrows were drawn, known as "pigs." When sufficiently cool, but still plastic, the iron in the several pigs was broken off from the iron in the sow. The iron in the sow was then broken up into a number of pieces of the length of the pigs. The pig-iron was now ready. Cast-iron articles were produced by ladling out the melted iron straight from the furnace and pouring

THE REVOLUTION IN IRON

it into moulds shaped it might be as chimney backs, or garden rollers or cooking vessels.

At the forge where bar-iron was made, the pig-iron was alternately heated and hammered. The heating was done in a forge called a " finery " or a " chafery " : an open hearth fed with charcoal and furnished with bellows. The pig-iron was reduced to the proper consistency in the finery, and then placed under a big hammer worked by a water-wheel, and beaten into a thick square or "half bloom." The heating and hammering were repeated a second time, and the product was then known as a " bloom," a square bar with knobs at either end. These knobs had to undergo more heating and hammering before they were turned into bars. The heating of these knobs was done at the forge, called the chafery.

When smaller bars or rods were required for the making of nails, the original bar was cut up at slitting and rolling mills. The slitting wheel, which was worked by water, broke or cut up the cold bar into short lengths; these lengths were then heated and when hot put under the rollers, also worked by water, and rolled flat. Finally they were put through cutters of different sizes. Coal could be used for the heating required in the slitting and rolling processes. When it left the slitting and rolling mills the iron was ready for the smith.

The production of iron employed several different categories of workers, from the charcoal burners, whose trade is still carried on by a few families in their turf cabins amongst Sussex coppices,[1] down to the workers in the metal industries such as nail makers and cutlers. A typical foundry would give employment to seven men; two keepers who controlled the charging of the furnace with ore or fuel, regulated the blast, and tapped the furnace when the metal was sufficiently liquid; two bridge servers who filled the baskets; two or three fillers who carried the baskets and charged the furnace. Women and children prepared the

[1] See Arthur Ponsonby, *The Priory and Manor of Lynchmere and Shulbrede*, p. 190.

ore and sorted out the cinders. At the forge "finers" or "hammermen" were employed to convert the pig- into bar-iron. These were the most highly skilled labourers. Each forge required at least two men and a boy, and a seven years' apprenticeship was usually demanded before a worker received the title of "Master of the Bloom." The master hammerman was a very important person, for there devolved on him "the varied functions of industrial leadership, technical training, and sometimes commercial dealing, in addition to the ordinary executive duties of the forge."[1] In the slitting and rolling mills a different set of workers were employed, but not much is known of their circumstances.

The dependence of ironworks, whether furnaces or forges, on woodlands, led to migrations from the Sussex weald long before the era of the great inventions. Measures taken by Elizabeth's Parliaments to save the diminishing forests of the weald drove Anthony Morley, a Sussex ironmaster, to set up works near Merthyr Tydfil. Ironworks and charcoal-burning were introduced in the Midlands and South Yorkshire, and district after district was stripped of its trees.[2] The growing of coppices for ironworks became a definite industry: in the north-west a more profitable industry than agriculture.

Ironworks needed water as well as woods: first, streams to provide the power for the bellows in blast furnaces and forges, for the hammers, and for the rolling and slitting mills; and secondly rivers or sea on which the bulky and heavy material could be transported. The Severn with its tributaries became the main waterway of the industry, and in the first part of the eighteenth century more than half of the domestic output of iron came from works connected with the Severn.[3]

The tendency of the industry to disperse in search of

[1] T. S. Ashton, *Iron and Steel in the Industrial Revolution*, p. 191.

[2] In 1727 a furnace was set up at Invergarry in the solitary wilds of the Highlands, where the abundant supply of wood was expected to compensate for the absence of every other advantage.

[3] Ashton, op. cit., p. 242.

fresh woods was counteracted to some extent by another tendency which brought forges, and still more, slitting and rolling mills, to the coal districts. For these forges and mills supplied the raw material for the smiths' industries, and the smiths' industries depended on coal, and flourished in districts where coal abounded. Consequently there was an early development of ironworks round the metal trade districts of Birmingham and Sheffield, as well as in the North East of England.[1]

[1] "About five miles from Newcastle are the iron-works, late Crawley's, supposed to be among the greatest manufactories of the kind in Europe. Several hundred hands are employed in it, insomuch that 20,000*l*. a year is paid in wages. They earn from 1*s*. to 2*s*. 6*d*. a day; and some of the foremen so high as 200*l*. a year. The quantity of iron they work up is very great, employing three ships to the Baltic, that each make ten voyages yearly, and bring seventy tons at a time, which amount to twenty-one hundred tons, besides five hundred tons more freighted in others. They use a good deal of American iron, which is as good as any Swedish, and for some purposes much better. They would use more of it if larger quantities were to be had, but they cannot get it. . . . They manufacture anchors as high as seventy hundred weight, carriages of cannon, hoes, spades, axes, hooks, chains, etc., etc. In general their greatest work is for exportation, and are employed very considerably by the East India company: They have of late had a prodigious artillery demand from that company. . . . As to the machines for accelerating several operations in the manufacture, the copper rollers for squeezing bars into hoops, and the scissors for cutting bars of iron—the turning cranes for moving anchors into and out of the fire—the beating hammer, lifted by the cogs of a wheel; these are machines of manifest utility, simple in their construction, and all moved by water. But I cannot conceive the necessity of their executing so much of the remaining work by manual labour. I observed eight stout fellows hammering an anchor in spots, which might evidently be struck by a hammer or hammers, moved by water upon a vast anvil, the anchor to be moved with the utmost ease and quickness, to vary the seat of the strokes. It is idle to object the difficulty of raising such a machine; there are no impossibilities in mechanics: an anchor of twenty tons may, undoubtedly, be managed with as much ease as a pin. In other works besides the anchor-making, I thought I observed a waste of strength."—Arthur Young, *Northern Tour* (1768), Vol. III, pp. 9-11.

The changes in the production of iron fall into three divisions: (1) Inventions connected with the name of Abraham Darby led to the use of coal in blast furnaces. (2) Inventions connected with the name of Henry Cort led to the use of coal in forges, and the introduction of the new processes of puddling and rolling. (3) Inventions connected with the name of James Watt led to the use of the steam engine to provide power for iron manufacture.

(1) **The use of coal in blast furnaces.** The scarcity of wood stimulated attempts as early as the sixteenth century to substitute coal for charcoal, the best known of the pioneers being the famous Dud Dudley. The difficulty about the use of coal was that its sulphurous fumes, though harmless in smiths' work, were bad for iron-ore in the furnace. It is now established that the man who learnt how to eliminate these bad effects was Abraham Darby the first, and not, as has often been supposed, Abraham Darby the second. The discovery was made as early as 1709. Abraham Darby (b. 1676) leased in 1708 an old blast furnace with some forges in Coalbrookdale, a Shropshire valley whose stream runs into the Severn. Before he came to Coalbrookdale Darby had patented a new method of casting pots in which sand was used instead of loam or clay. At Coalbrookdale he began to feed his furnaces with coal, and by using a particular kind of coal, and coking it, he produced satisfactory results in the making of iron for casting pots. A letter from the wife of the second Abraham Darby, published for the first time in Mr. Ashton's *Iron and Steel in the Industrial Revolution*,[1] gives a clear and authoritative account, which shows that though the first Darby used coal for making cast-iron goods, it was the second Darby who began to use coal about 1750 for making pig-iron of a quality that could be turned into bar-iron at forges. The family legend that Abraham Darby the second spent six days and six nights on the bridge of the furnace till the metal flowed out, when he was

[1] P. 249.

THE REVOLUTION IN IRON

carried off exhausted by his workmen, is probably connected with this discovery.

The Coalbrookdale Works grew rapidly from the single blast furnace with which the first Darby started, but the landscape still retained some of its beauty in 1776, when Arthur Young " viewed the furnaces, forges, etc., with the vast bellows that give those roaring blasts, which make the whole edifice horridly sublime."

" Coalbrook Dale itself " (he wrote) " is a very romantic spot, it is a winding glen between two immense hills which break into various forms, and all thickly covered with wood, forming the most beautiful sheets of hanging wood. Indeed too beautiful to be much in unison with that variety of horrors art has spread at the bottom ; the noise of the forges, mills, etc., with all their vast machinery, the flames bursting from the furnaces with the burning of the coal and the smoak of the lime kilns, are altogether sublime, and would unite well with craggy and bare rocks, like St. Vincent's at Bristol." [1]

Though the place " was very barren, little money stirring amongst the Inhabitants " when the first Darby arrived, his enterprises excited considerable opposition, opposition that was thwarted by the energies of the family and even by divine interposition, for

" a remarkable circumstance of awful memory occurs ; of a person who endeavour'd to hinder the horses which carried the Iron Stone and Coal to the Furnaces, from coming through a road that he pretended (he) had a right to oppose : and one time when he saw the horses going alone, he in his Passion, wished he might Never Speak More if they should Ever come that way again. And instantly his Speech was stop'd, and altho' he lived Several years after yet he Never Spoke More ! " [2]

The Darbys took out no patents, the second Darby refusing to " deprive the public of Such an Acquisition." [3] It is remarkable that a discovery so important attracted very little notice,[4] but the Darbys were quiet Quakers without

[1] *Annals of Agriculture*, Vol. IV, p. 168.
[2] From Letter of Mrs. Abiah Darby. Ashton, op. cit., p. 250.
[3] Ibid., p. 251.
[4] Sir J. Wrottersley, Member for Litchfield, said in the House of Commons, May 9, 1806, nearly 100 years after Darby's discovery and over twenty after Cort's invention : " Formerly and till within

advertising instincts, and the use of coal was only practicable at first in the casting branch of foundry work ; the second Darby learnt how to use it in making pig-iron, but for this purpose he had to choose particular kinds of coal.

Although Darby's discovery received little public notice it led to a great increase in the production of cast-iron wares, first in the Shropshire district, then in South Wales and Scotland. Cast-iron goods were cheaper than goods made of wrought-iron ; sometimes they were not only cheap but nasty. The Sheffield cutlers had good ground for their protests against the use of cast-iron to produce knives, forks, scissors and razors.[1] On the other hand, cast-iron was suitable for cooking-pots, stoves, firebacks, boilers and grates. It was at Coalbrookdale that the first iron rails were cast in 1767. They replaced wooden rails for wagon ways, and before the end of the century were largely used in collieries. The prejudice of the Office of Ordnance delayed for some time the use of cast-iron produced by coke and not by charcoal for munitions, but when this prejudice had been overcome, various firms, including the Carron Works in Scotland, the Walkers Works at Rotherham, and the Works set up in 1765 by Anthony Bacon near Merthyr Tydfil, derived great profits from Government contracts for the American War.[2] The first cast-iron bridge was built across the Severn in 1779, by the Coalbrookdale Company, who from conscientious scruples refused orders for war materials. Cast-iron was also used for water pipes, and, later, for gas pipes.[3]

(2) **The use of coal in forges.** The use of coal in forges, and the introduction of the processes of puddling

the last five or six years, wood or charcoal was the only material by which it was supposed that iron could be made ; but the ingenuity of the manufacturers led them to find a substitute in coak."— *Parliamentary Register.*

[1] G. I. H. Lloyd, *The Cutlery Trades*, p. 330 f.

[2] Ashton, op. cit., pp. 48 and 52.

[3] The Soho Works were first regularly lit with gas in 1803, and the first London Chartered Gas Company was formed in 1810. Smiles, *Lives of Boulton and Watt*, pp. 427 and 429 *n.*

and rolling are connected with the name of Henry Cort. Cort was born in 1740, and at the age of twenty-five was a Navy agent in London. Like Darby he had many predecessors, and of the patents taken out before his own, those of the Cranages and Peter Onions embodied principles of which he made use. Cort's right to be regarded as an inventor has been disputed; but even if it is true, as some writers urge, that he merely improved the inventions of others, he was at any rate the first to combine and co-ordinate these several improvements in a single process. His patents were taken out in 1783 and 1784. In Cort's method of making bar-iron the pig-iron when it came from the blast furnace was not put straight into the "finery," but was first heated in an intermediate furnace called a reverberatory furnace or air furnace, fed by common coal. In the door of the furnace there were holes through which the workmen could thrust bars and stir up or "puddle" the metal. The process has been thus described:

"When melted, it (the iron) spits out in blue sparks the sulphur which is mixed with it. The workman keeps constantly stirring it about, which helps to disengage the sulphureous particles; and when thus disengaged, they burn away in blue sparks. In about an hour after melting, the spitting of these blue sparks begins to abate (the workman stirring all the time), and the melted metal begins to curdle, and to lose its fusibility, just like solder when it begins to set." [1]

At the end of this process the iron was in clotted lumps called "loops"; these loops were then re-heated to welding heat and put under a forge hammer which hammered them into "half blooms" or small soft and ductile slabs. In the old method the half blooms would have been heated and hammered again; Cort re-heated them, but instead of hammering passed them under great rollers, afterwards called puddle rolls, which squeezed out the earthy particles:

"the slabs being extremely soft at the highest point of the welding heat, the force of the rollers consolidates the metallic parts into bar iron, and the dross is squeezed out and falls under the rollers." [2]

[1] *Annals of Agriculture*, Vol. XII, p. 370.
[2] Ibid., p. 373.

By this improvement Cort changed the whole history of the iron industry in England. Fifteen tons of bar-iron could now be produced in the time formerly required for producing a single ton, and, moreover, this could be produced by the use of coal in place of charcoal. Again the new bar-iron was of a superior quality, useful for every purpose except that of providing raw material for steel. In 1787 the Navy Board, after an elaborate test, decided to use Cort's iron instead of Swedish iron for its anchors.

Cort's personal fortunes followed a very different course. In setting up partnership with Samuel Jellicoe he had borrowed large sums from Samuel's father, Adam, and as security had handed over his patents and half the stock and profits. Now Adam Jellicoe was Deputy Paymaster of Seamen's Wages, and the loan to Cort came largely from public funds.[1] Adam Jellicoe died in debt to the Navy, and Cort's patents were taken as assets. Cort went bankrupt and lived from 1794 to 1800, when he died, on a pension of £200 a year. The patents in Government hands produced nothing. "As to the patents," ran the Official Report in 1805, "it does not seem that any opportunity has occurred, though endeavours have been used, to make it available to any profitable purpose." Whether this failure was due to official apathy or to the fear of litigation, is a disputed question. Thus Cort's inventions brought wealth to others and ruin to himself. Out of the vast fortunes they owed to Cort's brains, the ironmasters subscribed £871 10s. in 1811 for the benefit of his indigent descendants.[2]

[1] The use of public money by Paymasters for private purposes was common in the eighteenth century. Henry Fox, the first Lord Holland, amassed a fortune in this way.

[2] James Watt had given his opinion of the ironmasters as early as 1784. "Mr. Cort has, as you observe, been most illiberally treated by the trade; they are ignorant brutes; but he exposed himself to it by showing them the process before it was perfect, and seeing his ignorance of the common operations of making iron, laughed at him and despised him; yet they will contrive by some dirty evasion to use his process, or such parts as they like, without acknowledging him in it."—Smiles, *Industrial Biography*, p. 125 n.

THE REVOLUTION IN IRON

(3) **The use of the steam engine.** The third of the three great changes in the production of iron, the application of steam, should perhaps be associated with the name of John Wilkinson as well as with that of James Watt, for it was Wilkinson who devised a cylinder bored so accurately that no steam could escape. Steam power was applied to the actual processes of iron production in three ways : for the bellows, for the hammers, and for rolling and slitting.

The first use made of the steam-engine for the bellows was for pumping water to work them, but Wilkinson in 1776 used one of the first of Watt's steam engines for blowing blast furnaces directly, and this method soon became general. After Watt's invention of rotary motion in 1781, the steam engine was applied to working forge hammers, in 1782, and finally in 1784 it was used for the processes of rolling and slitting. The use of steam for these purposes made the iron industry independent of water-power, and from this time coalfields and ironworks developed side by side. The steam engine cheapened the production of coal, and the introduction of steam-blown bellows which improved the combustion, facilitated the substitution of coke for charcoal in the making of pig-iron and cast-iron articles. The use of steam, which made it easier to produce iron, increased at the same time the demand for cast-iron goods, since they were needed for the manufacture of steam-engines, and also for the machinery in the cotton and other industries which was worked by steam-engines.

The discoveries that reformed the production of iron were supplemented by a new process of steel manufacture invented by Benjamin Huntsman in 1740, between the discoveries of the first and the second Darby. Huntsman, born in 1704, and, like the Darbys, a Quaker, was a professional clockmaker, and also an amateur surgeon and oculist of considerable skill. He was discontented with the steel supplied to him for the purposes of his trade—perhaps also for the purposes of his hobby—and set to work to make an improved article. The ordinary method of producing steel was as follows : iron bars of good quality, coming as a rule from Sweden, were heated in a furnace with charcoal for twelve days ; this resulted in an increase in the carbon content, that is a certain hardening, and the product was technically called " blister steel " from the blisters or swellings on the surface. Blister steel was used for cheap goods.

To make better articles, this blister steel was broken up into small bits, bound up in faggots, and alternately heated and hammered to toughen it. The result was called " shear steel," and before Huntsman's discovery it was the highest quality obtainable. Huntsman, after many unsuccessful attempts, produced a superior article by taking blister steel and melting it in small clay pots or crucibles, in a furnace fed with coke to a heat so intense that all impurities were burnt away. The pots were then taken out with tongs, and the contents poured into iron moulds and afterwards forged into bars and slit up into convenient sized rods. This steel was called " crucible " or " cast " steel, and was close-grained, hard, tenacious, and yet flexible, suitable for watch springs, razors, knives and articles of the highest grade, whereas shear steel was used for ordinary cutlery and shears and edge tools.

Huntsman took out no patent for his discovery, but tried to keep his methods a close secret, an intention foiled, according to tradition, by the ruse of Samuel Walker, a neighbouring ironmaster, who on a cold and snowy night disguised himself as a homeless beggar and induced Huntsman's workmen to admit him to the warmth of the furnace.

The cutlers of Sheffield, with the conservatism of an old trade, were at first so prejudiced against the new steel that they refused to use it, and Huntsman found his market abroad, where French metal workers were quick to discover its advantages. After a futile attempt to prohibit the import of foreign articles made of Huntsman's steel, the cutlers accepted an invention that was to prove of immense importance to the history of their town and trade.

These changes introduced by the Darbys, Cort, Watt,

THE REVOLUTION IN IRON

Wilkinson and Huntsman led to a rapid expansion of the iron and metal industries. The output of pig-iron rose from 68,000 tons in 1788 to 125,000 tons in 1796, and 250,000 tons in 1806. At the beginning of the eighteenth century two-thirds of the bar-iron used in England came from abroad; in 1797 England was exporting bar-iron; by the late twenties of the nineteenth century the exports of British bar-iron exceeded the imports of foreign iron fourfold.[1] The growth of the industry due to technical changes and to improvements in organization received an unhealthy stimulus from the wars with America and France. The needs of the Government caused a great demand for English iron, followed when peace came by a slump and general distress. The industry had escaped the worst consequences of the slump at the time of the American Peace in 1783, because new uses were being found for cast-iron goods, and because, after peace, the American market for nails and hardware was reopened. But in 1815 the blow fell with full force; in many cases ironmasters were ruined and workers starved,[2] while

[1] Ashton, op. cit., pp. 98 and 99.

[2] A vivid description of the miseries of the Staffordshire iron workers was given in the *Annual Register* for 1816, p. 111:

"Within a small distance of my house is a large iron-work; the machinery of which extends for nearly half a mile. It was a noble manufactory. I passed by it one morning after its operations were suspended, and was exceedingly affected with the sight; a little before it was all animation and industry, affording the honourable means of livelihood to many thousands of my fellow-creatures; the silence that now pervades it spoke more eloquently and impressively to my heart than any language could possibly do; it was the silence of unmingled desolation. I visited a row of houses occupied by the workmen; the doors were used to be open, inviting the eye of the stranger to glance as he went along at their neatness, cleanliness, and felicity; little groups of healthful children were accustomed to appear about the cottages, full of merriment and joy, and the inhabitants, strong and healthy, saluted you as you went by. But the scene was lamentably changed . . . the cottages were closed —the inhabitants could not bear to have it known that they were stripped of their little ornaments—no children played around the doors—the very plants trained up in their windows had pined and died—one man only appeared, emaciated and ghastly, a living

the industry slowly readjusted itself to normal conditions, normal conditions meaning in this case a less violent succession of booms and slumps.

The changes that caused the rapid development of iron production led also to concentration of the several processes. As the industry made its home near the coalfields of the Midlands, Yorkshire, Derbyshire, and South Wales, it was easy to combine furnace, forge and mill in a single establishment. An early illustration of this concentration is given by Arthur Young in his *Tour through the North of England* (1768):

"Rotherham is famous for its iron works, of which it contains one very large one, belonging to Mr. Walker, and one or two smaller. Near the town are two collieries, out of which the iron ore is dug, as well as the coals to work it with; these collieries and works employ together near 500 hands. The ore is here worked into metal and then into bar iron, and the bars sent into Sheffield to be worked, and to all parts of the country; this is one branch of their business. Another is the foundery, in which they run the ore into metal pigs, and then cast it into all sorts of boilers, pans, ploughshares, etc., etc." [1]

Large scale organization became the rule. Ironmasters often owned their own collieries. In 1812 there were in the neighbourhood of Birmingham ten ironworks, each of which

spectre, as if the peaceful sepulchre had sent forth its inhabitants to fill with terror the abodes of the living.

"When I have told these poor creatures that the parish must find them food or labour, they have replied, 'Sir, they cannot do either;' and some who have fared the best when our manufactories were flourishing around us, have said: 'We would rather die, sir, than be dependent on the parish.'"

The ironworkers were reported to have an "excellent disposition" in spite of their privations; it was the colliers who supplied the "turbulent" element, but their turbulence was confined to harnessing themselves to wagons of coal which they dragged down South in some vague hopes of help. The ironworkers sometimes joined them. "They foolishly entertained the opinion that the Prince Regent could order them employment, and they prided themselves upon being willing to work for an honest livelihood." —Ibid., p. 95.

Vol. I, p. 115.

had cost over £50,000 to establish.[1] It is not surprising therefore to find a tendency to combine for purposes both of trade and politics that is in strong contrast to the scrambling individualism of the early cotton industry. For it required large capital to establish new ironworks, and it is obviously easier to secure concerted action in a trade which is in the hands of large capitalists than in one where a man with a hundred pounds can take his chances with good grounds for confidence. Ironmasters had begun early to co-operate in buying charcoal, and local groups would control prices; as the industry became centralized these local interests were fused and their organization was made stronger and more compact.[2]

An industry in such circumstances could exercise great influence on politics. The ironmasters played a large part in the defeat of Pitt's Irish Commercial Propositions in 1785, and they successfully resisted all attempts to raise money for the French War, out of which they were making large fortunes, by levying a tax on their prosperous industry. In 1796 Pitt proposed to put an Excise duty of 20s. a ton on pig-iron, with a corresponding Customs duty, but their agitation led him to drop the Excise, though the Customs duty, which, of course, they welcomed, remained. Ten years later, in 1806, the Ministry of All the Talents made another attempt to place some of the burden of the war on the broad shoulders of the iron trade; proposing an Excise duty of 40s. a ton on pig-iron. There was active opposition in Parliament, in which the ironmasters were supported by landowners and the several metal trades. It was contended, by some queer process of arithmetic, that the duty would be equivalent to a tax of 12s. on every horse employed in agriculture, that all manufactures would be injured, and "the comforts of the poor" diminished. The Government carried the proposal to the Committee

[1] Ashton, op. cit., p. 100.
[2] This process was made easier by intermarriage among the "dynasties" (as M. Mantoux calls them) of the iron trade.

stage, but there dropped it, beaten by the ironmasters' well-organized propaganda.[1]

The first cotton spinner families were largely of yeoman stock. The great ironmasters came, on the other hand, in many cases, from the secondary metal trades. Most of them had been blacksmiths, locksmiths, nailers, makers of hayrakes, spades and shovels, ironmongers, or brass workers.[2] Many of them were connected with the various Nonconformist societies that developed so rapidly at this

[1] " There were, at this time, 133 ironworks in Great Britain the proprietors of which met in the several districts, and deputed fourteen of their body to assemble in London, and arrange the information submitted to the committee of the House of Commons for imposing this tax."—Scrivenor, *History of the Iron Trade*, p. 97.

In the early eighteenth century, when England depended on foreign supplies of bar-iron, there had been struggles within the metal trades over import duties. The smiths wanted bar-iron to be free, with duties on the articles they manufactured; the forge masters wanted pig-iron to be free, and bar-iron to be taxed; the furnace masters wanted pig-iron to be protected. There were consequently vigorous controversies over the question whether bar-iron and pig-iron should be admitted from America in the early part of the century.

[2] Henry Darby, father of Abraham, was a locksmith; Aaron Walker a nailer; Crowley an ironmonger; Richard Reynolds son of an iron merchant; Anthony Bacon, who founded the Merthyr Tydfil works, had been an exporter of iron and ore; Crawshay, son of a Yorkshire farmer, ran away from home when 16, went up to London and got employment in an iron warehouse, where he succeeded his master and married his daughter. He bought the Cyfarthfa lease from Anthony Bacon, and made the works there the largest in the kingdom. He died in 1810 worth £1½ millions. C. Wilkins, *History of the Iron, Steel and Tinplate Trades of Wales*, p. 68.

Mr. Ness Edwards says that the capital for the development of the industry in South Wales came mainly from Bristol and London merchants, from English ironmasters who wanted to be nearer the seaports, and from financiers and stock companies. He cites as examples of the first the Bristol merchants who built works at Aberman, Tredegar, Risca and Dowlais; of the second the founder of the Guest family who went to Dowlais from Shropshire, and Homfray who went from Staffordshire. He traces the wealth of the Bristol merchants back to the slave trade. *Industrial Revolution in South Wales*, by Ness Edwards, p. 23 ff.

THE REVOLUTION IN IRON

time. Several were Quakers, some of whom refused War Office contracts, and forfeited large profits. Richard Reynolds, of Coalbrookdale, not only declined orders for cannon, but allowed his customers to fix a just price for his bar-iron, when the American War had disturbed the market. Thus the ironmasters included men who lacked the sharp and uncompromising business instinct that was supposed to characterize the successful leaders of industry. But as a rule they seem to have deserved the compliment that was paid them, that they were as unyielding as the material they manufactured. Austere and grim in their private lives they had little use for pleasure either for themselves or their workpeople. The great family of Lloyds opposed the project for a playhouse in Birmingham. John Wilkinson was perhaps a good type of the qualities that tradition connects with the dynasties of ironmasters. So far from refusing army contracts, he made cannon, if he is not traduced by the legends of the time, for the French Government, when England and France were at war. The great ironmasters invested their gains in coal mines, land, Government stock and finance ;[1] they passed like the cotton lords into the English aristocracy.

Cort's inventions and the introduction of steam-power increased the numbers and changed the character of the working population. The master hammerman disappeared. New classes were needed : puddlers, who stirred the liquid iron in the puddle furnace and then made it into what were called " puddle balls " : rollers, who dealt with the iron when it came to the big cylinders or " puddle rolls," after it had been through the puddle furnace and under the forge hammer, and various kinds of semi-skilled and unskilled

[1] Lord Foley, who died in 1766, left mines worth £7,000 a year, real estate worth £21,000 a year, and £500,000 in the Funds (Ashton op. cit., p. 226). Thomas Attwood, the famous Reformer, came from a family that combined iron production with banking. His father made a fortune in the iron trade. From the great iron and coal masters of South Wales came the families of the Guests and the Vivians.

148   THE RISE OF MODERN INDUSTRY

labour for the service of the trained engineers who superintended the new processes and managed the steam-power. This new population was collected from all parts; in early days furnace and forge were sometimes stopped in the summer for the workers who had been agricultural labourers to help with the harvest. When Ambrose Crowley established his ironworks at Sunderland he imported skilled workers from London and even from Liège.[1] When English ironmasters set up works in South Wales they brought with them skilled workers from Yorkshire, Shropshire and the Midlands.[2] The Carron Works in Scotland were started with English workmen " brought down at a great expense from Warwickshire, Staffordshire and Shropshire."[3] The work demanded strength and skill, and it was well paid.[4] Wages seem to have been fairly uniform, and to have varied little in time or place.[5] Hours were long, and in times of stress, irregular. In the early days Ambrose Crowley's men began at 5 a.m. and left off at 8 p.m., with two breaks of half an hour; towards the end of the century

---

[1] Ashton, op. cit., p. 197 f.
[2] Edwards, op. cit., p. 28.
[3] *Annals of Agriculture*, XXIX, p. 148 (1797).
[4] Wilberforce described the ironworkers as " mostly men of athletic make, and great bodily vigour, which was a consideration of no small consequence . . . since it had been too justly said that too many of our manufactures tended to deteriorate the physical constitution, and produce a feeble and degenerate race of men, without spirit or ability to defend their rights." House of Commons, May 9, 1806, in Debate on Pig-Iron Duty, *Parliamentary Register*.
[5] Mr. Ashton, op. cit., p. 190, gives these figures: the earnings of a furnace keeper, taken from the Wages Books at Horsehay, were in 1774 £2 9s. 6d. per month; in 1781, £2 16s. 7½d.; in 1797, £2 16s. 3d. Furnace labourers were paid 1s. to 1s. 6d. a day at Coalbrookdale and Horsehay. In 1826 the keepers at Horsehay had £1 a week; the fillers 15s.; the furnace labourers 14s. and the cokers and other unskilled labourers 2s. to 2s. 6d. a day. Payment by the piece, or time wages with a bonus, were the general rule in the foundry and forge. Arthur Young in his *Northern Tour* (1768) gives the wages at Walker's Iron Works near Rotherham: forgemen from 8s. to 20s. a week, average 12s. or 14s.; foundry men, from 7s. to 10s. a week.

THE REVOLUTION IN IRON 149

the hours at Coalbrookdale were from six to six, with an hour and a half off for meals. It must be remembered that before the introduction of steam-power, work was sometimes stopped altogether in the summer, when the water failed.

Tolerably full descriptions of the conditions of employment at the end of the period, in the ironworks of Staffordshire and Shropshire, South Wales and Scotland, are given in the *Report of the Children's Employment Commission*, published in 1842. Boys were employed in Staffordshire and Shropshire in the blast furnaces, at the puddle rolls and in the rolling mills ; young persons, that is boys between thirteen and eighteen, were employed in forging and as puddlers' assistants. The chief difficulty in the iron industry of this district arose in the blast furnaces. The work in most of these furnaces never stopped. The Commissioner gave a full account of it :

"The boys are employed in filling coke into baskets or barrows, and ironstone and limestone into what are called boxes, though a stranger would be apt to call them baskets. The young persons and the men convey these to the filling place at the top of the furnace. A certain proportion of each of the three is to be thrown on according to the orders which from time to time they receive, and to ascertain what is the proper quantity an acquaintance with coal, ironstone and limestone is necessary. A skilful and trustworthy person must see that the proper proportions are observed, and there are machines for weighing the ironstone and the limestone. As to coal or coke, the eye is sufficient, and the boxes or barrows are not weighed. There are generally two furnaces together, sometimes three, and when the people have put the charge into the one furnace they go on to put a charge into the next. There are never many minutes to rest, but occasionally time may be got to snatch something to eat and drink. Thus they go on all day until after four or five in the afternoon, and at that time the furnace is usually quite full. The boys and young persons then are allowed to go home and the blast is stopped for a time until the melted iron and the cinder be let off." [1]

On ordinary days one shift arrived at six in the morning and left at six in the evening, to be followed by a second

[1] Appendix to First *Report of the Children's Employment Commission*, Mines, Part I, p. 48.

shift which worked until six in the morning. But in order to enable the two sets to alternate, so that night-work should be done by each in turn, it was the custom to keep the shift that began to work on the Sunday morning until the Monday morning : a spell of twenty-four hours. The Commissioner reported that the ironmasters contended that to suspend the furnace would cause serious injury because the iron would set and pass into a solid state. Some ironmasters found it possible to stop the furnace for a few hours on Sunday : at Coalbrookdale and Horsehay the furnace was stopped for six hours from ten to four, at the Madeley Iron Works for rather longer, and a firm of the name of Addenbroke actually stopped the furnace for twelve hours on Sunday, though they reported that the consequence was the loss of a fourteenth of their product. The Commissioner held that the strain of the work was very severe, and the Commission said of the blast furnaces :

"This state of things, this perpetual and never-ceasing work, affects the physical and moral condition of the grown men, the young persons and the children, and this subject deserves particular attention." [1]

In the forge processes young persons acted as assistants to the puddlers at the puddle furnaces and to the men who worked the forge hammers. At the puddle rolls, or big cylinders, to which the iron was taken after being hammered, boys were employed to help the men rollers. A man stood at one end of the cylinders and one or two boys at the other end and the iron bar was passed to and fro between them. When it was sufficiently elongated the bar was set aside, and boys struck it from time to time with wooden mallets as it cooled to keep it straight. The Commissioner reported that the work at the puddle rolls was the most laborious work on which boys were employed in the ironworks of Staffordshire, and that as it could be done by men, there was no reason for using boys, except that they were

[1] Appendix to First *Report of the Children's Employment Commission*, Mines, Part I, p. 48.

THE REVOLUTION IN IRON

cheaper.[1] In the rolling mills, where the iron was again put through rolls or cylinders, the boys were employed as at the puddle rolls for the purpose of laying hold of the bar as soon as it had passed through the rolls, and passing it back again. The Commissioner reported: "They appear cheerful and able to go through with their work. Still they are exposed to great heat and breathe an atmosphere charged with effluvia from iron and coal." He found no immediate ill effects, but pointed out that it was not the place for "a boy to acquire strength of constitution."

The Commissioner employed in South Wales also described the Sunday working of the blast furnaces as one of the two worst abuses of that district, the other being the employment of young girls in the mines. In South Wales night work was the custom in the forges as well as in the furnaces, boys, young persons and men taking a shift from six to six. In the rolling mills young persons were employed at night, but not children. The children were as a rule employed and paid by the adult workers, who were often their fathers. One witness gave some figures of the earnings of adults, but they show such a wide margin as to be of little value. Founders, furnace men, puddlers and rollers earned, according to his account, from £1, £1 10s., £2, and £3 respectively up to £3 10s. The report contains statistics of the proportions of men, young persons and boys employed, but ironworks and collieries belonging to iron companies are not always distinguished.[2]

---

[1] Children's Employment Commission, *Report on Mines and Iron Works of Staffordshire*, pp. 51 and 52.

[2] The Report gives the following figures of persons employed in the Mines and Manufactures from which returns were obtained in Breconshire, Monmouthshire, Glamorganshire, Carnarvonshire and Pembrokeshire, p. 594.

	Males.	Females.
Adults (18 and upwards)	27,875	1,565
Young persons (13 to 18)	3,582	1,062
Children under 13	2,311	261
Total (36,656)	33,768	2,888

Of these, between seventeen and eighteen thousand were employed by the ironmasters of Monmouthshire.

In Scotland, where there were ironworks making marine engines, there appeared another type of boy worker, the rivet boy. Each squad of boiler-makers, consisting of three men, employed two boys, one to blow the fire in which the rivets were heated, the other to heat the rivets and pass them up to the boiler-maker with a pair of tongs. These boys began to work very early; some before they were seven. In other respects the conditions were much the same as in Wales.[1] An abuse here that was condemned in the strongest language was the negligence of the authorities about accidents. Coroners' inquests were not held, and a case of sudden death was only investigated if, owing to suspicion of manslaughter or murder, the attention of the Procurator Fiscal was called to it.[2]

When ironworks were set up in large centres of population like Birmingham and Wolverhampton, the changes in population and local life were comparatively gradual. In these places the growth of population was partly due to the development of the subsidiary metal trades that followed

---

[1] See p. 329. The Commissioner who reported on Scotland gave the following figures about the boys and young persons employed in foundries and ironworks.

Class.	Weekly earnings.	Day or Piece.	Paid by Master or Workman.
FOUNDRIES—			
Apprentice moulders	3s. to 12s.	P.	M.
Assistants	2s. 6d. to 6s.	D.	W.
Dressers	3s. 6d. to 6s.	P.	M.
Assistant dressers	2s. 6d. to 5s.	D.	W.
Rivet boys	3s. to 4s.	D.	M.
IRONWORKS—			
Pig moulders	2s. 6d. to 6s.	D.	W.
Catchers	6s. to 10s.	D.	W.
Straighteners, etc.	5s. to 8s.	D.	W.
Door drawers	4s. to 6s.	D.	M.
Puddlers' underhands	8s. to 12s.	D.	W.

See *Report on West of Scotland*, p. 336.

From another table on p. 328 it appears that catchers were aged from 12 to 16, straighteners from 12 to 14, door drawers from 10 to 15, and puddlers' underhands from 14 to 17.

[2] See p. 329.

THE REVOLUTION IN IRON

the revolution in the production of iron. Thus in Wolverhampton, when the Children's Employment Commission reported in 1842, there were very few large manufactures, but a very great number of small masters, such as locksmiths, key-makers, screw-makers, employing two or three apprentices apiece. Between 1801 and 1831 the population of Birmingham increased a good deal less rapidly than that of Manchester ; in the one case from 73,000 to 142,000, in the other from 94,000 to 237,000. The characteristic creations of the revolution in iron and steel were the settlements formed in country districts, where capital was applied on a large scale to coal mining and iron production. Canning, in opposing the suggested Excise Duty in 1806, gave an idyllic picture of these settlements :

"He also insisted that when a man had sunk a great capital in a business ; when he had established population in a place that was a wilderness before ; when he had settled a colony of dependents under him, the introduction of an exciseman to be, in a manner, the master of his establishment, would degrade and lessen the patriarchal authority which he was entitled to have over a family, as it might be called, which otherwise had none but him to look up to for support or countenance." [1]

There were cases in which Canning's phrase of a family was not altogether incongruous. Just as in the textile industries there were employers who provided libraries and dancing-rooms, so among the ironmasters there were benevolent employers like the masters of the Crowley Works near Newcastle. Here employer and workpeople co-operated to maintain a doctor, a clergyman, a schoolmaster and a contributory scheme of insurance against death, sickness and old age. But a very different picture is given in official reports of the Glamorganshire valleys and the iron districts in the West of Scotland, where vast bodies of men and women had been assembled from all parts of the country for work in the mines, furnaces and forges. There the power of the masters was absolute, and public spirit was

[1] House of Commons, May 9, 1806, *Parliamentary Register.*

at its lowest ebb. There were no shops, and the community bought what it needed at the stores set up by the employers. The abuses of the Truck system, bad enough in other districts, were rampant in South Wales. Parliament made an effort to control them. In 1749 the rule that wages should only be paid " in good and lawful money of this kingdom " was expressly extended from the woollen to the iron and other manufactures; in 1817 the provision was extended to the steel industries and to mines; in 1820 the law was stiffened. But the law was, for the most part, a dead letter. Before Boulton's coining presses were set to work, the masters could indeed plead that " good and lawful money " was hard to obtain, and it was not without reason that John Wilkinson issued his own coins and printed what were called his own " assignats " with which to pay his workmen. But the practice led to great oppression and hardship, and in the new districts redress was impossible, since masters and magistrates were the same persons. The Chief Constable of the Hundred of Caerphilly, writing from Merthyr Tydfil in 1827, lamented that in the whole district there were only two magistrates, one an invalid, the other a Member of Parliament,

"and these two Gentlemen are the principal individuals of two very extensive Iron Works, and employ from four to five thousand persons each, and they have very frequently to dispense justice among them, which I believe is very unpleasant." [2]

Lord Bute, Lord-Lieutenant of Glamorganshire, about the same time explained that owing to changes in the holding of property there were now in the manufacturing parts of the county only two Gentlemen, not proprietors of ironworks, qualified to be Justices of the Peace. " I find almost all the Iron Masters," he wrote, " in the Commission of the Peace." [3]

The workpeople were thus in a very disadvantageous position for defending themselves, because their masters controlled the price of provisions, owned their houses, and

[1] Ashton, op. cit., p. 228. [2] Home Office Papers, 52, 4.
[3] Ibid.

THE REVOLUTION IN IRON

administered justice on the bench. Moreover, the workpeople were a heterogeneous mass of immigrants, drunkenness was common, thrift was not encouraged, and, in a mixed population, where racial passions are never far below the surface, combination is difficult and quarrels frequent. There were strikes from time to time, but, as a rule, the Welsh ironmasters were more successful than their competitors in the Midlands in holding their workpeople down. In 1831, when the men's grievances were intolerable, there was open warfare lasting for several days in the Merthyr district, and the help of the 93rd Highlanders, the Glamorgan Militia and the Cardiff and Swansea Cavalry was needed before the workpeople submitted. In Merthyr itself the soldiers besieged in an inn killed fifteen people, and wounded sixty, in one volley, while outside the town a detachment of Swansea cavalry was disarmed by the workpeople who caught them in an ambush.

In the same year, stimulated by the example and the help of the National Association for the Protection of Labour, the ironworkers and colliers formed Union Clubs. The employers responded by turning off men who joined the union; the men met these tactics by brutal treatment of non-unionists. For month after month the struggle continued. When things were going badly with the men, the Union Clubs disappeared, and their place was taken by an organization known as "the Scotch Cattle." This organization consisted of the most violent men in the unions who, like the Irish moonlighters of a later date, attacked the blacklegs in their houses at night. It was found impossible to trace the authors of these outrages. The Commanding Officer of the district told Lord Melbourne that the Truck system was at the bottom of the trouble. This system was modified, and trade improved, with the result that the Scotch Cattle were not heard of again for a year. In 1834 trade unionism made another effort, the Union Clubs being restored and affiliated to Owen's Grand National Consolidated Trades Union of Great Britain and

Ireland. The ironmasters declared war at once, forcing their workmen to sign a document disowning the union, and, where necessary, closing down their furnaces. The union disappeared to make way again for the Scotch Cattle. The masters seemed to prefer brutal violence to organized combination, for the second limited their power, whereas the first, though it disturbed the peace and order of the district, and might imperil the lives of the leading ironmasters, was not so serious a threat to the profits of the industry.

Of the social conditions in the district of South Wales and Monmouthshire records have been left in official Reports as terrible as anything written in the English language. The district was surveyed and described for three different purposes : in 1842 by the Children's Employment Commission, in 1844 by the Health of Towns Commission, and in 1847 by the Commission on Education in Wales. The population, composed largely of immigrants, very many of them Irish exiles, were at the mercy of their employers. There was no public opinion outside the mines and the furnaces ; the great ironmasters and colliery owners ruled the countryside. The masters' shops supplied the wants of the workers ; their squalid huts supplied their shelter. Almost any passage taken at random from these reports will do as well as any other to illustrate the barbarous plight in which these men, who were making fortunes, placed and left the great settlements which Canning had described as their families. The Commissioners on Education gave this account of the housing :

"Even the physical condition of the people seems almost as if contrived for the double purpose of their degradation and the employers' profit. Some of the works are surrounded by houses built by the companies without the slightest attention to comfort, health or decency, or any other consideration than that of realizing the largest amount of rent from the smallest amount of outlay. I went into several of this class of houses in the north part of my district, and examined them from top to bottom. Men, women and children of all sexes and ages are stowed away in the bedrooms, without curtains or partitions, it being no uncommon thing for nine or ten people not belonging to the same family to sleep together

THE REVOLUTION IN IRON

in this manner in one room. In one instance I found three men sleeping in a sort of dungeon, which was nine feet by six feet in dimensions, without any light or air except through a hole in the wall, not a foot square, which opened into another room occupied by some women. . . . An immense rent in comparison to the accommodation is paid to the company or master for these miserable places. . . . There is neither drainage nor even light in the streets, although coal is close at hand. Nevertheless these places are little worse than others." [1]

In other places the Report described mud cabins, " in many instances a deserted cowshed converted into a human habitation " ; or beds used in turn by different sets of workers ; or houses in Merthyr, the centre of the iron trade, where " an open, stinking, and nearly stagnant gutter, into which the house refuse is, as usual, generally flung, moves slowly before the doors."

In these districts the citizen was so lost in the profit seeker that men who were founding great families sought to make fraudulent gain out of their shops, and even out of their schools.[2] They preferred their workmen to spend their money on drink, because they were afraid it might otherwise be used to strengthen their combinations.[3]

[1] *Report on Education in Wales*, 1847, Part II, p. 292.

[2] " Most of the large ironworks have their own schools connected with the establishment. The schools are often supported by a compulsory deduction from the wages of the labourers at the works. They are mulcted a penny or twopence in the pound, which frequently amounts to a very large sum per annum—a larger sum than is always appropriated to the school. . . . No account is rendered to the men, and the surplus money . . . may be pocketed by the firm and become a source of clandestine profit to the employer, without any possibility of detection."—*Report on Education in Wales*, 1847, Part II, p. 278.

[3] " Everything that would give the men foresight, prudence and discretion, and would teach them by teaching them to husband their means, would empower them in the strife and give them a vantage ground whereon to make their stand is discouraged by their masters. In order effectually to subjugate the men, and disarm them from power to strike, which is the great dread of the employers, they seem to strive to keep the men always at the end of their means, and their expenditure in advance of their income."
—*Report on Education in Wales*, Part II, p. 292.

South Wales gives perhaps the most complete picture of the worst features of the Industrial Revolution. There the economic man was not a mere nightmare of the new textbooks; he was an omnipotent force in a world existing for a single purpose. Where the revolution introduced the new system into a society with a past and a variety of interests, with inhabitants accustomed to the manners and outlook of citizens, its consequences were less sweeping. This was the case, for example, in Birmingham, where the Commissioners on Children's Employment in 1842 reported that there were more customary holidays, and that the hours of labour were shorter and less fatiguing than in any other large manufacturing town. In Manchester the Industrial Revolution was a more powerful force in the life and habits of the town, but Manchester had a history before the revolution, and, though its local government was scandalously unrepresentative and inefficient, great citizens, like Dr. Percival or Gould, the merchant, could find an audience for their warnings and their protests. From early days there was a society in Manchester which sought to enforce the observance of the Factory Acts. In Northumberland and Durham there were influences outside the great coal and shipping interests that could gradually modify the ruthless atmosphere of the new industry. In the early nineteenth century it was one of the scandals of the Northern coalfields that no inquests were held in the case of accidents. This abuse was redressed in consequence of the protest of a judge, a clergyman, and some local magistrates. In Staffordshire the Children's Employment Commission reported that some of the masters welcomed the inquiry.[1] In South Wales, on the other hand, the conditions were more like those of a newly discovered goldfield, or a plantation in tropical Africa; the restraints of tradition, of a common history, of experience in government, were all wanting. The

---

[1] "Mr. Alfred Darby said that it was a very proper inquiry, and that if they were doing any wrong it was right to point out to them that they might avoid doing so any longer."

Commissioner, reporting in 1841, could write as follows of deaths in the mines :

"When a man dies, the viewer looks at the body and sends for the coroner, and unless a case of suspicion is made out to the coroner, he does not come, but sends an order to the constable to bury, and frequently the coroner does not attend until there are five or six cases to clear."

Merthyr was the largest town in Wales and was thus described by the newspaper which represented the great ironmasters :

"The district through which our paper circulates is no longer an unknown nook, a petty hole and corner of the kingdom. It is the centre of important speculations and of great trade." [1]

As late as 1848 a writer could give this description of its streets and houses :

"The interior of the houses is, on the whole, clean. Food, clothing, furniture—those wants, the supply of which depends upon the exertions of each individual, are tolerably well supplied. It is those comforts which only a governing body can bestow that are here totally absent. The footways are seldom flagged, the streets are ill paved, and with bad materials, and are not lighted. The drainage is very imperfect ; there are few underground sewers, no house drains, and the open gutters are not regularly cleaned out. Dust bins and similar receptacles for filth are unknown ; the refuse is thrown into the streets. Bombay itself, reputed to be the filthiest town under British sway, is scarcely worse ! The houses are badly built, and planned without any regard to the comfort of the tenants, whole families being frequently lodged—sometimes sixteen in number—in one chamber, sleeping there indiscriminately. . . . In some of the suburbs the people draw all their supply from the waste water of the works, and in Merthyr the water is brought by hand from springs on the hillsides, or lifted from the river, sometimes nearly dry, sometimes a raging torrent, and always charged with the filth of the upper houses and works." [2]

A few miles away stood the palace of Cyfarthfa Castle, the home and monument of a man who had started life on

[1] The Monmouthshire *Merlin*, March, 1831, quoted Ness Edwards, op. cit., p. 73.
[2] C. Wilkins, F.G.S., *History of the Iron, Steel and Tinplate Trades of Wales*, p. 305.

the road to London " with all his fortune in his stout arm and his active brain," and had died worth a million and a half.[1] Never in the history of man had an age accepted with more headlong confidence the doctrine that private fortunes are the wealth of the State.

NOTES

Production of Pig-Iron in Great Britain

	Furnaces.	Output in tons.
1720 .	59	17,350 (more probably 25,000)
1788 .	85	68,000
1839 .	378	1,347,000

In 1835 France produced 290,378 tons.
In 1837 the United States produced 250,000 tons.

Distribution of Industry in Principal Centres

	1720. Furnaces.	1720. Output.	1788. Furnaces.	1788. Output.	1839. Furnaces.	1839. Output.
S.W. and South Wales . .	16	6,200	20	15,500	125	532,000
Staffs and Shropshire . .	8	3,100	33	31,800	142	453,000
Yorks and Derby . .	10	2,200	15	9,600	44	127,400
S.E. (Sussex, Kent, Hants)	15	2,000	2	300	None.	
Scotland. .	None.		8	7,000	50	195,000

See Scrivenor, *History of the Iron Trade*, pp. 57, 86, 87, 192, 266, 292, and Ashton, op. cit., pp. 98 and 235 ff.

---

[1] The Editor of the *Mechanic's Magazine* commented on some criticisms of the great ironmasters in a passage that sums up the philosophy of the age. " Persons in humble life should be the last —though, we regret to say, they are the first—to speak disrespectfully of the elevation of individuals of their own class, since in nine cases out of ten the individual is the architect of his own good fortune, and the rise of one man by honest means furnishes a ground of hope to all, that they may by a proper exertion of the powers which Nature has given them be equally successful."—Wilkins, op. cit., p. 85.

THE REVOLUTION IN IRON

Porter, *Progress of the Nation* (1851), p. 575, gives the following figures :

	British Iron made. Tons.	Foreign Iron used. Tons.	British Iron exported. Tons.	Hardware exported. Tons.	Remained for Home Use. Tons.
1806	258,000	27,411	36,925	4,629	243,857
1835	1,000,000	17,571	199,007	20,197	798,367
1848	2,093,736	20,437	619,230	18,105	1,476,838

Of the iron and hardware exported in 1835 the largest exports were to :

United States	63,000 tons.
Asia	29,000 ,,
Holland	15,000 ,,
France	15,000 ,,
Italy	13,000 ,,
Colonies of North America	12,000 ,,

See Scrivenor, op. cit., Table at end.

The price of bar-iron in different countries was given in 1825 by a French writer as follows :

France	£26 10s. per ton.
Belgium and Germany	£16 14s. ,,
Sweden, at Stockholm ; and Russia at St. Petersburg	£13 13s. ,,
England at Cardiff	£10 ,,

See Scrivenor, op. cit., p. 307.

CHAPTER X

THE REVOLUTION IN POTTERY

The making of pottery is older than the writing of history, and anthropologists use the potsherds on kitchen middens to reconstruct the life and mind of primitive man. For as soon as neolithic man took to shaping and baking clay into vessels to hold his food and drink, he liked to mould those vessels into forms that pleased his fancy. The pottery found in Lake Dwellings discloses in its rough geometrical patterns the instinct for design that was one day to produce the Sung Pot or the Greek Vase.

When men and women made their pots as they made their clothes, the articles they used, like the dress they wore, had an intimate association with their habits and ideas. The Industrial Revolution affected these two ancient arts in the same way, for the making of pots, like the making of clothes, became a factory industry; the output and range were so increased by invention, organizing power, the use of capital and skill, and by the development of the special natural resources of a particular district, that earthenware took the place of pewter in the plates and mugs of common life. Most people of the time would have considered the great dinner service made by Josiah Wedgwood for Catherine of Russia the greatest triumph of the new system. Catherine wanted each piece in the service to have a special decoration of its own, and Wedgwood met her wishes by providing a series of views of the seats of English country gentlemen. He had some misgivings about the scheme, for he thought he might offend those gentlemen who were either unrepresented in the collection or represented on the less distinguished pieces. This service was talked about all over Europe, but a more typical product of the new system was the willow pattern dinner set, produced by the thousand for the middle class household.

It is said that nine-tenths of the cotton spun in England is spun within eleven miles of Manchester. The home of English Pottery can be defined even more strictly. It is known all over the world that the Potteries are the Five Towns and the Five Towns the Potteries. From the beginning of the eighteenth century this part of Staffordshire, an area of twelve square miles embracing the towns of Burslem, Tunstall, Hanley, Stoke and Longton, had special advantages, and it so happens that though the industry has changed its character and methods, the district has always possessed the peculiar conditions that the industry needed in its new circumstances. Staffordshire itself has changed out of all recognition in the process, and no modern traveller could describe it as it was once described:

"when the little Pottery villages lying along a line of eight miles or more were divided by wide strips of green moorland; when the old timbered homesteads and stone-built country halls were surrounded by breadths of fields and gardens; when the country was extensively wooded; ... when the little streams which made their way from the higher gritstone were unsullied and unabsorbed." [1]

The natural advantages of the district were its coal and clay. Coal became important at the beginning of the eighteenth century as the supply of brushwood began to give out, and the clay, lying on the sloping base of a long chain of hills, had the qualities found in the clay of Samos and Etruria. These resources were at the service of the small potter, for Burslem had a population of enfranchised copyholders, men of initiative and independence, who could dig for clay and even for coal on the adjacent waste, while six miles away they could obtain the lead ore that they

[1] E. Meteyard, *Life of Josiah Wedgwood*, Vol. I, p. 97.

needed for glazing. Moreover, they had a good market in the neighbourhood, for Uttoxeter sent butter to London and used large butter pots for that purpose.

The industry that settled in this district in the seventeenth century was a peasant industry, and the equipment and establishments of the potters were so simple that primitive man would have found nothing very strange about them. All that the potter needed was an oven about 8 feet by 6, surrounded by a wall of clods or contained in a hovel roofed with clods and boughs, a few open sheds for drying the ware, and a sun pan, or open tank where the clay was first mixed and then left to evaporate until it was reduced to the right consistency. It was then kneaded like bread,[1] brought to the throwing wheel, and " formed as the workman sees good." The shaped article was then decorated with liquid clay and covered with a glaze of powdered lead before being put into the oven. The potters drew the cold oven on Monday, refilled it with new ware about Thursday, and fired it on Friday, giving it a last stoking up on Saturday morning, after which it cooled again till Monday. They were not abreast of the knowledge of the time, for they neglected the colouring properties of copper oxide, then in use throughout England. The ware was sold to travelling packmen who carried it about the country on horseback.

The conversion of this simple industry into a highly specialized and elaborate system was not due to some decisive invention or to the application of mechanical power. It was the result of a long series of improvements, great and small, both in the glaze and body of the ware and in the methods of manufacture and distribution, in consequence of which Staffordshire became the centre of the production both of earthenware and of china. Earthenware has a porous body covered with a vitrified non-porous

[1] For I remember stopping by the way
To watch a potter thumping his wet clay.
OMAR KHAYYAM

glaze; in rough pottery this glaze is apt to be defective and the vessel to leak. China or porcelain, on the other hand, is vitrified and non-porous throughout. In the latter part of the eighteenth century the Five Towns took the lead in the production of earthenware, but it was not until the early part of the nineteenth century that they took the lead also in the production of china.[1] With the first of these developments is associated the name of Josiah Wedgwood, with the second that of Spode.

Before the time of Josiah Wedgwood the local industry had made important advances. The introduction of tea drinking and the growth of clubs and coffee-houses in the seventeenth century increased the demand for good ware. The English pottery of the time could not match the best pottery of the Continent in quality or refinement, but at the end of the seventeenth century two Dutchmen of the name of Elers, said to have come over with William of Orange in 1688, taught English pottery to improve its primitive methods and to turn out ornamental red and black teapots of Staffordshire clay. One of the brothers stayed in London; the other established workshops and a kiln at Bradwell, where he worked in great secrecy. There was a legend that he had an elaborate speaking-tube from his house to the works, a mile distant, so that he might give warning of the approach of strangers. The legend is not without some basis, for voice pipes have been dug up in recent times designed to enable messages to be given from one part of the factory to another. But the secret, whether it was the Elers' own secret, or, as some said, a secret they had themselves stolen, was discovered by two local potters, who pretended to be very stupid and got taken into Elers' employment. Their names were Astbury and Twyford, and they, together with Dr. Thomas Wedgwood, built up the manufacture of salt-glazed stoneware which gave

---

[1] In the eighteenth century English china was generally made in London, Worcester or Derby. The Bow factory was started in 1744, Chelsea in 1745, Worcester in 1751, Derby in 1756.

the Potteries their reputation for the next half century.[1]

Salt-glazed ware was made by shovelling common salt through the top of the furnace on to the clay body, when it had been heated red hot in the oven. This gave the ware a coat, rather rough and pockmarked, of colourless glaze. The burning salt sent up dense clouds of black smoke, and by the middle of the century on Saturday afternoons, when the firing was going on, people had to grope their way about the streets of Burslem. Astbury introduced improvements of his own; for the body, made of local clay, was drab, and he whitened his ware by using white sand and also white clay that he brought from Devonshire. In 1720 he made another innovation, and one that the potter has good reason to remember. It was due, like so many inventions, to an accident. His horse, when he was travelling to London, suffered from an inflamed eye, and an ostler cured the horse by blowing into the eye a little fine powder, produced by putting a piece of flint into the fire, quenching it with water when red hot, and then pounding it. The potter, struck by the extreme whiteness of the calcined flint and the ease with which it was powdered, decided to experiment with it as a whitening ingredient. The results were wholly satisfactory so far as the ware was concerned, but the method that had cured the horse brought with this great technical improvement a lamentable evil, for the powdered flint is the cause of the terrible lung disease known as potter's rot. This disease attacked the men who crushed the flints as well as those who used the flint dust in their work as potters. The crushing process in its first form was so deadly that it was stated at the time that the healthiest and strongest man employed in it could not hope to live for more than two years, and that it was becoming difficult to find men who would undertake the task.[2] This process was made harmless by a London

[1] The introduction of salt glaze itself was probably due to the brothers Elers, but it is a disputed question.
[2] H. Owen, *The Staffordshire Potter*, p. 276.

painter named Thomas Benson, who was brought to Staffordshire with other workmen to decorate Lord Gower's house at Trentham. Benson patented in 1726 and 1732 a method for grinding the stones in a watermill.[1] He saved countless lives, but, like many inventors, fell himself into great poverty. Unhappily, no inventor appeared who could eliminate the fatal effects of the use of powdered flint body, and potter's rot or potter's asthma remained a scourge to the end of the nineteenth century.

The methods of making pottery, like those of most other industries, passed through a rapid succession of changes in the eighteenth century. Originally each piece was shaped separately by hand on the potter's wheel. This method was superseded in 1730 by the use of moulds into which the clay was run or pressed. The first moulds were made of porous clay from alabaster blocks, but about the middle of the century a more satisfactory material was found in plaster of Paris. This change led to the rise of new classes of pottery workers: carvers, designers and the men who forced the clay into the moulds. The last class, "flat and hollow ware pressers" as they were called, came to form the bulk of the men engaged in pottery work, for throwers were now only required for the most valuable articles. The smaller objects, such as handles, could be shaped by children. Mr. Arnold Bennett has given a description of the manner of their employment.

"In his new work he had to put a bit of clay between two moulds and then force the top mould on to the bottom one by means of his stomach, which it was necessary to press downwards and at the same time to wriggle with a peculiar movement." [2]

About the same time Enoch Booth introduced the custom of double firing, and substituted fluid lead glaze for the stone glaze that had been in fashion from the time of Elers. Under Booth's plan the ware was first fired, and then, in this state, which was known as a "biscuit" state,

[1] Meteyard, op. cit., Vol. I, p. 149 ff.
[2] *Clayhanger*, p. 31.

it was dipped into fluid lead glaze. The ware was then fired again in what was called a "glost" oven. This new lead glaze gave a smoother surface than the old salt glaze, and the process was cheaper, because there was less risk of damage in the oven. But Booth, like Astbury, had given a greater finish to the potter's ware at a terrible cost in human life and happiness; for, as Astbury had brought potter's rot, Booth brought the second of the curses of the trade, the lead poisoning which has given the Potteries so bad a name. The new glaze, being fluid, was less pernicious than the old dry powdered lead which was used before salt glaze was introduced, but the risks were increased by more complicated processes.

These several changes of method had made the complete reorganization of the industry on a capitalist basis inevitable. Astbury's improvements had led to the use and importation of clay from Devon and Cornwall, and from 1770 local clay was no longer used for the body, but only for the "saggers" or crates in which the ware was placed for firing. The demand for Staffordshire pottery had increased very rapidly, and an industry which imports and exports cannot be conducted on the scale of a peasant industry which uses local material and supplies a local market. The needs of the old industry had been served by master potters, each of whom had a single oven with six men and four boys, fired once a week, and drew a weekly profit of ten shillings, together with six shillings for his own labour. Before the middle of the century the more enterprising masters began to add oven to oven. Thus the factory arrived.

The Potteries had always found what they wanted. Nature had given them coal and clay when and where they were most useful; history had given them a society of enterprising freeholders, just when the industry demanded initiative and energy on a small scale; politics had sent them a Dutchman with technical skill just when the local art was at a standstill. Fate now brought on the scene a man who had all the gifts that were needed to organize

THE REVOLUTION IN POTTERY

the revolution in the life and transport of the Pottery district that was necessary to give full scope to this expanding industry.

For Staffordshire, with its rapidly growing trade, was still served by the roads that had served the peasant potters of the seventeenth century. These roads were narrow, rutty lanes, along which hard-worked horses and donkeys, muzzled to prevent them from eating the hedges, carried packs or panniers filled with crates of pottery or balls of clay. It is almost incredible that a hundred and fifty separate potteries employing 7,000 persons could import their clay and export their wares along such routes, for, according to the petition presented to Parliament in 1762, these wares were sent in vast quantities to London, Bristol, Liverpool and Hull, for despatch to America, the West Indies and almost every port in Europe. The clay and flints came to Liverpool and Hull. From Liverpool they were brought by the Mersey and Weaver to Winsford in Cheshire ; from Hull to Willington in Derbyshire. From Willington and Winsford they were brought on the backs of horses and donkeys to the Five Towns.[1]

The Potteries were rescued from this predicament by Josiah Wedgwood (1730–95), member of a notable and long-established family of master potters, who threw a great part of his remarkable energy and organizing power into the campaign for good roads and canals. He had a stiff battle, but he was admirable in agitation, and he was astute and indefatigable in pushing a Bill through Parliament. As a result of his efforts two turnpike roads were built which opened up the Potteries to the outside world, and enabled the potters to send their goods in carts, and in 1777 the Potteries were brought into touch with Liverpool and Hull by the Trent and Mersey Canal, and with Bristol by a branch connecting the canal with the Severn. The Potteries had good reason to thank Wedgwood at the

[1] See J. C. Wedgwood, *Staffordshire Pottery and its History*, from which book this account of the development of pottery is largely drawn.

time, and still better reason to regret him fifty years later, when the new Manchester and Birmingham Railway was kept out of the Potteries by the interests that he had defeated in the battle for the canals.[1]

Wedgwood was not less resourceful and untiring in improving the methods and organizing the commerce of the Potteries. He became famous at an early age for a cream-coloured ware, in which he used and developed the improvements of his predecessors. He delighted the taste of his time by his jasper ware, in which he imitated models from Greece or Rome, pressing white ornaments or figures on a coloured ground with remarkable skill. His reproduction of the Portland Vase is perhaps the best known example of his neo-classical work. His office and show-rooms in London became a fashionable resort.[2]

The changes in the manufacture of pottery in the last half of the eighteenth century were connected with the decoration of the surface as well as with the body and the glaze. Peasant ware had been decorated with liquid coloured clays called "slips" painted or brushed on the vessel before it was glazed and fired. Another method of decoration was enamelling. This was done by painting the surface when the ware was finished, and the painted pot had to be reheated in a small stove, till the glaze and paint were fused together. Enamelling was a separate trade and was sometimes done in a separate place; a shopkeeper

[1] "A hundred years earlier the canal had only been obtained after a vicious Parliamentary fight between industry and the fine and ancient borough, which saw in canals a menace to its importance as a centre of traffic. Fifty years earlier the fine and ancient borough had succeeded in forcing the greatest railway line in England to run through unpopulated country five miles off, instead of through the Five Towns, because it loathed the mere conception of a railway."—*Clayhanger*, p. 3.

[2] Messrs. Rackham and Read, in their notable volume on *English Pottery* (1924), give Wedgwood credit for evolving forms that combine fitness for purpose with undeniable beauty of line. "He had the insight to see that even under the factory system there was room for the exercise of an artist's intelligence.'

might keep an enameller to decorate his special cups and saucers. As the Staffordshire trade increased enamellers began to set up in the Potteries, and by 1750 enamelling was a regular trade in the district.

Wedgwood took great pains to obtain good enamellers, men and women; but hand painting was expensive for " useful ware," and in 1755 Saddler and Green of Liverpool invented a method of printing the outlines of a design on ware that was already glazed, leaving the colours only to be filled in by hand. Turner of Worcester found a more satisfactory process of printing in 1780, and his process, applied first of all to Worcester china, was introduced into Staffordshire by the first Spode. By this new process a coloured pattern was printed on the biscuit ware before it was dipped into the glaze, with the result that after the second firing the colours below took a rich soft tone from the surface glaze. " Blue printing " was specially successful, and the famous willow pattern was designed by the same Turner who had invented this process of printing under glaze. Blue printed ware became so cheap and popular that at the end of the eighteenth century it superseded all other forms of earthenware for " useful ware." The two potters most prominently associated with these new developments were the Spodes. The first Josiah Spode (1733-97) made his fortune out of " blue printed "; the second (1754-1827) introduced bone paste into the body of china and porcelain, and so made cheap china possible. He began to produce this new mixture in 1800, and North Staffordshire soon became the centre of the china industry.

The history of the Potteries illustrates several aspects of the Industrial Revolution. The whole life of the Five Towns was transformed. Instead of being a district living to and by itself, inconveniently connected with neighbouring districts, the Potteries came to take a brisk part in the economic system of a wide world. Whereas in the eighteenth century the roads were few and bad, and goods were carried on the backs of horses and donkeys, by 1818 there were eleven coaches passing through the Potteries each way, travelling between Liverpool or Manchester and London or Birmingham. The journey from Newcastle to London took fifteen hours.

Perhaps the most surprising fact about the development of the Potteries was that mechanical power played no part in it. Steam indeed replaced water-power for the flint and glaze mills about 1793, but otherwise the work was still done by human muscles.

"Up to the year 1845 the potting industry had remained almost completely unaffected by the scientific and mechanical improvements which had greatly modified some trades, and had revolutionized others. The whole range of mechanical science was almost solely represented in the manufacture of potting by the throwers' wheel —identical in mechanical principle, and practically so in form, with that used by the ancient Egyptians—and the turners' lathe." [1]

It was not, indeed, till the seventies of last century that mechanical power replaced human strength in the important process of flat and hollow ware pressing. The workers had been able to delay its introduction for more than twenty years.

But though mechanical power was not brought into use, the whole system of work had been changed and made more intricate. It was no longer the custom "for the journeymen potters to pass from one kind of labour to another, just as impulse or convenience prompted." Their world was now divided into definite and separate categories: the throwers, the turners, the oven men, the flat pressers, the hollow ware pressers, and the dippers, to mention only a few of the main classes.[2] Women began to find

[1] H. Owen, *The Staffordshire Potter*, p. 63.

[2] Arthur Young, writing in 1768, reported that about 6,000 people were employed in the potteries at Burslem; if preparatory work were included, about 10,000. Four years previously Wedgwood had introduced cream-coloured ware. The following were the wages: Grinders (of flints), 7s. Washers and breakers, 8s. Throwers, 9s.–12s. Engine lath men, 10s.–12s. Handlers (fixing handles, sprigs, etc.), 9s.–12s. Gilders—men, 12s.; women, 7s. 6d. Pressers, 8s.–9s. Painters, 10s.–12s. Moulders in Plaster of Paris, 8s.—*Northern Tour*, Vol. III, p. 252 and 254 f.

employment; children who had always been employed in the industry were employed in far greater numbers. Subsidiary and complementary trades grew up in the district, such as those of the crate-makers, the colour-makers, the lathe-makers, and it was difficult to recognize in the highly organized manufacture which exported by canal in 1836 not less than 73,500 tons of china and earthenware [1] the rough peasant industry which had so lately sent its rude goods to market on the backs of horses or donkeys.

How far had these improvements in technical skill and organization been followed by improvements in the condition of the workers ? Josiah Wedgwood, writing in 1783, declared that early in his life

"the inhabitants bore all the marks of poverty to a much greater degree than they do now. Their houses were miserable huts; the lands poorly cultivated, and yielded little of value for the food of man or beast, and these disadvantages, with roads almost impassable, might be said to have cut off our part of the country from the rest of the world, besides rendering it not very comfortable to ourselves. Compare this picture, which I know to be a true one, with the present state of the same country. The workmen earning near double their former wages—their houses mostly new and comfortable, and the lands, roads, and every other circumstance bearing evident marks of the most pleasing and rapid improvements." [2]

The second Josiah Wedgwood, sent up by his fellow master-potters to protest before Peel's Committee in 1816 against the suggestion to apply a Factory Act to the Potteries, declared it to be "a remarkably healthy, happy and contented district." [3] He did not add that the masters had

[1] In 1836 Stoke-on-Trent received by the canal 70,000 tons of clay and stone from Devon, Dorset and Cornwall, 30,000 tons of flint stone from Gravesend and Newhaven, 9,000 tons of timber, 4,000 tons of borax, cobalt, bone ash and colours, 7,000 tons of iron, steel and copper.—Wedgwood, op. cit., p. 165 f.

[2] From Josiah Wedgwood's *Address to the Young Inhabitants of the Pottery*, 1783.

[3] The hours at Etruria he stated to be from 6.30 a.m. to 6 p.m. in summer, from 7.30 a.m. to 6 p.m. in winter. In both cases one and a half hours were allowed for meals. Dippers, whose work was unwholesome, worked from 8 or 9 a.m. to 5 p.m. Men generally lost about a day a week, and made it up by working overtime till 9 p.m.

a short way of enforcing content. An agitation for Parliamentary Reform next year was promptly dealt with. " As soon as it was known that a Club was forming, the Master potters assembled and went to Massey's House and destroyed all the Books and papers."[1]

There were other aspects of the workers' conditions on which the employers were silent. The Pottery workers formed a union in 1824, which came to grief, and another, established by Doherty in 1830. This second union was encouraged by the best masters, and wages, pitifully low, were raised by 25 per cent. But in 1836 the masters combined in a Pottery Chamber of Commerce and a great struggle ensued in which serious grievances, in the method of hiring and the method of payment, were the chief subject of contention. Men were engaged at Martinmas, and were bound to make ware at a fixed price for the following year. If they broke their agreement they could be imprisoned. The employer, on the other hand, was under no obligation to provide adequate work. He could keep a man in a situation in which there was only work for one day a week, and a man who left that work could not get employment elsewhere without a written discharge. The second injustice was not less flagrant. The hollow ware pressers and throwers, the great mass of the workpeople, were paid by the piece, and they were refused payment for a piece which left their hands in good condition and was then spoiled in the oven. Even if a spoiled piece was afterwards sold at a reduced rate, the presser or thrower often received nothing.

The strike against these conditions was one of the most desperate in trade union history. Sheffield and Manchester sent £7,000 to the 20,000 potters on strike ; strike pay never exceeded 6s. for married and 4s. for single men a week. The winter was severe. The contest seemed hopeless, when several hundred men took all that was left of their clothes and furniture to the pawn shops, and paid

[1] Home Office Papers, 39. 76.

THE REVOLUTION IN POTTERY

into the strike funds the money they had raised in this way. These heroic measures kept the strike alive long enough to wring concessions from the masters, who guaranteed four days' work a week; undertook to pay for all ware damaged otherwise than by the maker and to break in the man's presence any article for which they refused him payment.

Unfortunately the struggle had been too much for the resources of the union, and the old evils soon returned. In 1836 the new Chamber of Commerce stated that the average wages of a man, which three years earlier had been 17s. to 21s., were now 21s. to 28s., of a woman 10s. to 15s., instead of 6s. to 11s., and of a child of fourteen 3s. 6d. to 4s. instead of 3s. to 3s. 6d. But these wages, which were probably an optimistic estimate, were eaten into by a bad system of allowances which was not abolished till 1844. The abolition of these allowances and of the truck system was the result of a new and more successful combination among the workmen, who conducted a newspaper called *The Potter's Examiner*.

The facts that were brought to light in these struggles were supplemented in the revelations of the Second Report of the Children's Employment Commission (Trade and Manufactures) published in 1843. In the seventy-nine principal manufactures or factories of porcelain and earthenware in Staffordshire there were 12,407 persons employed, of whom 7,192 were above twenty-one years of age, 3,715 between twenty-one and thirteen, and 1,500 under thirteen. In the first category there were 4,544 males and 2,648 females; in the second, 1,949 males and 1,736 females; and in the third, 978 males and 522 females. The children were hired by the journeymen. Apprentices were bound for seven years, as "twifflers," saucer-makers, printers and pressers, but most apprentices were only nominally indentured, because neither parent nor employer as a rule would pay the yearly stamp duty of £1. Consequently boys often ran away when half taught, to take work at wages below the good workers' wages; they could earn from 7s. to 18s. a week, and would find lodgings away from home.

Of the tasks left to children some, such as painting, burnishing, figure-making and engraving, were carried on in an airy and commodious room, and gave the children education in an elegant art. The case of the children employed in dipping and scouring was far different. In the first of these processes one or two adults would bring the ware in the biscuit state to the tubs and dip it. The article would then be passed to boys for shelving and drying. The fluid in which the article was dipped contained a considerable quantity of lead and sometimes of arsenic, and the employment was therefore unhealthy. In scouring, finely pulverized flint was brushed off the "saggers." The particles floated about the room and covered the young women employed in the process "as plentifully as flour the miller." But there were other classes of children whose lot was still worse. These were the "jiggers" and the "mould runners." Each man employed two children, one to turn the jigger or horizontal wheel, the other to carry the ware from the wheeler to the hot house in moulds. These children worked in a temperature varying from 100 degrees to 130 degrees. It was calculated that in a working week of 72 hours, a child would walk over seven miles a day, carrying 3,840 lb., besides the constant mounting of steps. Darius Clayhanger, it will be remembered, began his career as:

"'mould-runner' to a 'muffin-maker,' a muffin being not a comestible but a small plate, fashioned by its maker on a mould. The business of Darius was to run as hard as he could with the mould, and a newly created plate adhering thereto, into the drying-stove. This 'stove' was a room lined with shelves, and having a red-hot stove and stove-pipe in the middle. As no man of seven could reach the upper shelves, a pair of steps was provided for Darius, and up these he had to scamper. Each mould with its plate had to be leaned carefully against the wall, and if the soft clay of a new-born plate was damaged, Darius was knocked down. The atmosphere outside the stove was chill, but owing to the heat of the stove, Darius was obliged to work half naked. His sweat ran down his

THE REVOLUTION IN POTTERY

cheeks, and down his chest, and down his back, making white channels, and lastly it soaked his hair." [1]

The men worked by the piece and often idled in the early days of the week, making a great effort between Wednesday and Saturday. In these cases the child, instead of leaving his work at six, would be kept at it till nine or ten o'clock. One large employer said that many of the children in his works worked 15 hours a day, with $1\frac{1}{2}$ hours for meals. On the other hand, accidents were uncommon, as there was no machinery except at the grindery mills, and there was a general consensus of opinion that the children were seldom treated harshly. The average wage of the children was 2s. a week. Children's wages were much higher in Derbyshire (3s. a week under thirteen, and from 4s. 6d. to 10s. above thirteen), and in the West of England, where the youngest children received from 2s. 6d. to 4s. 6d. a week. The physical condition of the children employed as scourers, mould-runners, and jiggers was deplorable. "Not many scourers live long," and the mould-runners and jiggers, almost without exception, were pale, thin and stunted in growth. The places of work were divided into three classes. Recent buildings were large, airy, well ventilated and commodious. The older buildings, "by far the most numerous," some able to hold 800, others only 50, were, with very few exceptions, "low, damp, small, dark, ill-ventilated and unwholesome." The worst character of all was given to the rooms where Egyptian ware was produced. The sanitary conditions were disgraceful.

It was not till the sixties that the Factory Acts were extended, at the instance of Francis Wedgwood and some other masters, to the Potteries, and not until the end of the century that effective measures were taken against the deadly diseases which had followed the technical improvements of the eighteenth century, and had given the trade so infamous a name.

[1] *Clayhanger*, p. 29.

CHAPTER XI

THE REVOLUTION IN COTTON

OF all the changes in the world's economy that followed the great mechanical inventions, the revolution in the cotton trade was perhaps the most striking.

Down to the eighteenth century the manufacture of cotton was an Eastern industry, and it was mainly in the tropical countries that cotton clothes were worn. With the Industrial Revolution the industry becomes a Western industry, and Europe is largely clothed in cotton goods. At the same time the products of this Western industry are shipped in great quantities to the East. Thus Europe becomes the centre of a manufacture which draws its material from sources outside Europe, and sells its wares in countries where that raw material is grown.

As China was the early home of the silk, so India was the early home of the cotton industry. The exquisite skill and the delicate touch of the Hindu were so suited to its needs that this industry remained for centuries a chief source of India's wealth, although no improvement was made in the methods and implements that it used. India clothed a good part of Southern Asia. When the Portuguese came to India in the fifteenth century, India was sending calico and fancy goods, chintzes, handkerchiefs, cloths mixed with silk and woven with patterns to various parts of Asia, and muslins to Persia, Arabia, and Egypt. India's part in this export trade was passive, resembling England's part in the export trade in English wool in the tenth and eleventh centuries. At that time the English export trade was conducted, not by Englishmen, but by the merchants of the Hanse League. In the same way the Indian export trade before the arrival of the Portuguese was conducted, not by Indians, but by Chinese, Japanese, and Javan merchants. These merchants formed settlements in the Indian ports, and the Dutch and British merchants who formed settlements in these ports in the sixteenth century stepped into their place in the economy of India's commerce.

The circumstances under which the pushing Europeans who had found the new route to Asia were drawn into India are interesting and characteristic. The Spice Islands were of course the great attraction in the East, and cotton itself was very inferior to pepper as a prize of conquest or monopoly. But the Dutch bought the pepper and spices of the Islands with Indian cotton-made goods, for these goods played an indispensable part in the commerce of Asia, as a principal article of exchange. This cotton cloth the Dutch bought from merchants in Achin or Bantam, and they were charged exorbitant prices. To escape this imposition they decided to trade with India, and get their cotton direct from the Indian merchant. The English went to Gujarat partly for the same reason : they wanted to buy silk from Persia, and being shut out of the Spice Islands and unable in consequence to use spices in exchange, they had to find somewhere else an article of barter. Thus the Dutch and the English went to India largely in order to use cotton for trading in the East. The Dutch had of course a commanding position, and they were able to sell hides from the Spice Islands to Japan, and so to obtain from Japan silver with which to trade in India. England, being less fortunately placed for general commerce in the East, had even stronger reasons for wishing to develop direct trade with India.[1] France did not make any Indian connexions until much later.

[1] See Morland, *From Akbar to Aurangzeb*, p. 34. Yet the instructions issued to the Commander of the Third Voyage in 1607 show that the markets of the Red Sea were thought to be more hopeful than those of India. The fleet was to try for trade at Aden, but if Aden could not be reached in the trading season, the fleet was to make for Gujarat.

The Europeans did not merely continue the system that they took over from the Asiatic merchants and shippers to whose place in the Indian economy they had succeeded. The Portuguese, to whom the Pope had given India, extended the export trade to West Africa and to Brazil, where coarse Indian goods made suitable clothing for negro slaves, and to North West Africa, where muslins were made into turbans and girdles. The Dutch and English went further, finding markets in Western Europe for Indian cotton goods, and organizing production in their Indian settlements. It was the custom for the merchant to advance money to the weaver, and the Europeans developed this custom, collecting weavers into factories.[1] Indian fabrics became so fashionable in England and on the Continent that the woollen interests took alarm and tried, in most places with some success, either to exclude or to penalize Indian stuffs.[2]

This Asiatic cotton industry had already made some sort of a beginning in Europe. It was introduced into Spain by the Moors in the tenth century; by the middle of the twelfth century fustians made in North Italy and light cottons made in Piacenza were exported from Genoa, and in the fourteenth century fabrics containing cotton were produced in Flanders and round Ulm and Augsburg. England received the industry much later, for it was brought by Protestant refugees from Antwerp in 1585. As cotton was a new industry foreigners were allowed to practise it, and it was exempt from restrictions that regulated the woollen trade. By 1641 the industry was established in Manchester, an unincorporated town, and therefore free from the impediments that were to be found in smaller towns that possessed a charter.[3] Several kinds of coarse cotton goods, mainly fustians, were produced for domestic consumption and for export to the Levant. Still at the beginning of the eight-

[1] Unwin, *Indian Factories in the Eighteenth Century*, Manchester Statistical Society.
[2] E.g. Act of 11 and 12 William III, cap. 10.
[3] Baines, *History of the Cotton Manufacture*, p. 92.

THE REVOLUTION IN COTTON

eenth century the cotton wool imported was under 2,000,000 pounds, and in the middle of the century it was not much more. But the conditions in England were specially favourable for the development of the industry so soon as mechanical power came into use. Those conditions included a climate specially suitable for the spinning of cotton;[1] a number of streams flowing from the hills into the Ribble and the Mersey which supplied water-power for the first mills; coal in abundance and coal in the right place.[2]

The revolution that resulted in making the cotton industry the most important industry in England was due to a series of inventions in England, and one in the United States. Kay (1733) invented the flying shuttle, a device by which the weaver could pull a string and so send the shuttle on its course through the web, without throwing it himself by hand. This invention made it possible for one man to manage a wide loom, whereas previously a man had to stand on each side of the loom. By 1760 the flying shuttle was in general use for cotton weaving, and the weavers wanted more yarn than the spinners could supply. But the next three inventions revolutionized spinning, with the result that the yarn spun in England, instead of being inadequate to domestic needs, was so abundant as to become an important article of export. The first of these inventions was Hargreaves' multiplied spinning wheel, commonly known as the spinning jenny. This invention, patented in 1770, made it possible to work eight, and later as many as a hundred spindles by a single wheel, whereas the old spinning wheel worked one spindle and one alone.

---

[1] "The spinning districts of Lancashire are so suitable because they lie on the slopes of hills facing west, upon which the damp breezes from the Atlantic discharge their moisture, as they are driven to higher levels by the slope of the ground."—Chapman, *The Lancashire Cotton Industry*, p. 153.

[2] Knowles, *Industrial and Commercial Revolutions*, p. 27. Moreover the water in Lancashire is specially suitable to bleaching and calico-printing processes. C. R. Fay, *Life and Labour in the Nineteenth Century*, p. 290.

Neither weaving nor spinning had as yet passed into the factory. Both these inventions could be used at home and had merely increased the productive capacity of the weaver and the spinner working in their cottages. The man who made spinning a factory, rather than a domestic task, was Arkwright, who patented in 1769 and 1775 a roller spinning frame worked by water-power: the development of a process invented by Wyatt and Paul thirty years earlier.

The mule, invented by Crompton in 1779, was given its name because it borrowed features from the water frame and from the jenny as well, for it had both rollers and spindles. It was a most important invention, because as it produced a finer and stronger thread than the Arkwright frame it enabled Lancashire to rival the fine fabrics and muslins of India.[1] The first mules were worked by hand.

During the last twenty years of the eighteenth century, when the cotton manufacture was advancing, in spite of political opposition from the woollen interest, with a rapidity unprecedented in history, there were large mills where Arkwright's water frame produced warp, while Hargreaves' jennies and Crompton's mules were producing the weft, sometimes with the help of gin horses, in dwelling-houses or small establishments. But in 1785 another invention, Watt's steam-engine, was used for the first time in a cotton mill, and as steam-power displaced water-power, mules and spinning frames were more and more collected into factories and worked by the new power. Spinning thus became a factory industry in all its processes.

Weaving, on the other hand, passed into the factory more gradually. The first power-loom was invented by a parson, named Cartwright, brother of the reformer Major Cartwright, in 1785. His machine was useless at first, even after he

---

[1] "Thus in the invention of the mule may be found one of the chief causes of the transference of the seat of an industry to the Western from the Eastern world, where it had been situated from time immemorial."—Daniels, *Early English Cotton Industry*, p. 129.

THE REVOLUTION IN COTTON

had improved it in 1787, but his improved machine was further improved in 1803 by Radcliffe of Stockport, who invented a dressing machine, and by Horrocks, also of Stockport, who invented power-looms of iron the same year. In 1813 there were 2,400 power-looms in Britain; in 1820, 14,150; in 1829, 55,000; and in 1833, 100,000.

The inventions changed not merely the power but the character of the industry. Before the Industrial Revolution spinning and weaving were both cottage industries. The use of the term "spinster" on marriage certificates reminds us that spinning was the occupation of the normal woman, and the spinning in the cottages was done by women with their children helping in the subsidiary processes. The weaving on the other hand was done mainly by men. The Industrial Revolution brought a complete transformation. The machines that took the place of the women's skill were worked by men, the weaving machines were tended by women and young men: both in spinning and weaving the adults depended on the labour of large numbers of children.

This revolution in the methods of the industry caused of course an immense increase in its productive capacity; in 1764 England imported less than 4,000,000 pounds of cotton wool, in 1833 more than 300,000,000. Where did this vast quantity come from?

In the eighteenth century there had been a scarcity of raw cotton, and England and France competed for it.[1] But in 1793 the saw-gin, invented by Whitney, revolutionized the conditions of the industry in this respect also. Before that time the cleansing of American short-stapled cotton was a troublesome and expensive process, for in this plant the cotton adheres very closely to the seeds. Consequently the only cotton available for export was the long-fibred cotton known as Sea Island cotton which grew in a few specially favourable places. It is not surprising that under these circumstances English manufacturers had set little value on the thirteen colonies as a source on which to draw for

[1] Knowles, op. cit., p. 40.

raw cotton, holding that the West Indian Islands were in this respect, more important.[1] But Whitney's invention for separating the cotton from the seed removed all the difficulties that hindered the export of short-staple cotton, and the United States rapidly became the most important source in the world for the raw material of the new industry. In 1793 the United States exported less than half a million pounds of raw cotton; in 1795 over 6,000,000 pounds; in 1801 over 20,000,000; in 1803 over 40,000,000; in 1810 over 90,000,000, and in 1820 over 120,000,000 pounds; in 1832 over 300,000,000.[2] Of this export England took just under 220,000,000; France 77,000,000; in the same year Britain imported 37,000,000 from British possessions, of which 35,000,000 came from the East Indies and Mauritius; 20,000,000 came from Brazil, and 9,000,000 from Turkey and Egypt.[3] The price of the raw material in 1833 was less than one-fourth of its price in 1798.[4]

When it had become profitable to grow cotton on a great scale in her river beds, it was certain that sooner or later the United States would take to cotton spinning; the tariffs of 1828 hastened a development that was in any case inevitable. In 1800 America had two cotton mills; in 1810 102. In 1786 a model of Arkwright's first machinery was smuggled into the United States. By 1831 there were

[1] In 1786 our import of cotton (20,000,000 lbs.) was thus distributed: British West Indies, nearly 6,000,000; French and Spanish Colonies, 5,500,000; Smyrna and Turkey, 5,000,000; Portuguese and Dutch Colonies, 3,600,000.—Baines, *History of the Cotton Manufacture*, p. 304.

[2] Baines, op. cit., p. 302. Cairnes, *Slave Power*, p. 208.

[3] Baines, op. cit., p. 309. Mahomet Ali started growing cotton in Egypt in 1823. He began with long-stapled cotton, and in 1827 he imported the seed of Sea Island cotton. By 1825 he sent over 100,000 bags to England. He set up twenty-three or twenty-four cotton-spinning mills with great trouble, and got French and Italian artisans to teach his people the use of machinery, but the climate and other conditions were unfavourable.—Baines, op. cit., pp. 306 and 307.

[4] Baines, op. cit., p. 352.

nearly 800 mills working 1,246,000 spindles and 33,000 looms.[1] America was in much the same position as France, for whereas Britain consumed 234,000,000 pounds of raw cotton, the United States consumed 77,000,000 pounds, and France 74,000,000. The United States sent a third of their cotton manufactures to Mexico, and the rest to South America.[2] In 1832 our cotton exports to the United States were worth over £1,000,000, and to South American States over £2,000,000.[3]

Meanwhile the fortunes of war and politics had put the people that had taught mankind the old method of cotton manufacture in the power of the people that was teaching mankind the new. The last struggles between England and France in the East had ended. England was beginning to close her grasp on India when Crompton and Arkwright were perfecting their inventions. In the old days India, with its warm climate, had been a poor market for Western cloth, and one motive for the search for a North-West passage had been the desire to reach the temperate provinces of China where British cloth might find customers.[4] England was now producing something that India could buy. A British Government was not likely to treat a distant community that had come under its control more unselfishly than it had treated the British Colonies in America. Heavy duties were placed upon Indian cottons and silks in the home tariff, and when the Indian market, hitherto the monopoly of the East India Company, was thrown open in 1813, the duties imposed on cotton goods entering India were merely nominal. In 1831 a petition was presented from natives of Bengal, complaining without success of the British duty of 10 per cent. on manufactured cottons, and 24 per cent. on manufactured silks.[5] The effect of political control,

[1] Daniels, *Cotton Trade at Close of War*, and Ure, *The Cotton Manufacture of Great Britain*, Vol. I, p. xl.
[2] Ure, ibid.
[3] Ure, op. cit., Vol. I, p. 331.
[4] H. O. Meredith, *Economic History of England*, p. 206.
[5] Baines, op. cit., p. 81.

combined with the inventions, was seen in the figures of our trade with India. Very little yarn was sent to India in 1815; over 3,000,000 lb. in 1829; 800,000 yards of British cotton cloth in 1815; 45,000,000 yards in 1830.[1] In 1832 British cotton exports to the territories of the East India Company (which included China) were worth £1,500,000.[2] If India had been in the hands of a rival Power anxious either to develop a new cotton industry of its own, or to develop a native cotton industry in India, Lancashire would not have found so rich a market for her yarn and piece goods.

Thus Britain became the chief cotton power in the world, partly by skill, industry and enterprise, partly by the accidents of her position and the nature of her resources, partly by the issue of her struggle with France in America and India. If we want to appreciate the remarkable advance in human organization that this change represents, we have only to consider that a raw product grown in America was brought to England, worked into finished clothes, sent to India, and there sold in immense quantities, though the raw product was also grown in India, and the industry practised by Hindoos who had at once exquisite skill and the simplest wants in the world. An industry that clothed the poor could not maintain itself under these artificial conditions unless it had been conducted in every detail with the greatest efficiency.[3] One incident alone of this extraordinary history must strike the mind. Raw cotton condensed into compact bales by the aid of a hydraulic press was brought from the Atlantic States to England for one halfpenny to five-eighths of a penny a pound; from Egypt for three farthings a pound, and from Madras for a penny a pound.[4]

[1] Daniels, *Early English Cotton Industry*, p. 130 n.
[2] Ure, op. cit., Vol. I, p. 331.
[3] " In the year 1782 Arkwright's cotton twist of No. 60 exceeded the price of the raw material by 20s. a lb. or, in other words, he charged £1 sterling for spinning one pound weight of cotton into such yarn. In 1830 the charge for spinning one pound of such cotton yarn by the mule was only 1s. 6d."—Ure, op. cit., Vol. II, p. 424.
[4] Ure, op. cit., Vol. I, p. 144; Baines, op. cit., p. 317.

THE REVOLUTION IN COTTON

It is interesting to compare the completeness of this mechanism with the story told by Gibbon of Justinian's efforts in the sixth century A.D. to secure silk for his rich subjects. Before that time the silk from China was brought by a caravan journey of 243 days from the Chinese Ocean to the sea coast of Syria, and Persian merchants who frequented the fairs of Armenia used to deliver it to Roman customers. But these caravans were plundered by Tartan robbers and Persian kings, and then the merchants tried, without much success, another route over the mountains of Tibet and down the streams of the Ganges or the Indus. Justinian's problem was ultimately solved by two Persian Christian monks who brought the eggs of Chinese silkworms from China to Constantinople in a hollow cane and so introduced the silk industry into Europe.[1]

If we consider the perfection of machinery and organization that marked the conduct of this new industry, from the first of its operations to the last : the packing of the raw cotton, its final production in a thread so fine and delicate as to deserve, in the description of a writer of the time, the epithet bestowed on the robes of Dacca, " the woven wind," and the shipping of piece goods to China and India, we must regard the Manchester mills or the Liverpool Cotton Exchange or the ships making their way to the Far East with their cargoes, as the most spectacular proof of man's growing power over the conditions of his life. When we turn to the picture given by Francis Place of the consequences to the habits and cleanliness of the English people that followed the introduction of cotton clothing that could be washed, we see what a vast improvement the new industry brought with it in comfort, manners and health.[2] Unfortunately this series of triumphs has another and a more melancholy aspect, which must be considered in a later chapter.

---

[1] Gibbon, *Decline and Fall of the Roman Empire*, chapter xl.

[2] See M. Dorothy George, *London Life in the Eighteenth Century*, p. 60. But this improvement has its price, for it tied the woman to the washtub, since cotton clothes are washed much more often

NOTES

Some idea of the comparative progress of different countries is given in a table published in 1835 by the President of the Chamber of Commerce at Mulhausen:

"The manufacture of cotton-wool amounts, in—

	Kilogrammes
Great Britain, to	150,000,000
France	40,000,000
United States	18,000,000
China, being one-half the crop of India	15,000,000
Switzerland, Saxony, Prussia and Belgium	17,000,000
Total	240,000,000 "

By this calculation England's share of the total production of the world was five-eighths or about 63 per cent.[1]

In the year 1835 the cotton industry employed in the weaving and spinning factories 220,134 persons in the following classes:[2]

Male and female under 13	28,771
Male 13–18	27,251
Male over 18	58,053
Female over 13	106,059

Porter, *Progress of the Nation*, p. 193 (Edition of 1851), gives a table for the year 1839, from which the following details are taken:

	Males	Females
Under 13	7,106	5,221
13 to 18	41,287	56,810
Over 18	64,548	84,364
	112,941	146,395

than their predecessors. See on this point some remarks on the homespun clothing of the Greeks in Zimmern's *Greek Commonwealth*, p. 50 *n*. Another respect in which woman's work at the washtub was increased by the Industrial Revolution was the immense increase of smoke and dust in the air.

[1] Ure, *Cotton Manufacture of Great Britain*, Vol. I, p. lxxiv.

[2] Hutchins and Harrison, *History of Factory Legislation*, Appendix A, p. 304.

THE REVOLUTION IN COTTON

Porter (p. 192) gives figures abstracted from the Factory Inspectors' returns which show that there were 1,262 cotton factories in the United Kingdom in 1835, of which 683 were in Lancashire, 126 in the West Riding, 109 in Cheshire, 92 in Derbyshire, and 159 in Scotland.

The beginnings of the cotton factory system have been made the subject of important researches in recent years. *The Early English Cotton Industry*, published by Professor Daniels in 1920, threw a good deal of new light on this topic. The following year an invaluable set of early account books and other papers was discovered in the ruins of Oldknow's mill at Mellor, and the late Professor Unwin, with the help of his University colleagues, was able to construct from these papers a striking and illuminating picture of the career of this significant personage. See *Samuel Oldknow and the Arkwrights*.

PART III

THE SOCIAL CONSEQUENCES

CHAPTER XII
THE SHADOW OF THE SLAVE TRADE

OVER the history of English daring and enterprise in the new seas, there was from early days a terrible shadow. When the chief commerce of the world passed from the Mediterranean to the Atlantic a vicious system passed with it, and this system, developing rapidly and forming new vested interests, became in the eighteenth and nineteenth centuries the chief scandal in the life of Europe and of Europe's colonies. For this the English people had to bear in the eighteenth century the principal guilt, because the shame as well as the prize of this slave trade fell naturally to the power that came to the front in the rivalry of the sea.

The great African slave trade grew up because the masters of the new world wanted labour to develop its mines and plantations. To supply this labour they resorted to the device that had been used in mediæval as well as in ancient Europe.[1] In the thirteenth century the mamelukes, who had made themselves masters of Egypt, could not find at home all the men they wanted for their armies or the women they wanted for their harems. They consequently employed agents in different parts of the world, drawing especially on the races living round the Black Sea. Here the Genoese held the chief ports, Caffa and Tana, and the

[1] See W. Heyd, *Histoire du Commerce du Levant au Moyen-Âge*, Vol. II, pp. 555–563.

trade was controlled by the Genoese authorities, who ransomed any slave who said he was a Christian. But there was also a slave trade supplying the needs of Italy, for the Italians had acquired the habit of using slaves in their commercial colonies, and when they returned to Italy they brought slaves with them. Marco Polo had a Tartar slave. Venice and Genoa took the chief part in bringing these slaves to Italy; the Genoese law assigned certain ships to this service and laid down sanitary regulations against overcrowding. The price of slaves rose between the thirteenth and the fifteenth centuries, and before the fall of Constantinople there were complaints in Venice that slaves were becoming scarce. Apparently most of the slaves that went to Egypt were men destined for the army, and most of those who came to Italy were women destined for the pleasure or the service of their masters. In both cases the country round the Black Sea was the chief source of supply. Nothing perhaps illustrates the loss of European power and prestige at the fall of Constantinople more vividly than the clause in the commercial treaty between the Sultan and Venice which allowed Venetian traders to import Christian slaves, but forbade the trade in Mahommedans.[1]

The efforts of the Portuguese sailors and traders who explored Africa and crept down the coast in the early fifteenth century were animated partly by the desire to found a Christian Empire, and partly by the desire to import slave labour. The Portuguese used to buy slaves from the Moors, and they hoped, by acquiring possessions in Africa, to dispense with the middleman and supply themselves as Venice and Genoa had done. When therefore the Portuguese wanted labour for their distant American plantations, their mind turned easily to this expedient, and the slave trade in the New World was introduced in this way by the Portuguese and the Spanish. By a curious and tragical irony part of the responsibility for this terrible curse falls on the memory of a man whose long life was spent in a superb effort to

[1] Heyd, op. cit., Vol. II, p. 317.

protect the Indians from their new taskmasters. This was the great Las Casas, called anti-Christ by the Spanish settlers because of the heroic courage and resolution with which he combated, both in the Indies and at home, their cruelty and selfishness. Las Casas submitted a scheme for the solution of the problem created in Spain's new dominions, where the Indians were dying rapidly under savage ill-treatment, which included, together with many excellent provisions, a clause allowing a strictly regulated importation of negroes. Las Casas never ceased to reproach himself in later life for this advice.

England's share in the trade begins later. The first English slave trader was the famous Sir John Hawkins, who sailed to Sierra Leone in 1564, kidnapped negroes and exchanged them with Spaniards in San Domingo for hides and other commodities. Next year Elizabeth's Government lent him the "Jesus" for a second slave-catching expedition; on his return he was knighted and chose for his crest a negro in chains. But it was not until well into the seventeenth century that the English plunged into this commerce; the agent of the African Chartered Company, established in 1618, told a negro who offered him slaves, that Englishmen did not buy or sell "any that had our own shapes."[1] Unfortunately, though the English trade began late, it developed faster than the slave trade of any other country. For some time a Chartered Company, known as the African Company, enjoyed a monopoly, but in 1698 the trade was thrown open, and all British subjects were given the right to carry fire and sword into any African village and to kidnap the inhabitants. The importance attached by Governments to the trade was illustrated by the exemption granted to ships carrying slave cargoes from the general obligation to contribute to the maintenance of the forts along the coast. In the last twenty years of the seventeenth century 300,000 slaves were transported from Africa in British ships. In 1689 we had engaged ourselves

[1] R. Coupland, *Wilberforce*, p. 71.

THE SHADOW OF THE SLAVE TRADE

to supply the Spanish West Indies with slaves from our great slave market in Jamaica, and twenty years later we became, by an article in the Treaty of Utrecht (1713), the principal slave-trading nation of the world.

For one of the chief uses to which we put Marlborough's victories at Ramillies, Malplaquet and Blenheim was to secure for British ships the contract known as the *Assiento*, transferring to British subjects for thirty years the monopoly, enjoyed first by the Dutch and then since 1701 by the French, in the supply of slaves to the Spanish colonies.[1] The Government gave the contract to the South Seas Company and the greatest energy was thrown into the trade.[2] Colonial Parliaments were not allowed to prohibit or to restrict its operations. When South Carolina and Virginia passed measures for that purpose they were overruled. Bancroft estimated that in the hundred years preceding the prohibition of the trade by American Congress in 1776, 3,000,000 slaves had been imported into the European colonies and settlements on British ships. But the British slave trade continued for thirty years after this declaration of Congress, and it was most active during the war with France. Pitt, though he had made the most famous of his speeches on the wrongs of Africa, yielded to the panic of the hour, and so far from checking the trade, allowed it to increase. For every slave that was crossing the Atlantic under the British flag when he became a Minister, there were two crossing the Atlantic when he died.[3] Wilberforce, the slaves' indefatigable champion, was in despair.

In 1806 Austerlitz killed Pitt and brought his great rival to power. Fox, who was resolute in defying the vested interests and the honest fears that had been too strong for Pitt, was mortally ill, and a supporter of the trade rejoiced

[1] The *Assiento* was surrendered in 1750 for £100,000. C. Hayes, *Political and Social History of Modern Europe*, Vol. I, p. 312.

[2] The Company undertook to send 4,800 pieces of proper height and age annually for thirty years, the sovereigns of Spain and England each to receive a quarter of the profit.

[3] Lecky, op. cit., Vol. V, p. 342.

to watch the new Minister's legs swelling with the dropsy. But Fox lasted till the autumn, and in those few months, with death knocking at his door, he put this scandal at last out of our public life, thereby ensuring that it would sooner or later be put out of the public life of Europe.

Throughout the last part of those two centuries the British West Indies had played in the new world the part the island of Delos had played in the second century B.C. At Delos the slave merchants used to buy the wretched captives swept into the market from the countries washed by the Mediterranean and distribute them over the Roman world. In the West Indies the negroes brought from Africa were exposed for sale under the British flag and sent to serve European masters all over the new world. Rome paid for her leading share in the slave trade of the ancient world by the exhaustion of the springs of her life, for her agriculture declined, her peasants became mean whites, and the population of her capital a mob living on largesses.[1]

Great Britain did not pay so directly as this. Slaves never pushed Englishmen on this island from their work or their homes. In 1772, in a case brought before the courts by the courage and tenacity of Granville Sharp, it was decided that, though British merchants could make what profit they would by stealing men and boys in Africa and selling them as slaves to Englishmen in the West Indies, a slave who set foot on the soil of England ceased to be property in the eyes of the law. In this respect there is an interesting contrast between the cases of Rome and England. Rome imported slaves to work in Italy: Englishmen counted it one of the advantages of the slave trade that it discouraged the competition of British colonists with British manufacturers. For the slaves were chiefly needed for industries like sugar planting, in which Englishmen at home were not engaged.[2] Thus

[1] See Grundy, *Thucydides and the History of his Age*, chap. 4, on the similar effect of the employment of slave labour in Attica.

[2] " Were it possible for white men to answer the end of the negroes in planting, must we not drain our own country of husbandmen,

THE SHADOW OF THE SLAVE TRADE

it might be argued that England had escaped the fate of Rome and that she so used the slave trade as to make it a stimulus rather than a discouragement to native energy and skill.

Yet England did not escape the penalty. For it was under this shadow that the new industrial system took form and grew, and the immense power with which invention had armed mankind was exercised at first under conditions that reproduced the degradation of the slave trade. One of Aristotle's pupils collected all the causes of the destruction of human life and then showed how much more man had suffered from man than from nature. The Industrial Revolution would have served his purpose, and might have taken as its motto a reflexion of Cicero, " *Homines plurimum hominibus et prosunt et obsunt.*" The factory system was not like war or revolution a deliberate attack on society : it was the effort of men to use will, energy, organization and intelligence for the service of man's needs. But in adapting this new power to the satisfaction of its wants England could not escape from the moral atmosphere of the slave trade : the atmosphere in which it was the fashion to think of men as things. The West Indian slave trade was in this sense worse than the slave trade of the ancient world, for the slave brought from Delos to Italy was originally in theory an enemy whose life had been spared, but the slave carried to Jamaica was so much muscle to be appropriated and used by anybody who was strong enough to seize it. He was not a human being who had lost his rights in battle, but a piece of merchandise ; he had

mechanics and manufacturers too ? Might not the latter be the cause of our colonies interfering with the manufactures of these kingdoms, as the Palatines attempted in Pennsylvania ? In such case, indeed, we might have just reason to dread the prosperity of our colonies ; but while we can supply them abundantly with negroes, we need be under no such apprehensions ; their labour will confine the plantations to planting only."—*The African Trade,* by Postlethwayt, 1745, quoted by Cunningham, *Growth of English Industry and Commerce,* II, p. 315.

no more in the way of human rights than a bar of iron, or a mass of lumber picked up by a wanderer on the sea shore.[1]

An age that thought of the African negro, not as a person with a human life, but as so much labour power to be used in the service of a master or a system, came naturally to think of the poor at home in the same way. In this sense it was true, as Dr. Bridges once suggested,[2] that the steam-engine was invented too soon for the happiness of man: it was too great a power to put in the hands of men who still bought and sold their helpless fellow-creatures. The new industrial system was placed on this fatal foundation. In the days of the guilds the workman was regarded as a person with some kind of property or status; the stages by which this character is restricted to a smaller and smaller part of the working classes, and more and more of the journeymen and apprentices fall into a permanently inferior class have been described by historians. In the early nineteenth century the workers, as a class, were looked upon as so much labour power to be used at the discretion of, and under conditions imposed by, their masters; not as men and women who are entitled to some voice in the arrangements of their life and work. The use of child labour on a vast

[1] See De Quincey, *Works*, Vol. IX, p. 176 (edition of 1897). De Quincey points out that slavery assumed "a far coarser and more animal aspect" in the West Indian slave trade than in the Roman world. Men, women, and children were all viewed "in relation to mere prædial uses." Compare *Chapters from Baxter's Christian Directory*, edited by J. Tawney, p. 28. "How cursed a crime is it to equal *Men* and *Beasts* ? Is not this your practice ? Do you not buy them and use them merely to the same end, as you do your *horses* ? to labour for your commodity ! as if they were baser than you, and made to serve you ? "

In Rome slaves were of course artists, doctors, teachers, secretaries, as well as household or plantation slaves. In the houses of men like Pompey they resembled a staff of civil servants. It is significant that when transported felons and indented servants were put up for sale in Maryland, schoolmasters fetched a lower price than tailors and weavers. See M. D. George, op. cit., p. 147.

[2] See F. S. Marvin, *The Living Past*, p. 202.

scale had an important bearing on the growth of this temper.

The children of the poor were regarded as workers long before the Industrial Revolution. Locke suggested that they should begin work at three; Defoe rejoiced to see that in the busy homes of the Yorkshire clothiers " scarce anything above four years old, but its hands were sufficient for its own support." The new industrial system provided a great field for the employment of children, and Pitt himself, speaking in 1796, dwelt on this prospect with a satisfaction strange to modern minds, and disturbing even to some who heard him.[2] One of the most elaborate of all Bentham's fantasies was his scheme for a great series of Industry Houses, 250 in number, each to hold 2,000 persons, for whose work, recreation, education, and marriage most minute regulations were laid down. An advantage he claimed for his system was that it would enable the apprentices to

---

[1] " It is evident, in short, that the long hours of work were brought about by the circumstance of so great a number of destitute children being supplied from the different parts of the country, that the masters were independent of the hands; and that, having once established the custom by means of the miserable materials which they procured in this way, they could impose it on their neighbours with the greater facility."—Fielden, *Curse of the Factory System*, p. 12.

Fielden's view is corroborated by a paper drawn up by some employers at Burley, in 1802, who opposed legislation for the protection of apprentice children on the ground that " Free labourers cannot be obtained to perform the night work, but upon very disadvantageous terms to the manufacturers."—See *Town-Labourer*, p. 152.

[2] In asking the House of Commons to reject Whitbread's Minimum Wage Bill on Feb. 12, 1796, Pitt said: " Experience had already shown how much could be done by the industry of children, and the advantages of early employing them in such branches of manufactures as they are capable to execute." General Smith, speaking later, said: " As to employing the industry of children, such a measure, however apparently productive, ought not to be adopted without particular regulations. I have seen children, in some parts of the country, employed in branches of manufacture that were highly pernicious, whose wan and pale complexions bespoke that their constitutions were already undermined."—See Debrett's *Parliamentary Register*.

marry at "the earliest period compatible with health," and this was made possible by the employment of children.

"And to what would they be indebted for this gentlest of all revolutions ? To what, but to economy ? Which dreads no longer the multiplication of man, now that she has shown by what secure and unperishable means infant man, a drug at present so much worse than worthless, may be endowed with an indubitable and universal value." [1]

Infant man soon became in the new industrial system what he never was under the old, the basis of a complicated economy.

Most children under the old domestic system worked at home under their parents' eyes, but in addition to such children there were workhouse children, who were hired out by the overseers to every kind of master or mistress. Little care was taken to see that they were taught a trade or treated with humanity by their employers, and though London magistrates like the Fieldings did what they could to protect this unhappy class, their state was often a kind of slavery. The number of children on the hands of the London parishes was largely increased in the latter part of the eighteenth century, because an Act of Parliament, passed in 1767 in consequence of the exertions of Jonas Hanway, compelled the London parishes to board out their young children, and to give a bonus to every nurse whose charge survived. Until this time few parish pauper children grew up to trouble their betters.

The needs of the London workhouses on the one hand, and those of the factory on the other, created a situation painfully like the situation in the West Indies. The Spanish employers in America wanted outside labour, because the supply of native labour was deficient in quantity and quality. The new cotton mills placed on streams in solitary

[1] *Annals of Agriculture*, Vol. XXXI, p. 283 *n.* (1798). Bentham contrasted the happy lot of his apprentices with the fate of the sons and daughters of George III. "Princes unmatched, or late matched, or unprosperously matched, or incongruously matched. Princesses— five remaining—all ripe, but all too high, for happiness."

THE SHADOW OF THE SLAVE TRADE

districts were in the same case. The inventions had found immense scope for child labour, and in these districts there were only scattered populations. In the workhouses of large towns there was a quantity of child labour available for employment, that was even more powerless and passive in the hands of a master than the stolen negro, brought from his burning home to the hold of a British slave ship. Of these children it could be said, as it was said of the negroes, that their life at best was a hard one, and that their choice was often the choice between one kind of slavery and another. So the new industry which was to give the English people such immense power in the world borrowed at its origin from the methods of the American settlements.

When a London parish gave relief it generally claimed the right of disposing of all the children of the person receiving relief, and thus these London workhouses could be made to serve the purpose of the Lancashire cotton mills as the Guinea coast served that of the West Indian plantations. The analogy became painfully complete. In the *Assiento* the negroes are described as " pieces," and the description would be not less suitable to the children taken for the mills. Horner could tell the House of Commons of a contract between a London parish and a Lancashire manufacturer in which the manufacturer undertook to receive one idiot child with every twenty sound children. Romilly described their fate.

" It is a very common practice with the great populous parishes in London to bind children in large numbers to the proprietors of cotton-mills in Lancashire and Yorkshire, at a distance of 200 miles. The children, who are sent off by wagon loads at a time, are as much lost for ever to their parents as if they were shipped off for the West Indies. The parishes that bind them, by procuring a settlement for the children at the end of forty days, get rid of them for ever ; and the poor children have not a human being in the world to whom they can look up for redress against the wrongs they may be exposed to from these wholesale dealers in them, whose object it is to get everything that they can possibly wring from their excessive labour and fatigue. Instances have come to my own knowledge of the anguish sustained by poor persons, on having their children torn from them, which could not fail to excite a strong interest in their favour, if they were more generally known. Instances have recently occurred of masters, who, with 200 such apprentices, have become bankrupts, and been obliged to send all their apprentices to the poorhouse of the parish in which their manufactory happened to be established, to be supported by strangers, and by strangers who consider them as fraudulently thrown upon them for relief." [1]

How closely the apologies for this child serf system followed the apologies for the slave trade can be seen from Romilly's description of a speech made in the House of Commons in 1811.

" Mr. Wortley, who spoke on the same side, insisted that, although in the higher ranks of society it was true that to cultivate the affections of children for their family was the source of every virtue, yet that it was not so among the lower orders, and that it was a benefit to the children to take them away from their miserable and depraved parents. He said too that it would be highly injurious to the public to put a stop to the binding so many apprentices to the cotton manufacturers, as it must necessarily raise the price of labour and enhance the price of cotton manufactured goods." [2]

It was not until 1816 that Parliament would consent to reform this system of transportation. In that year a Bill that had been repeatedly introduced by Mr. Wilbraham Bootle passed both Houses, and it was made illegal for London children to be apprenticed more than forty miles away from their parish. But by this time the problem had changed, for steam-power was superseding water-power and mills could be built in towns; in these towns there were parents who were driven by poverty to send their children to the mills. In the early days of the factory system there had been a prejudice against sending children to the mill, but the hand-loom weaver had been steadily sinking from the beginning of the century into deeper and deeper poverty, and he was no longer able to maintain himself and his family. Sometimes too an adult worker was only

[1] *Life of Sir Samuel Romilly*, by himself (edition of 1842), Vol. II, p. 188.
[2] Ibid., Vol. II, p. 204.

given work on condition that he sent his child to the mill. Thus the apprentice system was no longer needed. It had carried the factories over the first stage and at the second they could draw on the population of the neighbourhood.

These children, who were commonly called "free-labour children," were employed from a very early age. Most of them were piecers: that is they had to join together or piece the threads broken in the several roving and spinning machines. But there were tasks less skilled than these, and Robert Owen said that many children who were four or five years old were set to pick up waste cotton on the floor. Their hours were those of the apprentice children. They entered the mill gates at five or six in the morning and left them again at seven or eight at night. They had half an hour for breakfast and an hour for dinner, but even during meal hours they were often at work cleaning a standing machine; Fielden calculated that a child following the spinning machine would walk twenty miles in the twelve hours. Oastler was once in the company of a West Indian slave-master and three Bradford spinners. When the slave-master heard what were the children's hours he declared:

"I have always thought myself disgraced by being the owner of slaves, but we never in the West Indies thought it possible for any human being to be so cruel as to require a child of nine years old to work twelve and a half hours a day." [1]

This terrible evil fastened itself on English life as the other fastened itself on the life of the Colonies. Reformers had an uphill struggle to get rid of its worst abuses. The first effort was made in 1802 when, after strong representations from a great Manchester doctor, Percival, Sir Robert Peel, father of the statesman, prompted by Owen and a Manchester merchant named Gould, carried a Bill limiting the hours of apprentices to twelve a day, forbidding night work and providing for visits to the mills by parsons and magistrates. The Act was a dead letter from the first. A second Act,

[1] *Town Labourer*, p. 160.

passed in 1819, applying to all children in cotton mills forbidding employment under nine and limiting working hours of children between nine and twelve to twelve a day, was equally ineffective.[1] An Act passed in 1831 brought all persons under eighteen within the provision for a 12 hours' working day, but the first Act that had any considerable effect was the Act passed in 1833 which provided for State inspection. This Act, applying to woollen as well as to cotton mills, forbade the employment of children under nine, limited the working hours of children between nine and twelve to 9 a day and 48 a week, and those of persons under eighteen to 12 a day or 69 a week. But though this Act was a notable advance, because it introduced the principle of inspection, it was easily evaded. The work of the children and that of adults was so closely connected that it was in practice impossible to protect the children except by a measure that would in fact limit the working hours of the whole mill. This was the plan that had been urged by the advocates of the 10 hours' day. The struggle from 1829, when Sadler first adopted this scheme, was between those who thought it so important to rescue the children that they were ready to limit the working hours of the mill, and those who held that it was so important to let the mill work to the utmost of its capacity that it was necessary to overlook the consequences to child life. The struggle ended at last in 1847 with the passing of the Ten Hours Bill, which limited the actual work of all between nine and eighteen to 10 hours a day, exclusive of

---

[1] See e.g. the Report about Wigan in Home Office Papers, 52, 5, from the two Lancashire Visitors of Cotton Factories appointed by Quarter Sessions in 1828. "The children go to work at 5 in the morning, and continue till 9 at night. Some few are allowed to go to their homes to breakfast and dinner, but by far the greatest number are not suffered to go out of the premises at all between the hours mentioned." The Visitors point out that it is impossible to enforce the Act as the Wigan magistrates are all cotton mill proprietors, and are forbidden to try cases under the Act.

meal times. The chief names associated with this reform are Sadler, Fielden, Oastler and Shaftesbury.

Throughout this long struggle the apologies for child labour were precisely the same as the apologies for the slave trade. Cobbett put it in 1833 that the opponents of the Ten Hours Bill had discovered that England's manufacturing supremacy depended on 30,000 little girls. This was no travesty of their argument. The champions of the slave trade pointed to the £70,000,000 invested in the sugar plantations, to the dependence of our navy on our commerce, and to the dependence of our commerce on the slave trade. This was the argument of Chatham in one generation and Rodney in another. When Fox destroyed the trade in 1806 even Sir Robert Peel complained that we were philosophizing when our looms were idle, and George Rose, that the Americans would take up the trade, and that Manchester, Stockport and Paisley would starve. They could point to Liverpool, which had been turned from a small hamlet into a flourishing port by the trade. For Liverpool was the centre of the commerce that throve on this trade. She shipped cheap Manchester goods to Africa, took thence slave cargoes to the West Indies and brought back sugar and raw cotton. In the eleven years from 1783 to 1793 Liverpool slaving ships carried over 300,000 slaves from Africa to the West Indies and sold them for over £15,000,000. In 1793 this single port had secured three-sevenths of the slave trade of Europe. A Liverpool Member said that nobody would introduce the slave trade, but that so large a body of interests and property now depended on it that no equitable person would abolish it.[1]

[1] It must not be forgotten that great Liverpool citizens like William Rathbone and William Roscoe were leading opponents of the trade. Roscoe having been elected M.P. for Liverpool in 1806 had the satisfaction of putting an end both to the trade and to his own career by speaking and voting for abolition. Muir, *History of Liverpool*, p. 205.

The argument for child labour followed the same line. In the one case the interests of Liverpool, in the other those of Lancashire, demanded of the nation that it should accept one evil in order to escape from another. Cardwell, afterwards the famous army reformer, talked of the great capital sunk in the cotton industry and the danger of the blind impulse of humanity. Sir James Graham thought that the Ten Hours Bill would ruin the cotton industry and with it the trade of the country. The cotton industry had taken the place in this argument that had been held by the navy in the earlier controversy. Our population, which had grown so rapidly in the Industrial Revolution, was no longer able to feed itself: the food it bought was paid for by its manufactures: those manufactures depended on capital: capital depended on profits: profits depended on the labour of the boys and girls who enabled the manufacturer to work his mills long enough at a time to repay the cost of the plant and to compete with his foreign rivals. This was the circle in which the nation found its conscience entangled.[1]

The life of man had been regulated before by the needs of a particular order or the pattern of a particular society: the government of king or church or lord had defined narrow limits within which a man was to run his course. The new master was a world force, for this economy could make its profits, so it was believed, where it chose, and when Englishmen rebelled against its rule it would seek its gains and bestow its blessings elsewhere. This way of looking at

[1] When the slave trade was abolished Liverpool did not decline. In 1806 she had 111 ships engaged in the trade; many thought that the destruction of the trade that had made her a great port would leave her with idle ships and deserted docks. But in 1810 her ships were busier than ever they had been in the most prosperous years of the slave trade (Baines, *History of Lancashire*, Vol. I, p. 188 f.). The experience of the cotton industry was similar, for after the passing of the Ten Hours Act all the sombre predictions by which it had been resisted for twenty years proved as false as the predictions of the fate of Liverpool.

the new industrial system put man at the mercy of his machines, for if the new power was not made man's servant, it was bound to become his master. If at every point the governing claim was not man's good but the needs of the machine, it was inevitable that man's life and the quality of his civilization should be subordinated to this great system of production.

A speech made by Burke on the Slave Trade in the House of Commons drew a contrast between a slave and a man, that has an apt application to the life of the times.

"Nothing" (he said) "made a happy Slave, but a degraded man. In proportion as the mind grows callous to its degradation, and all sense of manly pride is lost, the Slave feels comfort. In fact he is no longer a man. If he were to define a man, Mr. Burke declared, he would say with Shakespeare
'Man is a being, holding large discourse,
 Looking before and after.'
A slave was incapable of either looking before or after." [1]

It is interesting to compare with this description of the slave the description of the workman in the new industries given by some of the leading politicians of the time. Windham, defending popular sports in 1800, complained that magistrates were apt to act on the opinion that "common people ought only to eat, to sleep and to work." Nearly half a century later Sir James Graham gave this very description of the life of the worker, "eating, drinking, working and dying." [2]

Nobody could argue that the ordinary worker before the Industrial Revolution was a free man, whether he was a peasant in the country or a journeyman in the town, but the age which watched the change from domestic to factory industry in Lancashire and Yorkshire could see that a great many men and women lost what they had possessed of initiative and choice. For the Industrial Revolution gave a look of catastrophe to the final stages of a process that had been in train for centuries. Before

[1] *Stockdale's Parliamentary Debates*, May 12, 1789.
[2] House of Commons, March 3, 1847.

this time there had been fierce quarrels between master and journeyman. Professor Unwin describes a scene at Chester in 1358 when the master weavers, shearmen and challoners and walkers attacked their journeymen with iron-pointed poles during the Corpus Christi procession.[1] It is true, as he says, that from the middle of the fourteenth century there was to be found in every industrial centre of Western Europe a body of workmen in every craft who had no prospect before them but that of remaining journeymen all their lives, that there was constant friction between this class and the masters, and perpetual disputes over hours, wages and other conditions. The Industrial Revolution did not create the quarrels of class, nor did it create the wrongs and discontents that are inevitable in any relationship, where interests are sharply opposed and power is mismatched. But it made the disproportion of power much greater, and the immense extension of industrial life which followed came at a time when there was a general disposition to regard the working-class world as idle and profligate, and to regard industry as a system that served men by ruling them. Consequently the Industrial Revolution, if it did not introduce all the evils that were so acute in the earlier factories, gave them a far greater range and importance.

What happened at the Industrial Revolution was that all the restraints that the law imposed on workmen in particular industries, were standardized into a general law for the whole of the expanding world of industry, and all the regulations and laws that recognized him as a person with rights were withdrawn or became inoperative. The workman, as we have seen, lost one by one the several Acts of Parliament that gave him protection from his master in this or that industry. His personal liberty was circumscribed by a series of Acts, beginning with the Act of 1719, which made it a crime for him to take

[1] Unwin, *Industrial Organization in the Sixteenth and Seventeenth Centuries*, p. 49.

his wits and his skill into another country: a law that applied to the artisan but not to the inventor. At the end of the century the masters were given complete control of their workmen, by a Combination Act which went far beyond the Acts against combinations already on the Statute book. By the Combination Act of 1799 any workman who combined with any other workman to seek an improvement in his working conditions was liable to be brought before a single magistrate—it might be his own employer—and sent to prison for three months. This Act, of which the chief authors were Pitt and Wilberforce, was modified next year, when Parliament decided that two magistrates were necessary to form a court, and that a magistrate who was a master in the trade affected should not try offences, but these modifications did not affect in practice the power that the law gave to employers. Under cover of this Act it often happened that a master would threaten his workman with imprisonment or service in the fleet in order to compel him to accept the wages he chose to offer. In 1824 Place and Hume, taking advantage of the reaction from the worst of the panics produced by the French Revolution, managed to carry the repeal of the Combination Laws. Next year, after their repeal had been celebrated by an outburst of strikes, a less stringent law was put in their place. But the view of the new system as a beneficent mechanism which the mass of men must serve with a blind and unquestioning obedience was firmly rooted in the temper of the time, and thus anybody who tried to think of Englishmen in the spirit of Burke's description of a man, found himself strangely out of tune in a world where the workman was refused education, political rights and any voice in the conditions of his employment.

"At Tyldesley," it was said in a pamphlet published during a strike, "they work fourteen hours per day, including the nominal hour for dinner; the door is locked in working hours, except half an hour at tea time; the workpeople are not allowed to send for water to drink, in the hot factory : and even the rain water is locked up, by the master's order, otherwise they would be happy to drink even that." [1]

In this mill a shilling fine was inflicted on a spinner found dirty, or found washing, heard whistling or found with his window open in a temperature of 84 degrees. The men who were thrust into this discipline, however hard and bare their lives, had been accustomed to work in their own homes at their own time. The sense of servitude that was impressed on the age by this discipline, by the methods of government, the look of the towns and the absence of choice or initiative in the lives of the mass of the workpeople, was strengthened by the spectacle of the new power.

"While the engine runs," wrote an observer, "the people must work—men, women, and children are yoked together with iron and steam. The animal machine—breakable in the best case, subject to a thousand sources of suffering—is chained fast to the iron machine which knows no suffering and no weariness." [2]

These evils were not of course peculiar to England. Some opponents of reform argued that England could not shorten the working day of the mill because other countries would gain an advantage : an argument that recalled the apology for the slave trade that if England relinquished the trade, others, her rivals, would seize it. The factory system was called the English system, but as it travelled to other countries then and since it reproduced the same features.[3] A pamphlet published in 1833, describing the American factories, contained a passage that was cited by Fielden in his *Curse of the Factory System*.[4]

The author is imagining a visitor being shown over the American mills.

[1] *Town Labourer*, p. 20.
[2] See *Town Labourer*, p. 21.
[3] See for its latest illustration, Report of recent Commission on Child Labour in Shanghai.
[4] P. 71.

"He might see in some, and not unfrequent instances, the child, and the female child, too, driven up to the clockwork with the cowhide, or the well-seasoned strap of American manufacture. We could show him *many* females who have had corporeal punishment inflicted upon them; one girl, eleven years of age, who had her leg broken with a billet of wood; another who had a board split over her head by a heartless monster in the shape of an overseer of a cotton-mill. We do not pretend to say that all overseers are thus cruel, but we do say, that *foreign overseers* are frequently placed over American women and children, and, we are sorry to add, that sometimes *foreigners in this country* have employed American overseers to carry into effect their tyrannical rule in these mills."

Opponents of regulation drew from these facts the moral that England could not afford to shorten the long hours of the mill; Fielden, the moral that they made the case for reform all the stronger, because it was clear that France and America would make their working day as long as ours, even if they had to call in foreign overseers to enforce it. Ultimately the argument of Fielden prevailed, and Britain set the example in checking the worst abuses of the new system. But reform came slowly, and the traveller of 1830 who visited the mills of Lancashire, where cotton was spun and woven for the poor, would have seen under the same roof a mechanical genius that was inconceivable to the mind of the crusades, and men and women still as much the slaves of dire necessity as the men and women of the mills of Antioch and Tyre, whose weary fingers used to clothe in their dazzling raiment the princes and the bishops of the Middle Ages.

CHAPTER XIII

THE CURSE OF MIDAS

" 'Two centuries ago not one person in a thousand wore stockings ; one century ago not one person in five hundred wore them ; now not one person in a thousand is without them." This sentence from *The Results of Machinery* (1831),[1] one of the publications of the Society for the Diffusion of Useful Knowledge, illustrates a feature of the Industrial Revolution that made a profound impression on the imagination of the time. When capital was applied to production on a large scale, it gained its profits by producing in bulk ; producing, that is, for mass consumption. Energy and brains were now devoted to satisfying, not the luxurious taste of the classes that were served by the commerce of mediæval Europe, but the needs of the poor consumer.

Man's faculty for creation and self-expression develops when he can diminish the demand that the satisfaction of elementary needs for food and shelter makes upon his intelligence and his strength. Hence this vast improvement in the means for the provision of those needs marked a definite and startling advance in human history.[2] Man, in this

---

[1] P. 161.

[2] "It must, we repeat, be admitted that, despite all drawbacks, this enormous development of successful profit-making meant, at any rate for the time being, a vast increase in that part of the nation's earnings which may fairly be called its wealth. If wages were low, and the conditions of labour so bad as to be destructive of the people, the continual pressure for a cheapening of production —especially after the general removal of taxes upon commodities of common use—largely benefited the consumer. The profit-makers

sense, became freer than he had ever been; his *jus in naturam*, as Spinoza put it, was infinitely greater. This aspect of the new system struck many contemporary observers as its most important aspect; they were fond of showing that the poor of their time were better off in respect of the conditions of life than the rich of other times; the cottager than the noble.[1]

It was natural for the age that witnessed the first triumphs of the new system to worship production for profit. This great addition to the wealth of the world seemed to follow automatically when men were left to acquire at their pleasure. Swift success is a dazzling spectacle, and the new industrial system provided a new miracle every day. A visitor to a mill in Bolton or Preston watching the inventions of Crompton, Hargreaves, Arkwright and Watt, stood before a power that was conquering the world as no Cæsar or Napoleon had ever conquered it. To the generation that saw on the one hand the small farmer carrying the wool he had woven on his hand-loom at home to Leeds or Halifax on the back of his horse, and on the other the great mills at Blackburn or Rochdale sending out thousands of bales of cotton to be transported by rail and ship to the other ends of the earth, it looked as if progress that had dawdled through so many centuries was, now that man had learnt its simple secret, to follow a rapid

themselves found their greatest gains in increasing output and consumption by a continuous lowering of the price of commodities that every one consumed and of services that every one used. Combination among capitalists, in such a way as permanently to maintain prices above the cost of production, was practically unknown. The whole nation shared, through declining prices, combined with a reasonably stable currency and, on the whole, stable or even slightly rising rates of wages, in the ever-growing stream of commodities, and steadily widened the range and increased the quantity of its consumption."—Webb, *The Decay of Capitalist Civilization*, pp. 81 and 82.

[1] Cf. *Annals of Agriculture*, Vol. XXVIII, p. 392 (1797). "On the comforts enjoyed by the cottagers, compared to those of the ancient Barons."

and unbroken course; as if the society that surrendered itself to the control of private profit released a force that would regenerate the world. Any people into whose hands this power had fallen would probably have been plunged into the state described by Boulton as "steam-mill mad," just as any people that had first grasped the new wealth of America in the fifteenth century would have been as frantic as the Spaniards for gold and silver.

The English people, from the whole tone and cast of its thought and politics, was specially liable to be swept off its balance by this revolution. The positive enthusiasms of the time were for science and progress: for material development and individual liberty. The restraints of custom, tradition and religion had never been so frail over the classes that held power. In the Middle Ages the Church had laid a controlling or checking hand on manners; the Guilds had hampered individual enterprise by a corporate discipline. But the Church of the eighteenth century was merely part of the civil order, without standards, authority or conscience of its own; the Guilds were dead, and their successors stood not for corporate spirit, but for property and nothing else. Thus neither Church nor Guild survived to offer any obstacle to the view that headlong wealth was the sovereign good for society and for the individual, for cities and for men.

This view was powerfully encouraged by the philosophy of confidence which the eighteenth century had substituted for a religion of awe. Mediæval religion had watched man's instincts with anxious eyes, as instincts needing to be disciplined, coerced, held fast by Pope and priest; the Puritans, though they gave him different masters, were not less suspicious of the natural man. The new philosophy, on the other hand, regarded man's instincts as the best guide to conduct, and taught that left to himself man so acted as to serve rather than injure the society to which he belonged. Capital was a magical power; man was a benevolent creature. Thus so far as an age lives by a system of belief, this age drew its wisdom from a philosophy that found nothing but good in the new force to which it had submitted.

The state of politics was also congenial to this impulse. Neither Conservative nor Radical offered any distracting or competing motive, for while they disagreed about political and administrative reform, they did not disagree about the advantages of a system under which acquisition and profit-making were unimpeded. If it was the manufacturers who promoted the new system in industry, the landowners were equally active in promoting it on their estates. The most important force in making the English an industrial people was the destruction of the village. Nations that kept the peasant could never be completely absorbed in the new industrial system, and it was the landowner, often of course the new landowner, who had come from the world of finance and industry, who pushed the English peasant out.

The quarrel between Conservative and Radical did not raise any issue that was an obstacle to the new system. Their quarrel was political. Reform, both of Parliament and of local government, was long overdue. In a country where all initiative has been gathered, and power has long resided, in the grasp of a class, the instincts of authority and the habits of action enable that class to keep life in a bad system long after it has lost all claim to the support of those whose needs it once served. Such a class ceases in time to be a governing class, and becomes a garrison. Particularly is this true where, as in the case of eighteenth-century England, the governing class possesses the qualities of courage and resolution in a remarkable degree. Thus it came about that Parliament and local government, the administration of justice and of law were full of gross anomalies, and the defence of those anomalies was for a time the chief care of the Conservative party. A party that was engaged in the effort to keep what it held in the way of class privilege, and to protect property rather than custom, a system of inequalities rather than any large design of social harmony, did not offer to the sentiment or the sense of the English people any ideal that could discredit acquisition, as the leading motive of conduct. Lord Hugh Cecil has said of its purpose that it sought to preserve the sanctity of property ; property significantly interpreted as the right to the " undisturbed enjoyment of good fortune." [1]

If Conservatism offered no distracting aim, Liberalism gave active encouragement to the new system. In the eighteenth century Liberalism was a crusade against authority based on anything but consent. Its basis was individualism, for it regarded society as existing to enforce respect for rights that man brought with him into society : not as a community whose members and classes served different purposes, and stood in some organic relation to one another.[2] In this sense Liberalism was a revolt from an essential tradition of the Middle Ages. Mediæval society had attempted to preserve what mankind had kept of its inheritance of culture through the havoc of the Dark Ages, by a system that was a sort of caste system. This system was not new in Europe. Diocletian and Constantine had tried to overcome the dangers and difficulties of an exhausted Empire by attaching classes to occupations. By their time the peril of civilization was manifest and the rulers of the Empire had to devise methods for securing that the land should be tilled, the inhabitants of the towns fed, the revenue maintained, and the work of the world carried on.[3] Diocletian had created a class of hereditary seamen to guarantee the transport of corn for Rome ; Constantine bound the class of farmers known as the " coloni " to the soil. This caste system included other classes ; definite obligations and liabilities, for example,

[1] See *Conservatism*. The rejection of Whitbread's Minimum Wage Bill (1795 and 1800) on the invitation of Pitt showed how far the Conservative party had travelled from the earlier doctrine that capitalist power should be controlled.

[2] See H. J. Laski, *Political Thought from Locke to Bentham*, p. 284.

[3] See Heitland, *Agricola*, p. 451.

were imposed on the landowners who filled the *curia* in each district, and they were excluded from other careers. This principle was applied to all trades and professions whose members were subject to the capitation tax.[1] There was the same underlying idea in the social system of the Middle Ages. Different classes had different duties. As Chaucer's parson put it, "God has ordained that some folk should be more high in estate and degree, and some folk more low, and that everyone should be served in his estate and his degree."

This view of society would in any case have been obnoxious to Liberals, who refused to believe that a man's place and career should be fixed for him, for all time, by birth and custom. When it was attacked by Liberals in the seventeenth and eighteenth centuries, the system was in decay, and it survived in the main in the form of abuses. The Church, the town, the manor, the guild, represented a philosophy that once had life, meaning and purpose, but, with their decadence into the temper and methods of monopoly, the whole system of regulation to which they belonged had changed its character; instead of an arrangement to serve a rationally ordered and living society, it was become the entrenchment of a class. The mediæval idea, if it kept the poor in their place, gave them some protection and recognized that they had certain rights. In the eighteenth century the system had lost this character of social obligation; it had degenerated for the most part into a mass of idle and unearned privileges. The individualism of Locke, Adam Smith and Bentham in England was directed, like the individualism of Turgot in France, against authority exercised in the interests of the few, no longer seeking its justification in the idea of duty or function, claiming obedience on the ground of divine right.

---

[1] Bury, *Later Roman Empire*, Vol. I, p. 27. See also Dill, *Roman Society in the Last Century of the Western Empire*, p. 232; and Levasseur, *Histoire des Classes Ouvrières et de l'Industrie en France avant* 1789, Chapter VI.

The Liberals were thus attacking a great body of abuses and an arbitrary system of power. Their vigour and courage enabled them to strike effective blows. They made Parliament less unrepresentative, town government less corrupt, punishment less brutal, justice less unjust. But the philosophy that prompted this campaign did not quarrel merely with the abuses of the feudal society: it combated its underlying principles. It opposed to the idea of mutual obligation the idea of natural rights,[1] and these rights included the right to acquire and use property, as a right subject to no kind of qualification. For these minds one aspect of the Industrial Revolution overshadowed all others. That revolution had made it very much easier for the poor man with courage and intelligence to step out of his surroundings. The door had been thrown open to enterprise and thrift, and men could pass through it without asking leave of ruler or neighbour. The Liberal was chiefly concerned that this door should never be closed: he believed that in a world where exertion and perseverance can carry a man from poverty to riches, injustice will always be kept within tolerable limits.

Thus economic individualism occupied an essential place in Radical theory, and as the right of the capitalist was deduced from a theory, it was treated as a right that was absolute and independent of experience. It belonged for English Radical, as for French, like the right to life, or the right to liberty, to a series of natural rights, which society had no business to limit. It involved the right to take what interest and profit you could get; to buy and sell as you pleased; rights that had been controlled in the Middle Ages. Thus the Radicals tended to substitute

[1] Bentham rejected the philosophy of rights, but his Utilitarian philosophy took a direction, from his mistrust of authority, that brought his school to the same practical result. The individual understood his own interest best, and the good of the greatest number would be realized by allowing him complete freedom to pursue it.—L. T. Hobhouse, *Liberalism*, pp. 67–77.

for the divine right of kings the divine right of capitalist. They did noble work in abolishing injustices and oppressions, but they acknowledged a new power which was largely to determine the character of a civilization. For a people passing through such changes as those that accompanied the Industrial Revolution, this question, whether and at what point the claim of the capitalist to uncontrolled exercise of his power should be withstood, became the most important question in public life. England was on the eve of a great expansion of resources, numbers, wealth and power. What were the new towns to be like ? What their schools, their pleasures, their houses, their standards of a good life, their plans for co-operation and fellowship ? What the fate of the mass of people who did not feel or force their way through the doors thrown open to enterprise ? To all these questions the Industrial Revolution gave the same answer : "Ask Capital." And neither Conservative nor Radical, the man defending or the man attacking bad laws and bad customs, thought that answer wrong. But that answer meant that the age had turned aside from making a society in order to make a system of production.

This new power then descended on a society in which the intellectual and political atmosphere inclined the age to give it a free rein. Restraint of every kind on the acquisition and the use of wealth was discredited ; the doctrine that the man who seeks his private gain finds the public good was accepted like a discovery of Newton's ; progress was regarded as constant, and it was believed that the Industrial Revolution was making the problems of life not more but less complex. For the ascendancy of the mathematical sciences had encouraged abstractions dangerous from their simplicity. The economist dismissed moral and religious impulses, finding in selfishness the driving power of industrial enterprise. The world seemed to be organized in such a way that the capitalist's desire for profit was really the best guarantee that the consumer and the workman would benefit by his activities.[1]

One other circumstance about the place and time of the Industrial Revolution is not without importance. The most famous societies of the past had been made in countries where the physical conditions did not demand a great effort for the maintenance of life. The food and clothing of the Greeks were frugal and simple ; the Roman slept naked and wore only a tunic indoors ; the legions fought on a diet of spelt.[2] In the English climate the actual needs of life are more exacting, and this, of itself, at a time when a nation was entering on an elaborate economy in which organized production and exchange came to regulate all life, and to make themselves, so to speak, responsible for the livelihood of a people, tended to push from men's minds those aspects of civilization that were outside man's immediate necessities. This tendency was encouraged by the calamity that during twenty of these critical years England was engaged in a deadly war, from time to time facing scarcity, fearing famine.

The effect of this concentration is seen in the towns of the age. They were left, like everything else, to the mercy and direction of the spirit of profit. Town planning was not an unknown art ; at different times in the world's history it had served the purpose of defence, of religion, of display, of commerce. Rulers with their eyes on the needs of war had planned towns like Stockholm ; others, thinking of their personal glory, had planned great reconstructions in Paris or Rome. The English town of this period, which looked like the product of a tired age that had lost its stride, was really the product of an age full of energy, that had no care for order, space or plan. Public beauty

[1] " The benign and wise Disposer of all things, who obliges men, whether they will or not, in pursuing their own selfish interests, to connect the general good with their own individual success."— Burke, *Thoughts on Scarcity*, Works, Vol. VII, p. 384. Burke went so far as to say that a monopoly of capital was a great benefit, and a benefit particularly to the poor.

[2] See Zimmern, op. cit., p. 48 ; and Salvioli, op. cit., p. 128.

seemed to have been banished by the new science. The England of the first industrial age was richer than most ages in painters and poets, but the great achievements of its literature, the galleries of its private mansions, the elegant taste of its aristocracy, all these served to emphasize the significance of the deliberate exclusion of beauty from its common life. The humanism of Shelley, the passion of Byron, the piety of Wordsworth, the imagination of Scott, were all in a sense protests against the industrial spirit ; the mind that had any feeling for the large spaces of fancy or of history turned away from it. What there is of beauty in the age belongs either to the lingering charm of an aristocratic culture with its agreeable ease and self-satisfaction, or to the desire to picture a past or future as unlike the present as dreams could make it. All that belongs to the new life of the nation bears a character as unmistakable as the character given to a mediæval town by its handsome buildings. The chimneys of Lancashire represented energy, initiative, ambition : qualities that had given to Manchester the grasp of a larger and richer world than that from which Tyre or Venice, Antwerp or Amsterdam had drawn their lavish wealth. The random and squalid buildings of the new Manchester where 200,000 people lived without a single public garden, were not less eloquent ; they spoke for the discredit into which man's life outside this system of production had fallen, the poverty that had stricken the social consciousness of the race.[1]

Mankind did not admire wealth for the first time ; but the rich merchant of Bruges, Genoa or Norwich, like the rich Pope or the rich noble of the Middle Ages, or the rich Senator of the Roman Empire, had regarded the beauty and culture of his town as a sign of his own importance

[1] See the discussion in C. Delisle Burns, *The Contact between Minds*, p. 101. "Indeed it seems as if the perception of beauty as well as the creation of beauty in art is essentially social ; because the great periods of art have been precisely those in which the social consciousness was highly developed."

and success.[1] Vespasian, frugal as he was, did not hesitate to begin the restoration of the Capitol, though he had inherited a debt of over three hundred million pounds. The private citizen who gave Bordeaux an aqueduct costing £160,000, or the benefactor who spent £80,000 on the walls of Marseilles, the soldier who provided free baths for slave girls at Suessa Senonum, the civic dignitaries who gave temples and theatres,[2] these typical figures of the early Roman Empire would have been astonished to learn that in the districts of South Wales, where men had risen in a few years to such wealth as would have rivalled the wealth of Atticus or Herodes, the poorer classes had to go a mile for water, waiting in a queue a great part of the night; that the chief town of this rich district had neither public lighting nor drainage.

Yet the Industrial Revolution which had given these men their fortunes had made it much easier to supply the needs of the towns that sprang up beside their great establishments. One of the products of that revolution was gas lighting; the Soho Works were lighted with gas in 1802 to celebrate the Peace of Amiens. Great factories at Manchester and Leeds soon followed the example of Boulton and Watt. Another product was the cheap water-pipe. At the end of the American War English ironmasters were exporting water-pipes to Paris and New York.[3] The Romans had no cheap water-pipes made by the help of mechanical power, but they could supply their towns with clean water, whereas the people of Merthyr Tydfil, their streets echoing by day and night with the clamour of forge and furnace, had to drink whatever the river brought them.

[1] Professor Ashley points out that the great increase of wealth in the fifteenth and early sixteenth centuries was followed by the building of our most famous town churches. See *Economic History and Theory*, Vol. I, Part II, p. 51. See also Gretton, *The English Middle Class*, p. 86.

[2] Dill, *Roman Society from Nero to Marcus Aurelius*, pp. 225 and 227.

[3] Ashton, op. cit., p. 140.

Augustus' Rome, with its undeveloped mechanical arts, would not have looked more primitive to the Lancashire of Arkwright or Crompton than nineteenth-century Manchester, with its random and formless streets, would have looked to the Rome of Vitruvius, the architect of the first century B.C. who set the classical tradition, to whom the task of deciding where a town should place its temples, its circus, its forum, its amphitheatre, and how it should organize its water supply and its drainage seemed the most urgent of the tasks of a civilized society.[1] Great wealth has been prized for different reasons at different times. It has been coveted by men who liked power or display, who sought to satisfy the generous impulses of their religion, or to lay to rest its haunting fears. Perhaps the most comprehensive account of the attractions of wealth was that given by a man of religious temperament, who believed himself to have been guided by Providence to the discovery of the new World, and did not foresee the havoc its prizes would play with the finer impulses that had inspired his courage. It occurs in the letters of Columbus.

"Gold constitutes treasure, and he who possesses it has all he needs in this world, as also the means of rescuing souls from purgatory, and restoring them to the enjoyment of Paradise."[2]

Columbus himself wished this new wealth to be used for another crusade, for the recovery of the Holy Sepulchre, and he spent long hours with the Bible and the early Fathers seeking for light on this project. The eager world of which he was one of the founders would have deplored such dissipation of time and energy. In the new industrial age, more emphatically than in any other, wealth was prized as an end in itself: the rich spinner or the rich ironmaster believed that the way to save your soul was to become richer.

An original and interesting writer, discussing the signi-

---

[1] See Lanchester, *The Art of Town Planning*, Chapter II.
[2] Raleigh, *English Voyages of the Sixteenth Century*, p. 28.

ficance of different types of architecture, remarked that "only what can be got out of life can be put into art." Thus he traced definition and the sense of ideas in Greek art, energy and passion in Gothic art, the recovery of the balance and order of intellectual composure in the art of the Renaissance.[1] The town of the industrial age, without beauty or method, marked the spirit of this age just as truly as St. Paul's Cathedral marked the spirit of the Renaissance, or the cathedral of Durham the spirit of the Crusades. It expressed a concentration in which religion, beauty, leisure, the life of the spirit, or the life of the senses, were all held to be rivals to the stern life of selfish duty. The purpose of man's life was not to fight or to pray, to contemplate or to create, to enjoy or to become, but to make profits, profits for himself, if a master, profits for another, if a servant. This was man's duty, and it was the duty of society to put no obstacle in his way. The Greek view of life, as the expression and exercise of many faculties, has been threatened by the asceticism of the seeker after salvation, and by the asceticism of the seeker after profits; of the cotton spinner, who lived and worked like a slave, and ruled like a slave driver, it was as true as it was of St. Simon Stylites on his pillar that he sacrificed the whole to the part of a man's life. The rage for production had swept England, as the rage for piety had swept the age of the monachists. And production had taken a form that was intensely isolating; the successful man kept his secrets, tried to find his neighbours' secrets, strove for personal gain, took personal risks, made his way by personal initiative and personal enterprise.[2]

This concentration led to the complete neglect of the most urgent of the tasks of the age. In the first twenty years of the nineteenth century the population of Manchester increased from 94,000 to 160,000; of Bolton from 29,000 to 50,000; Leeds more than doubled its population between

[1] L. March Phillipps, *The Works of Man*.
[2] Limited Liability was not introduced until 1856.

1801 and 1831; Bradford, which had 23,000 inhabitants in 1831, grew grass in its streets at the end of the eighteenth century. Oldham, which had 38,000 inhabitants in 1821. had three or four hundred in 1760. In the twenty years from 1801 to 1821 the population of Lancashire grew from 672,000 to 1,052,000; in the next twenty years it grew to 1,701,000. The population of Merthyr increased from 7,700 to 35,000 between 1801 and 1841, and that of the two counties of Glamorgan and Monmouth from 126,000 to 305,000.[1] Industry was accumulating dense masses of people into particular districts, where the workman was shut up in melancholy streets, without gardens or orchards. England was passing from a country to a town life, as she passed from a peasant to an industrial civilization. What this meant is clear if we compare the state of the towns as revealed in the health statistics, with that of the country districts. In 1757 Dr. Percival put the death-rate for Manchester at 1 in 25, for Liverpool at 1 in 27. In Monton, a few miles from Manchester, the ratio was at that time 1 in 68, at Horwich, between Bolton and Chorley, 1 in 66, at Darwen, three miles from Blackburn, 1 in 56. The Industrial Revolution was to spread the conditions of town life over places like Monton, Horwich and Darwen.[2]

The problem of arranging and controlling the expansion of the towns was thus the most urgent of the problems created by the Industrial Revolution. Its importance was illustrated by a picture of some cottages near Preston published by the Health of Towns Commission in 1844. These cottages stood in two rows, separated by little back yards, with an open sewer running the whole length. The picture was given as an example of dangerous and disgusting drainage. But this is not its chief significance. One would suppose that these huddled cottages, without gardens of any kind, were built in a crowded town, where not an inch of space

[1] Ness Edwards, op. cit., pp. 29 and 30.
[2] Quoted by L. W. Moffitt, *England on the Eve of the Industrial Revolution*, p. 271.

was available for amenities. They were in fact in the open country. Clearly then there was more here than a problem of drainage, for if it were left to private enterprize to develop this district, under the guidance of an uncontrolled sense for profit, these rows would spring up all round, and Preston would have another slum on her hands. This is what happened in the new industrial districts. When the Health of Towns Commission investigated towns like Manchester, they were told that the worst evils were not the evils of the past, for new Manchester was reproducing the slums and alleys of the old, and spreading them, of course, over a far wider surface.[1] Of no other problem was it so true that neglect by one generation tied the hands and the mind of the next.

One of the few to grasp this truth at once was Southey, who, recalling the teaching of Sir Thomas More, summoned his age to make provision for this development on wise and generous lines. An ant heap, he remarked, is just as orderly when it is large as when it is small. " The Augean Stable might have been kept clean by ordinary labour," he said, in another passage that comes bitterly

[1] " In the last decade of the eighteenth century, it could be said by a medical man that ' in some parts of the town, cellars are so damp as to be unfit for habitations ' ; that there is one street in which ' is a range of cellars let out to lodgers which threaten to become a nursery of diseases ' ; that ' near the extremities of the town . . . the lodging-houses . . . produce many fevers . . . by want of cleanliness and air.' Thirty years later all these kinds of nuisances were found in undiminished intensity with the important difference that, instead of one such street or group of underground dwellings or lodging-houses there were, in 1830, literally thousands in the same awful state. This meant that the wretched inhabitants of these cellars and tenement houses had become, not only more densely crowded together, but also increasingly hemmed in, so that their whole lives were passed in the slums. The growth of Manchester, together with the corresponding transformation of Salford, Stockport, Stalybridge, Hyde, Ashton, and other townships, had, for miles in every direction, defiled the atmosphere, polluted the streams and destroyed the vegetation."—Webb, *Statutory Authorities*, p. 400.

home to succeeding generations, " if from the first the filth had been removed every day ; when it had been accumulated for years it became a task for Hercules to cleanse it."[1] Unfortunately Southey had few disciples ; Macaulay's shallow and contemptuous criticism was significant of the welcome his ideas received. A people governed as the English people was governed at the beginning of the century was singularly ill-fitted to manage this vast problem. The country districts, and those districts that were country one day and town the next, were under the rule of squires, who were men of great personal courage and self-confidence, but quite incompetent to initiate or to suggest great constructive schemes. The towns were, for the most part, in the hands of little oligarchies, seldom public-spirited, and often corrupt. Many of these oligarchies were abolished by the Municipal Corporations Act of 1835, but that Act, though it substituted popular bodies for the little groups that had drawn town government into their hands, gave very limited powers to the new Town Councils. It was still the rule to leave most public services to special bodies like Improvement Commissioners set up by private Act of Parliament.

The first few years of the reformed Parliament were years of great activity in respect of inquiry into abuses. This energy was due largely to the influence of Bentham. It has been well said that there were two schools of *laissez faire*. There were men like Melbourne, who wanted to leave things alone : there were men like Bentham, who wanted to remove laws or abuses that hindered individual development.[2] Bentham's general aim was to substitute science for custom in law and administration, and for this purpose it was essential to make the facts of social life known and understood. But the energy with which Parliament inquired into one set of facts after another was due also to the agitations led by Owen and the Chartists, for the

[1] Southey, *Colloquies on Society*, I, pp. 111 and 113.
[2] See *Life and Labour in the Nineteenth Century*, by C. R. Fay, p. 44.

upper classes were anxious to disarm criticism and to remove the most flagrant scandals. In consequence of this influence the practice, initiated to its credit by the unreformed Parliament, of setting up inquiries was used to great effect by reformers at this time. A few doctors, led by Southwood Smith, a few officials, led by Chadwick, a few Members of Parliament, led by Normanby, Ashley and Slaney, were able, with the powerful help of Dickens, to bring this machinery into use in the cause of public health.[1] For one moment it looked as if the English people was about to take in hand the most urgent of its new tasks.

In 1840 a Committee of the House of Commons recommended a series of reforms of a drastic and far-reaching character, and the Government of the day, represented at the Home Office by Normanby, a Minister who was in earnest, introduced Bills to give effect to its porposals. This Committee regretted that there was no general building law in force at the beginning of the century, " the fulfilment of one of the first duties of a humane government," and called for a general building law, a general sewage law, the setting up of a Board of Health in every town, with instructions to look after water supply, burial grounds, open spaces and slums. Cellar dwellings and back-to-back houses were to be forbidden. The importance of preserving amenities, footpaths, and something of the look of the country was impressed on Parliament. The most significant comment on the neglect of these proposals is to be found in the recurring complaint that runs through all the Reports on Health and Housing that were issued in the nineteenth century Town planning never found its way into an Act of Parliament until the twentieth century, and back-to-back houses (made illegal in 1909) were built in great numbers two generations after Normanby's Bill had proposed to forbid them. The Commission which sat

[1] These men were the successors of three doctors, Thomas Percival, John Ferriar and James Currie, who led an earlier crusade for sanitary reform in Manchester and Liverpool.

THE CURSE OF MIDAS

in 1867 found in existence the main evils that were revealed by the Committee of 1840 ; the Commission of 1884 found in existence the main evils that had been revealed by the Commission of 1867. In many towns the death-rate was higher in 1867 than in 1842, and Cross, speaking as Home Secretary in 1871, could match the terrible revelations by which Chadwick had tried to rouse the indignation and fear of the Parliaments of Melbourne and Peel.

Before each Commission the large towns disclosed the same difficulties. The law did not enable them to control expansion, or to prevent the creation on their circumference of the evils they were trying to suppress at the centre. The Committee of 1840 had pointed out that back-to-back houses were being introduced into towns that had been free from them. Town Clerks told the Commission of 1867 that whole streets were still being built on " a foundation composed of old sweepings, refuse from factories, old buildings and other objectionable matter." Parliament passed Public Health Acts and set up authorities with sharply limited powers, but the fatal blindness to the character of the problem, as a problem in the organization and planning of town life, which marked the early phases of the Industrial Revolution, persisted. England learnt sooner than other countries how to cleanse her towns,[1] but towns still continued to grow at the pleasure of the profit seeker. Each generation looked wistfully back to its predecessor as living in a time when the evil was still manageable, and over the reforms of the century could be inscribed the motto " the Clock that always loses." For the creed of the first age of the Industrial Revolution, that the needs of production must regulate the conditions of life, and that the incidence of profits must decide in what kind of town, in what kind of streets, and in what kind of houses a nation shall find its home, had cast its melancholy fatalism over

---

[1] " This nation has shown the way to all others in means for the removal of filth by drainage, and for the supply of pure water." Leathes, *The People on its Trial*, p. 122.

the mind of the generations that followed. The trouble was not merely that the evil was greater when a town had a quarter of a million of inhabitants instead of a hundred thousand. It was that men still saw with the eyes of their grandfathers, and that they were busy polishing the life of the slum, when a race that was free and vigorous in its mind could have put an end to it. With the consequences and the traditions of this neglect industrial civilization is still fighting an up-hill battle.

The other task that became immensely more important with the Industrial Revolution was the task of education. Adam Smith had pointed out that the division of labour, though good for production, was bad for the mind of the labourer. Men, women and children lost range, diversity and incentive in their work, when that work was simplified to a single process, or a monotonous routine. Life was more versatile and interesting when craftsmanship was combined with agriculture. Under the new system a boy or youth learnt one process and one process only ; a great part of his mind was never exercised ; many of his faculties remained idle and undeveloped. Moreover, apprenticeship was declining, and thus an important method of education was passing out of fashion.

Nor were these the only reasons why popular education was needed more urgently in this than in previous ages. Men learn from their leisure as well as from their work. Now the common life of the time was singularly wanting in inspiration, comparing in this respect unfavourably with the life of the ancient or that of the mediæval world. The Greeks and the Romans put a great deal of beauty into their public buildings ; they made provision, in some cases barbarous provision, for public amusement ; they did not isolate art and pleasure for the delight of a small class.

" The free enjoyment of sumptuous baths, of good water from the Atlas, the Apennines, or the Alban Hills, the right to sit at ease with one's fellows when the *Pseudolus* or the *Adelphi* was put upon the boards, the pleasure of strolling in the shady colonnades of the forum or the market, surrounded by brilliant marbles and frescoes, with fountains shedding their coolness around ; the good fellowship which, for the time, levelled all ranks, in many a simple communal feast, with a coin or two distributed at the end to recall or heighten the pleasure—all these things tended to make the city a true home, to some extent almost a great family circle." [1]

Life in Manchester or Merthyr was very different. Mr. and Mrs. Webb, who have described the work of the several bodies of Improvement Commissioners at this time, remark that even the most energetic among them made no provision for parks, open spaces, libraries, picture galleries, museums baths, or any kind of education.[2] The workmen put it that their sports had been converted into crimes, and their holidays into fast days. Rich men in the Roman Empire spent their money on things that were for common enjoyment as rich men in the Middle Ages spent their money on things that were for common salvation. Pliny gave to his native Como, a library, a school endowment, a foundation for the nurture of poor children and a Temple of Ceres with spacious colonnades to shelter the traders who visited the great fair. The wealthy Herodes Atticus, tutor of Marcus Aurelius, gave a theatre to Athens with a roof of cedar to hold 6,000 persons, another theatre to Corinth, and a race-course to Delphi. Such gifts were common in the days of the Antonines. But in the England of the early Industrial Revolution all diversions were regarded as wrong, because it was believed that successful production demanded long hours, a bare life, a mind without temptation to think or to remember, to look before or behind. Some Lancashire magistrates used to refuse on this ground to licence public-houses where concerts were held. Long hours did not begin with the Industrial Revolution, but in the Middle Ages the monotony of industrial work was broken for the journey-man by frequent holidays, saints' days and festivals ; for mediæval Europe, like Rome, gave some place in common life to the satisfaction of the imagination and the senses.

[1] Dill, op. cit., p. 233.
[2] See *Statutory Authorities,* p. 246 n.

Perhaps nothing served so directly to embitter the relations of class in the Industrial Revolution as this fashionable view, that the less amusement the worker had, the better. The love of amusement has a place of special significance in the English character.[1] If the English workman stints himself for his holiday week at Blackpool, as the Scottish peasant stints himself to send his son into the Ministry, or the Irish or French peasant stints himself to own a little property, it is not merely because he sets his holiday high among the enjoyments of life. The satisfaction of this desire is connected with his self-respect. The football field and the holiday resort represent a world in which the poor man feels himself the equal of the rich : a corner of life in which he has not bargained away any rights or liberties. It might be said of the early Radicals, that they sought to extend to his view of politics, and of the early Socialists, that they sought to extend to his views of property, the spirit that ruled the workman's outlook on his pleasures : that they sought to make him resent in those spheres the inequalities he was so quick to resent, when employer or magistrate tried to keep from him amusements that other classes enjoyed.

The need for popular education became in these circumstances specially urgent. The reading of print is one way of using and exercising the mind, and its value at any moment depends on circumstances. In the days of pageants and spectacles, when story-tellers went from village to village, when pedlars and pilgrims brought tales of adventure or war or the habits of foreign countries, a man might be unable to read or write, and yet take a share in the culture of the time. Buildings, plays, music, these may be greater influences on the mind than book or pamphlet

[1] Chamberlayne's *Angliae Nototiae*, published in 1660, has this description : "The common people will endure long and hard labour, insomuch that after twelve hours hard work they will go in the evening to football, stockball, cricket, prison base, wrestling, cudgel playing, or some such like vehement exercise for their recreation."

or newspaper. But the youth of the early nineteenth century who found no scope for initiative or experiment or design in his work, found no stimulus or education for his fancy from the spectacles and amusements provided for his recreation. Science was improving the mechanical contrivances of life, but the arts of life were in decline. To take advantage of these improvements, the power to read and write was essential. In a world depending on newspapers the man who cannot read lives in the darkest exile; when the factory was taking the place of the craft, the newspaper the place of the pageant, illiteracy was the worst disfranchisement a man could suffer.

Horner, reporting in 1839 that a population of over a hundred thousand persons in a district of Lancashire comprising Oldham and Ashton was without a single public day-school for poor scholars, the Commissioner who said of South Wales in 1842 that not one grown male in fifty could read,[1] both spoke of an age in which the story-teller had left the village, and the apprenticeship system was leaving the town. Adam Smith had argued that as the division of labour deprived the worker of opportunities of training his mind, the State ought to provide opportunities by public education. The ruling class argued, on the contrary, that with the new methods of specialization, industry could not spare a single hour for the needs of the men who served it. In such a system education had no place. A few far-seeing men, like Price, Paine, Whitbread and Brougham, had pressed for the public provision of education.[2] Whitbread carried a Bill through the Commons in 1807 under which each parish would have had its elementary school. Brougham incessantly urged the claims of education. But politicians were prepared to leave the nation to a hopelessly inadequate provision made by voluntary societies, and it was not until 1833 that education received any help from the public funds. The great majority of the ruling

[1] Ness Edwards, op. cit., p. 47.
[2] Turgot and Condorcet had pressed the same policy in France.

class believed, as one of them put it, that the question to ask was not whether education would develop a child's faculties for happiness and citizenship, but whether it " would make him a good servant in agriculture and other laborious employments to which his rank in society had destined him." [1]

Thus England asked for profits and received profits. Everything turned to profit. The towns had their profitable dirt, their profitable smoke, their profitable slums, their profitable disorder,[2] their profitable ignorance, their profitable despair. The curse of Midas was on this society: on its corporate life, on its common mind, on the decisive and impatient step it had taken from the peasant to the industrial age. For the new town was not a home where man could find beauty, happiness, leisure, learning, religion, the influences that civilize outlook and habit, but a bare and desolate place, without colour, air or laughter, where man, woman and child worked, ate and slept. This was to be the lot of the mass of mankind: this the sullen rhythm of their lives. The new factories and the new furnaces were like the Pyramids, telling of man's enslavement, rather than of his power, casting their long shadow over the society that took such pride in them.

[1] Davies Giddy, House of Commons, 1807, quoted *Town Labourer* p. 57.

[2] " During the rapid increase of this town (Merthyr) no attention seems to have been paid to its drainage, and the streets and houses built at random as it suited the views of those who speculated in them."—*Report of Commission of Inquiry into State of Large Towns*, 1845.

The average period of life in Merthyr was 18 years and 2 months. See N. Edwards, op. cit., pp. 45 and 46.

CHAPTER XIV

WORLD IN DISORDER

WHEN Rome seized the treasure of the East, the temptations of plunder overwhelmed the virtue and simplicity of this small and hardy people, and threw, first the Roman people, and then the growing world that they controlled, into confusion and civil war. Yet Rome has gone down to history as a noble example of the power of man to create a civilization, for the pirate Empire became the law-giving Empire, the great brigand the great statesman. The tide turned with Augustus, and so far as the recovery has a philosophy, the solemn and urgent note of obligation was sounded by Cicero in a book that served for centuries as a sermon to mankind.

The circumstances of its composition give a peculiar pathos to the treatise *De Officiis*. At once a patriot and a humanist, Cicero had passed his life in a society that was in violent and fatal discord, and a discord that seemed to involve in its ruin the destinies of the civilized world. The latest event in that long strife was the assassination of Cæsar, an event hailed by Cicero with precipitate confidence as the prelude to the restoration of the Republic When he composed this book he was disillusioned; a wanderer flying from the wrath of Antony he knew that Cæsar's death had settled nothing. In this atmosphere of private suspense and public disappointment he gave the world his meditations on the duty of man and the duty of nations, reviewing with a calm and noble courage the conduct and the prospects of the people that he loved.

Cicero argued in this book that the Roman Empire had

been at one time a " patrocinium " rather than an " imperium " ; maintaining itself by services rather than by violence ; that injustice had set in with the career of Sulla,[1] and that this injustice had brought ruin on foreign peoples, on Rome's allies, and, lastly, on Rome herself. What was the capital mischief that had caused this collapse ? The abuse of power by the State, by politicians, by traders, by men of property. Self-control had gone, yet men and States could only live by duty, for to live otherwise was to challenge nature. Civil society depended on the recognition of obligations, and those obligations were not bounded by the family or even by the nation, for the man who admitted obligations to fellow-citizens but not to foreigners " would destroy the universal brotherhood of mankind." The honourable State and the honourable man refused to take advantage of a neighbour in order to become powerful or rich.

This plea was addressed to a people whose whole life had been thrown into disorder. All the settled customs that control man and keep his feet on some traditional basis of virtue had vanished in violent strife and civil war. In such a society everything depends on the sense of honour, or of shame, or of pity, or whatever that emotion or principle is called, which prompts a man to be better than his circumstances and surroundings compel him to be. Cicero appealed to such a sentiment of honour ; in battle it was no defence of cruelty that the State with which you were contending was your enemy ; in commerce it was no defence of sharp practice that you had kept within the law. In business relations, concealment, or misrepresentation, or taking advantage of your neighbour's ignorance were wrong ; the

[1] Compare Plutarch, *Sulla*, 12, where Plutarch draws a contrast between Sulla's behaviour to the Greeks and that of his predecessors. Modern historians would give an earlier date for the beginning of the decline. Compare Toynbee, in *Legacy of Greece*, p. 314, on the war with Hannibal and the awe with which Lucretius spoke of its horrors a century and a half later. Cf. J. S. Reid, *Municipalities of the Roman Empire*, p. 74.

doctrine that selfishness was public spirit, because private fortunes were the wealth of the State, was dangerous and misleading.[1] Cicero's philosophy was not original or profound, for it was mainly an interpretation of Greek thought to the Roman temperament, but his message was significant because of the man who delivered it and the people who received it. The greatest master of the Roman language recalled to the people, into whose hands the world had fallen, the teaching of the Greeks, that the difference between the right and the wrong use of power, between the use that disregarded and the use that respected the claims of others, was the difference between civilization and barbarism. The word "respublica" stood to such a mind as "nomos" or "polis" stood to the Greeks, for a body of truth, custom, law, common inheritance and common duty, which could not be shaped to the will of a single man or a single generation.[2] It was because this idea contained a principle that Rome could assimilate, that Roman history, after giving the world a great example of plunder, gave it also a great example of public law.

When the discovery of the Atlantic routes brought distant peoples within the reach of Europe, events followed the same

[1] He held, for example, that a man selling a house that was insanitary or had vermin in the bedrooms was bound to make these facts known, or that a corn dealer, bringing corn into a port where there was famine, was bound to make it known that a cargo of corn ships was just behind him.

[2] Herodotus (VII, 104) gives the Greek conception in the answer of a Greek to the Persian King: "They are free, O King, but not free to do everything. For there is a master over them named law, whom they fear more than thy servants fear thee." Compare the contrast in Sophocles' *Antigone* between "the Citiless man, and the High Citied man holding the City's law and the Oath of God in his inmost soul supreme."

See an eloquent description by Ferrero of the significance of the word respublica in Roman history. The gradual control of arbitrary power is seen in the progressive legislation for the protection of slaves, under Nero, Domitian, Hadrian, the Antonines and Alexander Severus. See Lecky, *History of European Morals*, Vol. I, p. 307, and Vol. II, p. 62.

course. The daring of sailors, travellers, and traders from every nation in Europe; the devotion of Franciscan and Jesuit missionaries, who faced danger of every kind for the sake of races strange to them in language, mind, habit, and colour; the new and bold ideas that inspired the intellectual life of Western Europe; these successes seemed to show that man could rise in imagination and spirit to any task that might be set him within the wide spaces of his new horizon. As the epic voyages touched with a new romance the delight that the recovery of learning had brought to the world, there came through new windows an air larger and more generous than the atmosphere of old Europe. In our language the word "Elizabethan" stands for valour, initiative, creation, the greatest name in our literature, the greatest events in the history of our drama.

It might have been expected that Europe would use these opportunities more nobly than Republican Rome had used the mastery of the East, and that the courage of men like Diaz, and Vasco da Gama, Columbus and Magellan, Drake and Raleigh, would redound to some great common purpose. Europe had learned many steadying lessons since the days when Lucullus and Pompey brought home their dangerous spoils. The aims, though not perhaps the history of the great Councils of the Church, the life and spirit of the mediæval universities, the passion for a civilizing unity that had given to art, letters and scholarship an inspiration so sublime: all these were signs of a temper that could look beyond material power and wealth for the purpose of human effort. Unhappily, though these forces created or preserved Europe's culture, they scarcely counted for more in her distracted politics than the Amphictyonic Council had counted in the distracted politics of ancient Greece. The events and figures of the time made this tragically clear. The father of the Church, who assigned the New World with a stroke of St. Peter's pen, was not an Augustine, or an Ambrose, or a Gregory, but a politician who pursued his ambitious ends, and a man of the world who pursued his

A WORLD IN DISORDER

guilty pleasures with less shame and scruple than others. Constantinople had fallen to the Turk because there was not enough common loyalty to defend the tradition of the Eastern Empire. Italy, helpless victim of her discord, was the prize of a bloody war between the King of France and the Emperor of Germany, and three years before Pizarro led his brave rovers to the treasures of the Incas, a motley army of Spaniards and Germans, in the name of the Holy Roman Empire, had plundered the treasures of Rome more savagely than any Goth or Vandal in the past.

The discovery of the New World by such a Europe was followed by numberless and irreparable evils: the extermination of the tribes of Hispaniola by the Spaniards,[1] the massacres in Mexico and Peru, the atrocious cruelties of the Puritans, a great extension of piracy, half private and half public on the sea, a long and exhausting series of wars, a slave trade that rivalled the evil fame of Delos, a ruthless pillage in India, such as the ancient East had suffered at the hands of Rome. More's Utopia, published in 1516, and the writings of Las Casas, who struggled for a lifetime with the greed of the settlers and the divided conscience of the Spanish Court, showed what might have been made of this new world if the age had been guided by its noblest minds. But so far from making a better world, Europe made a

[1] "Twelve years after the first landing of Columbus the five great tribes of Hispaniola were all but exterminated. Many of the Indians perished by the sword, many under the lash of the Spanish task-master; others died of hunger in the mountains, or took their own and their children's lives, to escape from the cruelty of Spain. The successive names of the island—Hispaniola, San Domingo, Hayti—embody its miserable history. The gentle and generous designs of Queen Isabella gave way to a persecution worthy of the fierce St. Dominic, and when the Indians were dead, " by sundry kinds of death," the island was peopled with imported negroes, under whose government at last it fell. In the full Nineteenth Century, the gold-laced officials of the Black Republic have been known to retire by night to the mountains, to celebrate their magic rites, attended by human sacrifice."—Raleigh, *English Voyages of the Sixteenth Century*, pp. 25 and 26.

worse. Spices, silver, slaves, and markets: these prizes had tempted the bold and adventurous into outrage and cruelty, ever since man had sailed the seas. But the scale was greater; the theatre was wider; Governments entered on a brigandage that was commerce and a commerce that was brigandage, in order to build power on the wealth they could seize or keep from a rival. In the rivalry of the Mediterranean, Venice and Genoa had often encouraged piracy; in mediæval Europe there was traffic in slaves between the mamelukes of Egypt and Italian merchants; but nobody could compare the petty and occasional corsairs of the Levant to the established buccaneers who made their headquarters in the West Indies, and harried the New World in the sixteenth and seventeenth centuries; nor the Genoese trade in slaves with the huge cargoes that crossed the Atlantic in the eighteenth century. Piracy and slave trading were much more like incidents, and less like principles of the life of mediæval Europe. In the seventeenth and eighteenth centuries they were so much a part of politics that it is no flight of fancy to declare that the new seas flew the black flag as man was passing from the age of the City State to that of the great nation.

To the world that was ringing with the reckless violence of this new strife, a grim and significant ghost returned from the shadows. As men talked of its great exploits, their minds went back, not to some generous cavalier who had rescue rather than bloodshed in his heart, or to some conqueror whose fame rests on achievements nobler than conquest. John Stow, wishing to praise the bravest of the knights of this age of high mettle, said of Drake that he "was as famous in Europe and America as Tamburlaine in Asia and Africa." When Marlowe set upon the stage, in his swift and ruthless drama, the passions that had slipped from man's guarding reason, he chose for his hero this same nomad "scourge and terror of mankind," who welcomed new discoveries because he longed to set his savage heel upon the wide face of the world.

Europe learnt slowly to check this violence : to think of something beside plunder ; to bring to this Empire ideas of duty, law and government. The Spanish regulations, however limited their effects at first, for protecting the natives from settlers [1]; the heroic life of Las Casas, and the work of the monks who followed in his noble footsteps ; the career of Warren Hastings, alike in the high purpose it pursued, and the sincere blame that fell upon it ; the blows struck by Pitt, Fox, Burke, and Wilberforce in English politics, by Voltaire, Raynal, Mirabeau, and Condorcet in French ; the self-devotion of French and Spanish missionaries, the teaching of the Friends, Unitarians and Evangelicals ; the suppression of the buccaneers [2] ; the crusade that outlawed first commerce, then property in slaves ; the triumphs of Franklin, Washington, Jefferson and Alexander Hamilton in creating a new civilization : these are all stages in a recovery such as Rome had made. Thus into the pushing and scrambling world of Albuquerque or Drake, there came, however slowly and timidly, the feeling for order, self-control, and conscientious government.

The two chief nations brought, each of them, some special quality to the task of organizing a civilized life. The French exhibited from early days in North America the quality that has given them their chief distinction as a governing people : the intellectual sympathy that can enter into the

[1] "The Spanish government, after the barbarities of the first colonists had shown the necessity for interference, stepped in to protect the Indians by a whole code of regulations, the main object of which was to prevent the exploiting and extermination of the population on which the prosperity of Spain in the New World was seen to depend. These regulations, which exhibit the Spanish system in its best aspect, have no parallel in the early colonial schemes of any other nation. The scheme of protection, humane and tender as in many points it was, involved, on the other hand, perpetual tutelage for the protected, and was in no way educative."
—*Cambridge Modern History*, Vol. VII, p. 99.

[2] The age of the Buccaneers came to an end with the Peace of Ryswyk, 1697. E. A. Benians in *Cambridge Modern History*, Vol. V, p. 691. See the Treaties of Ryswyk and Madrid.

imagination of a distant race, Indian or Arab, seizing its outlook, appreciating its play of taste and mind, and accepting its history as a significant background in the life of man.[1] The English established in an India, distracted first by the quarrels of Asia, then by those of Europe, a system of government in which integrity, efficiency, patience and self-possession were to achieve whatever successes those qualities can achieve in the government of one race by another. The French and the English developed and displayed, in this way, the complementary elements of the civilization that Rome had given to a great part of the world : the French contributing a form of equality, the English a sense for impersonal justice.

The Industrial Revolution must be seen in a perspective of this kind : as a departure in which man passed definitely from one world to another, as an event bringing confusion that man is still seeking to compose, power that he is still seeking to subdue to noble purposes. Some critics argue that the term " revolution " is misleading, and it is true that it might seem to imply changes sharper and more abrupt than the change that came over the English people at the end of the eighteenth and beginning of the nineteenth century. Mediæval society, with the life of manor and guild, and their system and principles of social order, was not extinguished by a sudden stroke, like that which converted into a man of property the peasant across the channel, who had scarcely lost the stooping shoulders of the serf. Capitalist direction, a dominating force in the new system, so far from being a new feature, was the form industrial organization had begun to assume in the textile industries, and the form it had taken from the first in the industries connected with coal and iron. The intellectual

[1] The difference between the French and the English colonists in North America in this respect is well described by the late Miss Bateson in Chapter III, Vol. VII, of the *Cambridge Modern History*.

principles that guided the new age had been finding body and coherence ever since the days of Locke. Nature was beneficent ; men had rights bestowed by Nature ; the pursuit of private gain was the best way to serve the public interest ; restraints on profit-seekers defeated their own end ; capital and labour ebbed and flowed in harmony with the ebb and flow of public needs. This set of doctrines had been growing into a system from the sixteenth century, the " watershed," as it has been called, of our economic history.[1]

But if these ideas were not new in themselves, they became the basis of a new society at the Industrial Revolution, just as ideas that were older than 1789 became the basis of a new society at the French Revolution. It is in this sense that the two events changed the mind and outlook of mankind. For when the fullest account has been taken of all the qualifications that the case demands, it remains true that what happened at the Industrial Revolution could not justly be described by any phrase with less of catastrophe in its sense and sound. Societies can pass through important changes that leave the customary life of the mass of the people very much as it was. Such changes may include a change of masters. As states or nations rose or sank in the competition of war or commerce in mediæval Europe, or the Europe of Philip II or Louis XIV, there were great numbers of people whose daily lives were little altered by the revolutions of high politics. They suffered indeed, since they paid in greater misery for the follies of their rulers ; poverty and cold had sharper edges at one time than another ; but the plan and compass of their lives remained the same while dynasties or governments were winning and losing empires. This was not the experience of Englishmen when the economy that governed the life of the village, part peasant, part textile, was merged in the new system of capitalist agriculture and the new system of factory production. A man's life was profoundly altered in

[1] See R. H. Tawney, *Religion and the Rise of Capitalism.*

its reach, its habits, its outlook, its setting, when, from being some kind of a craftsman or a peasant with various tasks and interests, he became a unit in a series of standardized processes. The lives of women were not less intimately affected. In the economy by which the family was provided with food and clothing before the Industrial Revolution, woman's share was definite and visible. Women spun and wove in their homes, brewed the ale, looked after the pigs and fowls; their functions, if different from those of their husbands, were not less important. Specialization extinguished this life, and the women who helped to spin and weave the nation's clothes under the new system, left their homes for the factory, where they found themselves involved in competition with men, working under disadvantages so easily exploited by their masters that the law treated them as young persons in order to protect them.[1] Thus for men and women alike the Industrial Revolution destroyed a great body of significant custom. Large numbers of men and women lost their chief shelter, for in the eighteenth century custom was the shield of the poor, as the law was the weapon of the rich. The poor were thrown into an unfamiliar world where they had neither experience nor tradition to help them.

This impression of the age as an age in revolution, as a migratory society, is not less vivid, if we turn from the poor to the new rich: to the men who wielded the new power. Under what conditions did they exercise their authority? England had neither civil service nor police force at the beginning of the nineteenth century; magistrates and judges, with a few noble exceptions, represented the prejudices of a privileged class in a panic; what public opinion existed was the opinion of a small class which held the doctrine, so mistrusted by Cicero, that the more quickly a man makes his fortune the more certainly is he benefiting

[1] For the importance of this change see *The Disinherited Family*, by E. F. Rathbone, and *The Working Life of Women in the Seventeenth Century*, by Alice Clark.

A WORLD IN DISORDER

his fellows. In this unorganized world a series of discoveries had given to enterprise and capital opportunities, even richer than those offered two centuries earlier by the discoveries of Da Gama, Columbus and Magellan. And in this revolution, as in the other, man began by extending the abuses of the world he was leaving behind : making a great system of factory serfdom out of the cruelties inflicted on pauper apprentices, as his ancestors had made the Atlantic slave trade out of the worst traditions of Genoa and Venice.

For the men, to whom these opportunities fell, were as little tempted to think of social obligations, or of the reactions of their conduct on the life and liberty of the world, as the first Dutchman who pushed his way into the Spice Islands, or the first Englishman to step ashore at Gujarat. They were immersed in a single passion. In their surroundings there was nothing to compel them, or indeed to prompt them, to think of anything but making profit. There were among them men of noble and generous disposition who disliked, modified, and ultimately reformed, the system ; but their existence and their behaviour did not alter the fact that this world was a society with the morality of a world in revolution. In such a world there is a virtue that takes the place of a public conscience : the virtue described by the Greek word " aidôs," shame or sense of honour.[1] There were spinners and manufacturers with " aidôs " : men like Owen, Fielden, John Wood, the Ashtons, the Strutts and the Gregs.[2] But the powerlessness of public opinion or settled law is illustrated by two incidents of the time : a hundred men could be killed in a colliery accident in Northumberland without a coroner's inquest ;[3] the apprentice children who had been collected in a Lancashire mill could be cast adrift on the sands by their master to beg

[1] Murray, *The Rise of the Greek Epic*, p. 80.

[2] Cunningham pointed out that John Bright, though, unlike his family, an obstinate opponent of factory reform, ran his mills at a loss in the Civil War rather than put his workpeople out of employment. *Modern Civilization*, p. 186.

[3] *Town Labourer*, p. 25.

or steal or starve among strangers, without the intervention or notice of magistrate or law.[1]

For this new England was a migratory society : one of those worlds where men live, not by the slow and sober time of law, but at the rapid and reckless pace that revolution sets. The Industrial Revolution had not merely created a new mechanical power, of which man had to be master or victim ; it had brought into violent play all the qualities that had sent Drake or Pizarro across the seas; for it produced the same absolute types, men of genius and determination seeing and seeking a single end in life. A second Marlowe might have made of this new revolution a drama like that in which Tamburlaine and Faustus had symbolized this demonic force in the theatre of the sixteenth century. Shakespeare in that century and Dickens later made these qualities serve the purposes of great literature, putting them in their place in a complex composition, giving a picture, not of a world of fantastic energy, uncontrolled by reason or conscience, but of a world in which life and conduct display all the subtle and various elements that compose man's character. The Industrial Revolution set to the statesmanship of man the problem these minds had solved in art : the problem of bringing into harmony and discipline those rude forces that either destroy a civilization or give it new power.

[1] *Town Labourer*, p. 147.

CHAPTER XV

THE BEGINNINGS OF A NEW SOCIETY

An Italian historian has said that all through history you can watch the struggle between those who produce wealth and those who seize it from them. It is only the theatre that changes. This is one aspect of history. Southey has described the horror with which he listened to the careless remark of a mill owner who was taking him over his factory, that a great proportion of the children never reached the age of twenty, because they worked under such unhealthy conditions. "He spoke of this with as little compunction as a General would calculate the probable consumption of lives in a campaign."[1] This mill owner was exploiting the weak in the most direct and palpable form, but he was not a new figure; there have always been men like him on the sky line of history: the lord oppressing the villein, the usurer oppressing the debtor, the trader following the Roman legion to Pontus, the adventurer from Europe descending on the helpless Indian village. For every form of organization, social, political, religious, may be made a contrivance for exploiting the passions or the terrors or the weakness of man, in the interests of a person, or a class, or a people, or a scheme of government in Church or State.

But the struggle that runs through history may be seen in another aspect. Progress has been described as the gradual escape of man's mind from the relation of use to the relation of fellowship.[2] The first relation in its crudest

[1] Hodder, *Life of Shaftesbury*, Vol. I, p. 146.
[2] See a powerful chapter in *What is the Kingdom of Heaven*, by the late A. Clutton-Brock.

simplicity leaves a man blind to beauty, purpose and truth in life, for nothing has any value to him apart from the use he can make of it : the second, when it reaches its highest expression in religion, gives a sublime sense of sympathy with the universe, in which everything has a beauty, purpose and truth of its own. In the intercourse of mankind there is the same antithesis. Power or circumstances enable some men and some peoples to treat others as if they had no end in life except to serve the strong ; if this opportunity is taken, the world becomes in their hands, not a fellowship where free men and women help each other to achieve what beauty and purpose they can in their lives, but a system of government, or a system of plunder, or a system of war, or a system of production. It is the mark of such a system that the mass of men are limited in their lives by the needs of those who use them, whether their masters are soldiers or capitalists, merchants or kings. Seen simply in this relation of use, man can never be a creature holding large discourse, as Shakespeare saw him, for he serves, not the universal purpose of God, but the particular purpose of his master.

Still there persists throughout history the second impulse : the impulse to make a society in which men co-operate : equals in the sense that no one of them is merely a means to other people's ends, and that all of them share in some common inheritance of truth and beauty. The basis of this society is fellowship. At some moments in the world's history this sense of fellowship has found its fullest expression in art, at others in religion, at others in politics. Where it is active and passionate, it dominates the whole life of a society. If we compare the way in which Tamburlaine thought of a fellow Tartar, and Pericles of a fellow Athenian, or the way in which Ginghis Khan on the one hand and St. Paul on the other thought of a fellow man, we see the difference between the two impulses, the difference between the outlook of the robber who exploits and that of the artist who creates, between the predatory and the sympathetic temperament. If, in one aspect, history records

THE BEGINNINGS OF A NEW SOCIETY

a struggle between the strong and the weak, in another it records a struggle between the robber and the artist in man : between qualities and forces that do not follow any dividing line of class or nation or religion or circumstance, since every man and every society is both robber and artist, divided between possessive and generous instincts, between the delight in power for the sake of power, and the desire for sympathy for the sake of a deeper satisfaction. The same age may produce the divine grace of the Parthenon and the gross crimes of the Peloponnesian War, the delicate visions of Blake and the savage cruelties of the Slave Trade ; for in every society and every age man trembles between the light that touches his imagination, when he sees the world in the wide mystery of fellowship, and the shadows that close about it, when he sees the world in the hard and narrow circle of ambition or avarice or fear.

At the Industrial Revolution this conflict was resumed on a larger theatre, for the new inventions increased the power of both these instincts. They increased the power of the robber, for they enabled the few with capital and talent to use the minds and muscles of the many more effectively, more directly, more continuously, and with greater profit than ever before in history. The new cotton mill recalled the silk mills in which Syrian capitalists collected their hands in the time of the Crusades; the great coal fields recalled the plantations or the mines in which slaves from Thrace or Africa or Gaul had worked for their Roman masters. The form of this organization, with its great mass of labour, obedient to a single authority, unprotected yet by law or custom, inevitably encouraged the impulse to think of men only in terms of use.

"Over a large surface of the Industrial Community" (wrote Shaftesbury in 1842) " man has been regarded as an animal, and that not an animal of the highest order: his loftiest faculties, when not prostrate, are perverted, and his lowest exclusively devoted to the manufacture of wealth."

"I regard their degraded conditions" (wrote the Government Commissioner who visited Monmouth in 1847) "as entirely the fault of their employers, who give them far less tendance and care than they bestow on their cattle, and who, with few exceptions, use and regard them as so much brute force, instrumental to wealth, but as nowhere involving claims to human sympathy."[1]

Nor was this spirit confined to the employing class. The whole life of the industrial districts was absorbed in this system: husband, wife and child were all in its power; their habits as well as their livelihood were governed by it; their homes and their towns dwelt in its shadow; their minds moved in its narrow orbit. "There is as much craving for gain among the men as among the masters," wrote the same Commissioner, describing the naked class conflict in South Wales, "they struggle with each other in the worship of their common idol."[2] In Lancashire, long after reform had begun, the worker still considered it the natural thing that his child should be taken from school at twelve, for work in the mill. England lagged behind Germany and Switzerland later in the century in raising the school age, because the infant half-timer was regarded as an essential part of the industrial economy by employer and employed alike.[3]

Again, the relation of a craftsman to his craft was like the relation of a creator, that of a factory worker to his task like that of a servant in a process. The new inventions seemed to give man greater mastery over matter if you thought of the inventor; but the man or woman who followed a routine occupation had less sense of initiative and power than the craftsman whom the factory had dispossessed.[4] For the factory system had intensified the moral loss which Adam Smith had detected as a drawback to the division of labour.

[1] *Report of Commission of Inquiry into State of Education in Wales*, Part II, p. 293.
[2] Ibid., p. 292.
[3] Charles Russell, *Social Problems of the North*, p. 46.
[4] This loss is described with feeling in *The Wheelwright's Shop*, by George Sturt.

THE BEGINNINGS OF A NEW SOCIETY

It is significant, as Mr. Chesterton has said, that the word "master" ceased to mean a man who was master of his craft and came to mean a man who was master of others.

Yet it is clear that man's new command of nature gave a greater scope to the artist as well as to the robber in man. Bacon's dictum that " truth is the daughter of time and not of authority," if it has to be grasped again with each new system that man contrives, takes new power with every new discovery. In this sense men were made freer by Watt as they had been made freer by Newton, Galileo, Caxton or Columbus, or by the men who invented paper and writing in earlier ages. Moreover, under the new conditions it was easier to spread and to share knowledge : to bring minds together across boundaries of race and sea [1]: to increase the margin of leisure, and to extend the range of spiritual experience and self-expression. All this was made easier, though it was only made easier for a society that was bent on using this power for such purposes.[2]

This struggle was complicated by the disadvantages of war. It is tempting to think that the French Wars are responsible for all the evils that followed the Industrial Revolution, and that its course would have been wholly beneficent if these wars had not brought confusion, passion,

---

[1] It is reasonable to believe that the League of Nations will prove a more effective force than the international institutions which sought to check the quarrels of City States and feudal societies.

[2] The optimist about the prospects of this struggle might have pointed to two incidents in the life of Sir Humphry Davy : (1) During the war with France he received a prize from the Institute of France for his discoveries. (2) He refused to take out a patent for his safety lamp, sacrificing thousands of pounds—" his sole object being to serve the cause of humanity." The pessimist might have pointed to two incidents in the life of Whitney : (1) The invention of the saw gin was the direct cause of the great increase in slavery in the Southern States, by making the growing of cotton in the river beds immensely profitable (Cairnes, *The Slave Power*, p. 208). (2) Like many other inventors Whitney went bankrupt ; he retrieved his fortunes by inventing a firearm.

and material ruin. This view would overlook important elements in the problem : the temperament of eighteenth century England, the social antecedents of the revolution, and the disturbances that would have been caused in any case by these vast changes in custom and social life. The state of the early factories and the early workhouses does not suggest that the French War found the ruling class sensitive and left it brutal. But the war had undoubtedly a disastrous influence. It accelerated an industrial expansion that would in any circumstances have been too rapid. England would have been happier, stronger, freer, if industrial power had advanced with slower stride ; if other countries had taken a larger part in the satisfaction of the needs of the new world ; if the war had not given England so preponderant a share in the new economy and the new wealth.

In the second place, though the war did not fill the imagination of the times as the last great war filled the imagination of Europe between 1914 and 1918,[1] the fear and hatred roused by the French Revolution, greater than the fear and hatred roused by the Bolshevik revolution, since France was closer to our shores, undoubtedly helped to poison the relationships of class. The complacent arrogance of the time, the view that the great mass of the people were, in Wilberforce's phrase, " that valuable portion of the community whose labour is so essential to the social system under which we live," was not the product of the French Revolution, it was the eighteenth century atmosphere. But the Jacobin scare added terror and bitterness to this temper, and it was a catastrophe that the French Revolution and the Industrial Revolution came together.

Writers have sometimes speculated on the course the Industrial Revolution would have taken if it had come

---

[1] It has often been remarked that the wars are hardly mentioned in Miss Austen's pages. It is still more significant that the needs or special circumstances of the war were not mentioned by speakers in the debates on the Combination Acts in 1799 and 1800.

in some other society: if the great discoveries had been made by an age or a people with a strong sense of beauty,[1] or a strong habit of democratic conduct, or a strong tradition of corporate life. In some respects the Revolution was unfortunate in place as well as in time. Rich and poor were sharply divided in eighteenth century England; the traditions of co-operative action had almost faded from the mind; the mechanism of government was bad, its spirit narrow and exclusive; the leading philosophy of the time despised the steady truth that is half hidden in memory and custom, forgetting, in its dread of the shadows, the light that lay over the past. It was under such conditions that mankind began once more the perpetual task of finding the formula that will turn chaos into order, and the multitude of wills into a deliberate society.

But England, the first nation set down face to face with this task, was not left entirely to its own resources. The industrial world was new, but the English were an old people. The conditions resembled those that might be looked for in some distant continent exposed to the greed and cruelty of strength, but the inhabitants had been bred in the traditions of Europe and lived in its atmosphere. The Romans, caught in a storm that nearly wrecked their civilization, could use the spiritual wisdom of the Greeks; the English in the same way could draw inspiration and guidance from the constructive statesmanship of other ages.

For education had given to the English governing class an insight into a civilization in which the conduct, the relations, the difficulties and the purposes of social life had been the subject of endless experiment, of penetrating discussion, and of the most exquisite compositions in history,

---

[1] "In the textile industries her [England's] vast superiority of mere producing power was accompanied by a grade of beauty and design that was often woefully low. Here France was her mistress, and parts of Germany at least her equals."—*Cambridge Modern History*, Vol. X, p. 755.

philosophy, poetry, and drama. The best representatives of that class were steeped in the humanism of the classics. Students, it is true, might derive from that literature impressions and moods which tended to limit their courage and their sympathy. For some minds, no doubt, the social injustices of the eighteenth century seemed still less intolerable, when thrown against the background of a brilliant and critical society living on the labour of slaves. But the same complaint could be made of the study of any literature in the world; the wider its compass, the closer and the more significant its contact with life, the more diverse and the more perverse are the lessons that may be drawn from it. Theologians so little in agreement as the Spanish Catholic historian of the sixteenth and the Puritan settlers of the seventeenth century held alike that the grossest cruelty to the American Indians was justified or even demanded by the teaching of the Bible.[1] A literature makes its effect by the atmosphere of awe or generous hope into which it puts imagination and memory, by the sense it gives a man of the place and significance of an age or generation, in a vast procession of forces and persons, ideas and events. If you ask of education that it should teach how man has tried to make societies, how far his experiments have succeeded, from what causes they have come to catastrophe, the study of the life and literature of Greece and Rome is an experience possessing a completeness that no other culture can provide : it is like contemplating a vast tragedy on which the curtain has dropt.[2] The value of this culture was evident even to the leaders of a rival civilization who still had reason to dread its enslaving charm.

[1] The learned Sepulveda pressed this argument at the Junta convened by Charles V at Valladolid in 1550 to debate " whether a war of the kind that is called a war of conquest could be lawfully undertaken against the nations of the New World, if they had not committed any new faults other than those they had committed in the times of their infidelity."—Helps, *Life of Las Casas*, p. 265.

[2] See Toynbee's brilliant chapter on " History " in *The Legacy of Greece*.

THE BEGINNINGS OF A NEW SOCIETY 253

In the fourth century, when Christians were being drawn back into Hellenism, and many of the Fathers of the Church held that this seducing literature should be put under a ban, the wisest minds of the time, like St. Jerome and St. Augustine, took the braver view that it should be used for the training of Christian youth.[1]

For the English statesman of the eighteenth century this literature was specially important, because it was an education for politics and not only for the management of a man's life. It reflected the anxieties and the temptations of peoples struggling with problems closely resembling the problems of his own age. Chatham, like Cicero, saw the stolen treasure of the East corrupting the politics of his day; Fox and Burke, denouncing the misgovernment of India, spoke as pupils of Thucydides and the Greek tragedians, as men for whom history had rehearsed the scenes that moved before them, and inspired minds had interpreted their meaning. At the climax of the greatest of the speeches by which he charmed the senses of the House of Commons, the younger Pitt turned to the stately music of Virgil's hexameters as naturally as Bright would have turned to the solemn cadences of the Psalms. For it was from the classics that men of liberal temper derived their public spirit, their sense for tolerance, their dread of arbitrary authority, the power to think of their nation in great emergencies as answering nobly or basely to some tremendous summons.[2] Religious teaching did not touch their imagination or their conscience, because the fashionable Church had no light of its own for the awakening or the guidance of the age.

Yet mediæval Christianity, the other great steadying and constructive force in the past of Europe, was not unrepre-

[1] Dill, *Roman Society in the Last Century of the Western Empire*, p. 387.
[2] See Macaulay's letter to his father. Trevelyan *Life and Letters of Macaulay*, Vol. I, p. 69 (edition of 1923). "My opinions, good or bad, were learnt . . . from Cicero, from Tacitus, and from Milton."

sented in the governing class. The religious revival, which touched this world at first only on the margin, had this in common with the spirit of Aquinas, that its standard was not the reigning standard of profit. Wilberforce, denouncing the Slave Trade, was the pupil of that tradition. Shaftesbury, the greatest name in that revival, little as he liked some aspects of mediæval Christianity, looked on a world that made wealth its god, with the stern eyes of a noble and passionate monk. The Tractarian movement recalled a Church with a wider and more spiritual horizon than the well-bred and self-satisfied Church of the eighteenth century. Thus within the governing circle, though its outlook as a whole was that of a spoilt class clinging to its privileges, education had kept alive the humanism of Cicero and the compassion of Christian teachers like St. Francis or Las Casas, Sir Thomas More or Latimer, who had scourged " the steplords " in the first of the enclosures. The English were thus not a raw people, facing an emergency without help or guidance or warning from the wisdom or experience of the past.

Nor again was this England without a share in the mind of contemporary Europe. The intellectual relations of England and France were particularly intimate in the eighteenth century. Adam Smith had meant to dedicate the *Wealth of Nations* to Quesnai, if Quesnai had been still alive. The general movement of the time towards a new and in some respects too confident simplification of social life was perhaps more French than English. Men like Bentham, Romilly, Brougham and Mackintosh, who banished savage anomalies from English justice, and sought by popular education to extend the most important of personal rights, were the friends and allies of the reformers who gave directly to France, and indirectly to a good part of Europe, the blessings of the great Code of the Revolution. The new compassion and the new tolerance which redeemed so many of the vices of the eighteenth century were strong moral forces in both countries; there were indeed more distin-

THE BEGINNINGS OF A NEW SOCIETY 255

guished names in the *Amis des Noirs* in France than in the Abolitionist Committee in England.[1] England first faced a problem that was to engage the mind of one people after another ; but we have only to think of Wordsworth, Shelley, Byron, Mill, Bentham, Southey, Coleridge, Carlyle, pupils of French Liberals and German mystics, to see that the English people could borrow from the new truth that Europe was giving to the world, as well as from the old truth that Europe had inherited from her past. Perhaps English thought has never been less insular.

By the middle of the nineteenth century it was possible to discern the chief contributions that England was to make to the task of creating a society out of this new chaos. Those contributions were Factory Law, the Civil Service,[2] and Trade Unions. By these influences this new revolutionary world was brought gradually and reluctantly to acknowledge the civil order. The mill owner, who had been told by philosophers and politicians that the mill was his own province, and that he could do what he liked on his own premises, had to open his doors to the representative of the civil authority. A series of Factory Acts set definite limits to the use a man might make of his power over others : limiting in short his right to give play to his predatory instincts and compelling him to behave as a good citizen to whom the men and women he employed had rights that he was obliged to recognize. This represented a long step from the day when philosophers argued that if a man wanted to exploit his neighbours, God had so arranged the world that he could not help serving them.

The most important feature of the Factory Acts was the provision of inspection ; the employment of skilled and responsible men to visit and examine factories, to report abuses, and to suggest reforms. From this time the ardent

[1] See Coupland's *Wilberforce*, p. 147. At one time it seemed likely that the two nations would co-operate in abolishing the slave trade.

[2] It is interesting to note that the Roman recovery was largely achieved by the establishment of a skilled Civil Service.

self-centred life of industry was explored and partly regulated by men for whom the world was older than the steam-engine : for whom Euripides and Shakespeare had lessons to teach mankind, not less important than those taught by the eager merchant selling cotton piece goods on the Manchester Exchange. In this way the English people turned to their resources of culture and tradition, in order to bring a standard of conduct into a world that was just as little of a society to the men into whose hands it had fallen, as the Spice Islands had been a century earlier to the hardy traders who had crossed the Indian Ocean.

The first capitalists used Lancashire as a source of rapid and unthinking profit. By the time of the Chartists, deplorably barbarous still in respect of its towns, its houses, its education, its culture, Lancashire was no longer merely this. Civilization had begun slowly to raise its head above the smoke ; government and institutions had begun to bear some kind of relation to the needs of life outside the needs of profit. The cotton industry was in this sense the pioneer, for the districts where coal and iron had marshalled great and sudden populations were far behind. In the towns of South Wales improvement had not yet begun; it was still the worst watch of the night. For there no gleam had penetrated the raw confusion of the new system ; the callous rule of profit was still unchallenged except by the sporadic violence of its victims, whose methods showed in what school they had been bred. As late as 1847 the visitor to Monmouthshire would have had no reason to hope that a self-respecting society would ever scramble through the enveloping mud and stand upon its feet.

The institution of Factory inspection by the Act of 1833 was a stage in the development of a new kind of Civil Service. English administration had been in the hands of a ruling class, applying its desultory and unscientific methods to problems that were novel and complex. The public spirit of this class was active and honourable, though it broke down as in the case of the Game Laws and the early

Factory Acts, where its prejudices and its interests were too sharply engaged. But it had few skilled servants, and neither devotion nor intelligence were expected from the officials who owed to a vicious system of patronage their opportunity of displaying either of these qualities. Bentham's passion for substituting science for custom, his view of administration that it was a skilled business, had in this instance results that were wholly satisfactory: under his inspiration England created a staff that brought to its work training and independence; unlike the English Justice of the Peace the new Civil Servant had knowledge; unlike the French *intendant* he was not the mere creature of a Government. The English people learnt to use educated men on terms that preserved their independence and their self-respect.[1] This was perhaps its chief contribution to the success or the survival of Parliamentary government, for a nation with a Civil Service that represents administration, rather than this or that set of rulers, combining tradition with efficiency for this or that particular task, can turn the sharpest corner without revolution or violence. For the moment, the chief occupation of this educated class was to throw a searchlight on the disorder of the new world. Nobody can study the history of the generation that followed the passing of the first Reform Bill, without being struck by the part played by lawyers, doctors, men of science and letters in exposing abuses and devising plans.[2]

These were the contributions of the governing classes, but the governed classes on their part were bringing a moderating force to bear on the confusion into which the revolution had flung the English people. In the Middle Ages arbitrary power had been gradually curbed by the growth of a body of custom that protected the villein.

[1] This was the result of the system of open competition, and the tradition that grew up with it: this system owed its most important features to Macaulay and Sir Charles Trevelyan; it was finally established by Gladstone in 1870.

[2] Consider the part played by such men as Lyon Playfair, Leonard Horner, de la Beche, Sir John Simon.

The new cotton lords and the new iron masters were not checked by any such influence; they ruled a new world where custom was a shadow or a memory. But by the middle of the century the governed world had established its trade unions, and thus brought a steadying force into the world of industry. Their progress can be traced through a succession of heroic ambitions and sensational failures: the efforts of leaders like Owen and Doherty, the work of the cotton spinners' unions, the great national movements of 1833 and 1834[1] and the agitations for the Charter. By 1850 some progress had thus been made towards setting up custom and combination as regulating influences in this revolutionary society.

In this development it is possible to trace the influence of the French Revolution and the spirit that it expressed or inspired. That spirit had in it the fierce quality of enthusiasm on which the eighteenth century had looked at once with fear and with contempt. When men come to think of the world as a universe in which their lives count, in which their individual minds are associated with a great harmony of functions and purposes, their response to this new vision has a kind of mystical force. There is in the atmosphere of the French Revolution as in that of the early Christian societies, the rapture of confidence and expectation. The word " citizen " meant to this movement what the word " Christian " had meant to the other: it brought into men's minds a driving power such as could be brought by no mere sense of wrong; men were eager to die for it; they became, unhappily, scarcely less ready to kill for it. The secret of happiness and virtue, it was a word to send armies to encounter every kind of peril from one end of Europe to the other. It is just this quality in revolution that makes it at once so intoxicating and so terrifying. Minds take sudden light from it, and a power that teaches by flashes is a dangerous master. Enthusiasm turns to fanaticism and under its spell men are better and worse than their fellows.

[1] For these phases see Cole's *Life of Owen*, chapters xv. and xvi.

In the French Revolution politics are at once sublime and brutal, generous and savage, surpassing the most ardent hopes of the age, outrunning its wildest fears. " Men are born free and equal and with equal rights. Free and equal they remain." The first article of the Declaration of the Rights of Man sped on wings of passion from the study to the Assembly, from the Assembly to the streets of Paris, from the streets of Paris to the battlefields of Europe.

This generous heat did not set the English people on fire, partly because many of the personal rights that the Revolution proclaimed were already, on paper, the rule in England, and partly because the poorer classes, to whom the Revolution brought its emancipating message, were not easily influenced by foreign ideas. The classes most amenable to foreign influence were not drawn to democracy but driven into reaction by the Revolution. Yet it encouraged idealist forces, inspiring in particular a new ardour for education. In all ages there are minds that think of education instinctively as a means of making one class more useful to another, and this was naturally the fashionable view at the time of the Industrial Revolution. But amid the gross inequalities of the age, the other view of education as a spiritual force, serving a master purpose and not merely the convenience or profit of a system, was not without its spokesmen. To such minds education is the means of making a man or woman freer, of enabling the poorest person, in St. Augustine's phrase, to carry within him his own fate. The vision of a vast world of ideas and knowledge from which nobody is an exile or an outlaw, excites the sense for fellowship with a passionate and infinite hope. Men like Brougham, Place, Lovett, and Owen, widely and angrily as they differed from each other, all had something of this religious spirit about education. In estimating the influences that gradually brought a constructive spirit into this predatory world, an important place must be assigned to this impulse : the impulse that produced the first Chartist societies, and the several projects that took shape in Owen's noble and discursive reveries.

A movement that was directly hostile to the French Revolution had none the less indirectly an influence of the same stimulating kind. The Methodist movement was conservative: it sought to make people contented with their material lot, looking with indifference on the savage inequalities of life. But it necessarily gave to a number of simple men and women a new conception of their place in the universe. The Industrial Revolution treated men in the mass; the Christian revival treated them as individual souls. The central Christian doctrine that all men are equal in the sight of God, assumes a new and eager significance in times of excitement, for those times bring back a Christianity that resembles the Church as it was, " a civilization of the proletariat," and not what it became when it passed into partnership with the Roman Empire. Thus in the ardent sects that were born at this time, men and women were seized with an ecstasy not unlike the ecstasy of the early Radicals and the early Chartists. As some minds were taken out of themselves and their surroundings by contemplating a fellowship where men of simple fortunes could walk in the company of Dante and Galileo, of Shakespeare and Newton, so these minds were taken out of themselves and their surroundings by contemplating a fellowship where the despised and the outcast could bear themselves proudly as brothers of the Redeemer of Mankind.

The temptations that had led men at different times to make of their power a system of plunder had led them in this revolution to make of it a system of production. The artist in man, who has revolted in all ages when the wide purposes of human life have been bent within a narrow compass, revolted against the injustice and cruelty of this new oppression, and the disfigurement it spread over the habits of man and the face of cities. In this struggle he found help from those earlier struggles, for England's rulers and teachers could learn from the famous civilizations that had overcome the chaos of Europe and set up a shelter for the ambitions in which man clothes his self-respect. No names stand higher in this conflict than names so native as those of Cobbett, Owen, Shaftesbury and Dickens, but there were other reformers of whom it is hard to say whether they gave more or owed more to the ideas that produced the Encyclopædia in France and the Liberal movement in England. The French Revolution, if it darkened the world with a new despair for many a generous mind, gave Radicals like Lovett a sense for human dignity as passionate as the rapture which lit up for a Methodist weaver the gloom of the workers' life. All these forces inspired and animated the effort that now began to engage the English people: the effort in which the impulse to make a system, and the desire to make a society, the impulse to pursue wealth and the desire to create a civilization were matched against each other in a struggle as old as the history of man.

An ancient myth taught that the life of the world is divided into definite ages, and that the birth of a new age is marked by some astonishing sign from heaven. The steam-engine was the symbol of a new age; an age seeking a new freedom, learning a new truth, creating a new power, living in a new cycle of hope and fear. The sense of escape from a dead past gives to the imagination a daring simplicity. Just as the philosophers of the French Revolution thought that when three words had scattered the old order of king and subject, noble and serf, privileged and simple, justice had no mocking question left to ask mankind, so the philosophers of the Industrial Revolution thought that if once man broke free from the elaborate bonds he had forged for mind and will, he would step into the outer air, lord, by his native light, of wisdom and of truth. It was only by slow disenchantment that the age came to learn that, when man leaves behind him the fading dusk, it is to set his face towards a doubtful dawn. For this perhaps is what we mean by progress, that man attempts his unending task on a more ambitious plan, finding a wider world for experiment and initiative, using and creating forces that increase the power of good and evil, of science and magic, of the artist and the robber, making success a more resounding achievement, and failure a more widely flung calamity. Thus the Industrial Revolution takes its place in the infinite rhythm that the life of man obeys, whether it is passed under Cæsar or Khan, under Emperor or Pope, under lord of war or lord of wealth, in the golden hope of the Renaissance or the deep shadows of the Dark Ages, beneath skies that are radiant with the first beauty of Greek column or Gothic spire, or beneath skies from which God's light is fled, that look on cities given to the flames, and ships sailing for plunder across remorseless seas.

CHAPTER XVI

THE WORLD ECONOMIC CRISIS OF THE TWENTIETH CENTURY

Since this book was published the whole world has been involved in an economic disturbance, the consequences of which have left no people quite untouched, however primitive its habits and manners, however remote its life from the main centres of commerce and finance. This phenomenon has been examined and discussed in a hundred aspects. It is perhaps worth while to take advantage of the publication of a new edition of this book to study one of the lessons of this crisis which has a special bearing on the problems considered in these pages.

Twice in the history of Western civilization there has grown up an economic system so extensive and all-embracing as to make the term world-wide appropriate. The first example was provided by the Roman Empire; the second by nineteenth-century Europe. The first came to an end with the Roman Empire; the second is to-day in a state of dangerous confusion. The decline of the first was marked by failure of food, of energy, of initiative: the confusion of the second by unemployment and a maladjustment of goods and needs so preposterous as to compel nations to destroy the food they grow. What light does that first great experiment throw on the second; what light does the fate of the first throw on the prospects of the second? That is the theme of this present discussion.

Commerce begins where civilization begins, for it is a form of intercourse between tribes or peoples, and civilization is the art of social life. Its activity implies a certain surplus of wealth and a certain power of communication. It is not surprising therefore that the peoples who were the first to write and make beautiful things were the first to find contact with the world outside. The Tigris, the Euphrates, and the Nile, are the sources of the wealth and the culture of Summerians, Babylonians, Egyptians, and Assyrians. The first civilizations are these river civilizations with two great centres, Mesopotamia and Egypt, exporting and receiving various products of agriculture and industry. We are only now learning from the researches of Sir Leonard Woolley and others how rich and versatile a life the Summerians were living by 4000 B.C. and how important were their relations with the outside world. Professor Myres has painted in *The Dawn of History* a brilliant picture of this stage in the development of commerce, with the desert taking the place that the sea takes to-day. The nomad Arabs knew the desert, its wells, its landmarks, and its dangers, and they organized caravans, set up bazaars and formed desert cities, sometimes at places where the desert touches a river as at Deir, sometimes where it touches the sea as at Suakin. The caravan is like the ship; the Arab trader is like the Dutchman who sails over the seas of the world in the seventeenth century or the Briton in the nineteenth.

The river civilizations are followed by the maritime. The Cretans, of whose history little was known until lately, inaugurated a new phase, in which the Mediterranean becomes the source of wealth and power. Sir Arthur Evans has made the pottery, the sculpture, the painting, the textiles, the gem and ivory work of the Cretans speak to the modern world of a commerce that brought Egypt, Sardinia, Mycenæ, and the Hellespont, into touch with one another. The Cretan age which began somewhere about 2500 B.C. and lasted till the sack of Knossos about a thousand years later, was followed by the rise of the Phœnicians. The Phœnicians had set up trading cities on the edge of the sea at Tyre, Sidon, Beyrut, and Aradus, just as the

Arabs had set up trading cities on the edge of the desert. From these they sent out colonists making settlements in Sicily, Sardinia, and Africa. The most famous of these settlements was Carthage founded by Tyre before 800 B.C. Carthage in her great days had a land trade with Central Africa; trade in slaves, ivory, metals, and precious stones, with all the Mediterranean peoples; copper mines in Spain; and her ships coasted along Portugal and France in quest of tin. For four centuries the Phœnicians monopolized the sea commerce of the world. At the time when Telemachus is asked by Nestor, in the *Odyssey*, whether he is a trader or a pirate, much as he might have been asked whether he was a painter or a poet, the Phœnicians were famous in both those characters throughout the Ægean. But they soon had rivals in the Greeks; first the Ionian cities of Asia Minor, then the cities of the Greek mainland. The Greeks spread colonies in Sicily and Italy, and Massilia (Marseilles) founded on the coast of Gaul gave them for a time access to the Spanish markets. But Carthage and the Etruscans combined against them, and in the sixth century they had to sign a treaty leaving the Spanish markets to the Phœnicians. On the other side they opened up the Black Sea trade, and after the conquests of Alexander the Great they developed trade over Central Asia and India.

If we look at commerce in its social and political character, we notice two things about this history. Commerce, though a constant cause of war, is also a cause of peace and friendship. The Greek traders carried over the world the Greek civilizing idea of city life. The relationships established by commerce, and the penetration of distant countries by traders, helped to create the Hellenistic kingdoms in the Empire left by Alexander, with all their influence on the mind of man. Even a world in which the man who lands on your shore is as likely to be a pirate as a merchant has its standards of good faith. Rivals enter into commercial treaties, and Greek trades with Phœnician as in the Middle Ages Christian trades with Saracen.

The second fact is this. The progress and expansion of all these civilizations is arrested by war, piracy, and political strife. We talk of Greek settlements in Italy and Sicily as we talk of British or French settlements in North America or the Indies. But there was an important difference. The terms British and French imply a relationship of sympathy between men of the same race and culture. The term Greek has not this significance, for the Greek settlements were often at war with each other. Even the common danger from Carthage could not teach Athens and Corinth to lay aside their quarrels, and the event in the history of Sicily that lives most vividly in literature is the defeat at Syracuse of Greek by Greek. So poor had been the progress towards political unity that a Greek city in that world corresponds to a European nation in this.

The Romans, so inferior to the Greeks in the life of the mind, succeeded where the Greeks failed in the life of the State. The Greeks could not make a political unity of Greece; the Romans made a political unity of almost the whole of the world known to them. The Greeks could not keep the peace in the Ægean Sea; the Romans kept the peace in all the seas over which their traders sailed. For two centuries after the founding of the Roman Empire, which we may put for these purposes at 27 B.C., the world had peace, order, and something like free trade, over an immense area. We get an excellent idea of the political character of this world from Professor Toynbee's description of it as the federation of a thousand city states,[1] for the basis was the old city state of the Greeks. We get again an excellent idea of the relationship of peoples under its ægis in the description given by Toutain.

"In the first centuries of the Christian era Italy was surrounded by a Roman Gaul, a Roman Spain, a Roman Africa, a Roman Greece, a Roman Egypt, but in these double names each term kept its own

---

[1] *Study of History*, III, p. 487.

value and the special characters of the peoples did not disappear under a dull uniform façade." [1]

But the unity that Rome had created was not confined to the shores of the Mediterranean basin, for the Empire had extended its boundaries to the Atlantic, the English Channel, the North Sea, the course of the Rhine, and part of the course of the Euphrates. Over this vast area, once the scene of war and brigandage, a man could travel now in relative safety.

This aspect of Roman civilization made a profound impression on the teachers of the new universal religions. " Cæsar seems to provide us with profound peace," wrote Epictetus the Stoic, who lived first in Phrygia, then in Rome and then in Epirus ; " there are no wars or battles any more ; no great bands of pirates or robbers : we are able to travel by land at every season and to sail from sunrise to sunset." " The whole world has peace, thanks to the Romans," wrote Irenæus the Christian, a native of Asia Minor and Bishop of Lyons in the second century, " and we can walk along the roads and sail the seas wheresoever we please without fear." [2]

Within this world-wide political order there grew up a world-wide economic order, so active and extensive that it had no parallel in history until the nineteenth century. There was brisk interchange within the Empire of foodstuffs, raw materials, and manufactured goods. Corn was supplied by Sicily, Egypt, and Africa ; oil by Africa and Spain ; wines by Gaul, Dalmatia, Syria, and Asia Minor ; flax by Egypt ; leather by Britain, Gaul, and Spain ; cloth stuffs by Spain, Gaul, Asia Minor, Syria, and Egypt ; pottery,

---

[1] Toutain, *Economic Life of the Ancient World*, p. 252. Compare the description in Tacitus, " jus apud cives, modestiam apud socios." Annals, I, 9.

[2] The great achievement of Rome was described in a single sentence by St. Augustine : " Condita est civitas Roma per quam Deo placuit orbem debellare terrarum et in unam societatem reipublicae legumque longe lateque pacare." *De Civit. Dei*, xviii, 22.

glass, terra cotta, jewels, perfumes, parchment, and papyrus, were all found within the Empire ; more distant countries sent amber, frankincense, spices, precious stones, and ivory. Silk travelled all the way from the Pacific to the Atlantic ; from China to Spain.[1] Roughly speaking we may say that the Roman Empire went abroad only for its luxuries; its needs—so various were its peoples and its climates—could be supplied within its own family. For this distant trade, for which it paid mainly in specie, ship-owners were combined in colleges and merchants in guilds in the different ports and cities of the Empire.

A man walking to-day in the streets of London or Manchester or Bordeaux, glancing at the offices of great shipping agencies and exporting houses, would think at once of all the resources on which international trade depends ; the telegraph, the telephone, the wireless services, aircraft, ships so powerful that they can ride any sea, so huge that they can carry great masses of food or raw material. None of these advantages were enjoyed by the Roman Empire. There was no quicker means of communication than the use of horse or ship ; for five months of the year the storms of the sea were dreaded with reason by sailors whose ships were usually not of more than 250 or 300 tons displacement. Pliny went so far as to say that ships were sometimes overturned by the quails that settled on them.[2]

The Roman Empire, then, owed little to invention ; almost the only discovery of importance that was made at this time was the discovery of the changes of the monsoon. It owed everything to political success. That success can be best described in three words that sound wistfully in our ears to-day, Peace, Free Trade, and Disarmament. It is true that civil war and rebellion were not unknown even in its two prosperous centuries. The death of Nero in

---

[1] See G. F. Hudson, *Europe and China* (pp. 70 and 71), where there is an excellent summary of the causes of commercial expansion under the Roman Empire.

[2] Quoted by M. P. Charlesworth, *Five Men*, p. 143.

A.D. 68 was followed by a terrible year of strife; there were rebellions of the Jews in A.D. 66–70 and A.D. 131–135, rebellion in Britain in A.D. 61, and rebellion in Belgium in A.D. 69. But in contrast to earlier and to later times this was a great spell of peace in the history of the world. It was also an era of Free Trade. The only handicap to trade within the Empire was the customs duties imposed on the borders of each province, and these duties were never very high, varying between 2 and 5 per cent. with $2\frac{1}{2}$ per cent. as the normal standard rate. When the question of annexing Britain was under discussion, it was argued by opponents that a military occupation would not pay its way because the additional revenue to be raised by direct taxation would be largely offset by a diminution of customs receipts. At the beginning of the third century Caracalla, in proposing to marry the daughter of the King of Parthia, argued that if Rome and Parthia were one land and one power, they would have the common unhindered enjoyment of the tapestries and carpets of the one and the metals of the other.[1]

To Peace and Free Trade the Roman Empire added the blessing of Disarmament. The Battle of Actium in 31 B.C. had put an end to naval warfare. Piracy, for so long a most flourishing trade and a most important part of war and civil war in the days of Mithridates and Sextus Pompeius, was now suppressed, and the Mediterranean was effectively policed by two naval squadrons. A historian of the second century said that Rome kept guard over her vast extent of land and sea as easily as though it were a modest farm. Between Rome and the Rhone there was only a single military unit, a *cohors urbana* of 1,000 men at Lyons. Professor Toynbee finds good reason for concluding that the total strength of the armed forces of the Empire,

---

[1] Charlesworth, *Five Men*, p. 160.

For this paragraph see Rostovtzeff and Toutain, Charlesworth, *Trade Routes of the Roman Empire*, Tenney Frank, *Economic History of Rome to the End of the Republic*, and the work of E. H. Warmington on the Eastern Trade.

frontier forces, metropolitan garrisons, Imperial Guards, and naval squadrons, was probably not above 300,000 men during the two centuries for which the Augustan Peace lasted. " For the first time after centuries of unceasing wars the civilized world enjoyed a real peace. The dream of the leading spirits of the ancient world for century after century was at last realized." So wrote Rostovtzeff. What was the dream of the ancient world is for the twentieth century a lost and envied golden age.

After the breakdown of this great Roman achievement the world never presents the spectacle of a system of peaceful exchange conducted over so vast an area until the nineteenth century. The collapse of Rome puts an end to the cultural and political unity of the Mediterranean world. The centre of gravity shifts to the East with the great Arab revival after the rise of Islam ; a revival that makes the Arabs the great traders as well as the great fighters of their age. They master Syria, Mesopotamia, Persia, Egypt, Sicily, and Spain. The seventh and eighth centuries belong to them. In the eleventh century the Normans drive them out of Sicily, and the Crusades bring back the initiative to Europe. But it is a very different Europe from the Europe ruled by the Roman Empire, for the Papacy could give Europe a unity of culture but not a unity of politics. Europe passes from the rivalries of the city state to the rivalries of the great nation, and after the fall of Constantinople and the discovery of the New World the great nations begin to expand overseas and the Western world enters on the process which is to create again in time a world economic order.

But when we turn to this second example of a world economic order we notice at once a striking contrast. In the case of the Roman Empire a world economic order grew up within a world political order. Peace, Free Trade, Disarmament, and the Roman reputation for integrity, provided a great field for economic expansion. Our modern world economic order has followed a different course, for the economic order has preceded the political. The advantages by which it has made its rapid progress are just the advantages that Rome lacked : the advantages of technical skill. The starting-point is the discovery of the New World which, by giving commerce a new importance and a new character, stimulated in time a series of inventions. It is these inventions that brought the whole world into a single economic system.

The description and discussion of those inventions fall outside the scope of this sketch, but a reference may be made to one chapter in their history in order to bring out the close relation of the economic to the political order. The sensational improvement of transport has brought a revolution into international politics by upsetting the life and economy of almost every people. It is easier to-day to supply the English market with corn from the Middle West and meat from Australia than it was to feed Rome from the cornfields of Lombardy. Nobody who considers how the modern world feeds and clothes itself can fail to see that so all-enveloping an economic system demands of the States that live by it some respect for their common interest, if the whole system is not to fall into confusion.

In the half-century that separates the wars of Napoleon from the Franco-German war of 1870, the need for a larger view of economic policy to meet these new conditions was urged on the British people by an important school of thinkers and statesmen. This school developed and applied the ideas of Adam Smith. Adam Smith had tried to teach his age that nations were injured by the obstacles to their mutual trade that were set up from motives of ambition, and that the acquisition of territory if selfishly pursued and selfishly enjoyed was a hindrance and not a help to national welfare. Cobden, his greatest pupil, looked out on the world half a century later when every warning that he found in *The Wealth of Nations* had grown infinitely more urgent with the changes that the Industrial Revolution had brought and was bringing into the habits and relationships of men and societies. When Adam Smith died in 1790 the steam-engine was a new toy; when Cobden entered the House of Commons in 1841 steam power was carrying men and goods round the world, over land and sea. The discovery of the New World in the fifteenth century was followed, owing to the ignorant and violent politics of the age, by two centuries of strife which made the Atlantic as lawless a sea as the Mediterranean had been in the savage days of Mithridates. If nations treated their new discoveries in the same selfish and short-sighted spirit, the Industrial Revolution was bound to lead to another series of wars, for access to raw materials and markets became more and more important as that Revolution increased the wants of man, and the power of man to satisfy them. Whether the new opportunities caused friction or spread friendship depended on the temper and the wisdom of politicians. Cobden appreciated better than most of his contemporaries the close relationships that the new system would create, and he hoped and believed that they would of themselves foster a spirit of social unity. He held that by adopting Free Trade England would serve her best interests, but he believed also that if she renounced monopoly and threw open her markets, she would educate the whole world by the example of her success. It was this that put such passion and confidence into his crusade for Peace, Disarmament, and a liberal spirit in trade. He was a man with a faith, and not merely a man with a policy.

During this time Great Britain's influence on the Continent, if measured by her initiative, her capital and her skill, was predominant. Her contractors were everywhere, her engineers were everywhere, her artisans were everywhere, her money was everywhere. She was building mills, railways, docks, harbours, waterworks, gas works, for the whole world. This was natural, for she had half a century's start of Europe. She alone had had a considerable industrial revolution before the railway age. If we take 1830 as the date of the beginning of that age, we find that England had already 1,000 cotton factories and cotton exports worth twenty millions a year. England was thus equipped before the rest of Europe with capital and skill for spreading the Industrial Revolution. In the early forties, when railways ran in four directions from London to the sea, only a few short scattered lines had been laid in France, her nearest competitor.[1] At one time Brassey, the great contractor, had railways and docks under construction in five continents, and half the capital subscribed for French railways before 1847 came from British pockets.

It is not surprising that British ideas made progress in a world so full of British energy, so conscious of British success. Adam Smith had had pupils outside his own country, among them Napoleon and the statesmen of Prussia.[2] His view that Great Britain owed her prosperity largely to her internal Free Trade had been shared by Turgot, and Napoleon accepted and applied it to the problems of France. In Prussia statesmen like Stein, Bulow, and Maassen abolished the sixty-seven tariffs that obstructed internal trade in 1818. This Free Trade process continued. In 1834 seventeen States combined in the German Zollverein and the Zollverein made commercial treaties with Holland in 1839, with Great Britain in 1841, and with Belgium in 1842. Adam Smith was making his mark on the map of Europe.

In the next twenty years the world travelled much further and faster. In 1846 England abolished the Corn Laws and in 1849 the Navigation Laws. The chief industrial State threw open its markets to the trade of the world. It was an immense event bound to strike the imagination of the age.[3] And if we look at the great figures in the politics of

---

[1] As late as 1880 Russia had not as much railway on her huge surface as there was then in the British Isles. Clapham, *Economic History of Modern Britain. Free Trade and Steel*, p. 212.

[2] Fay, *Great Britain from Adam Smith to the Present Day*, p. 15.

[3] "To expect, indeed, that the freedom of trade should ever be entirely restored in Great Britain, is as absurd as to expect that an Oceana or Utopia should ever be established in it." *Wealth of Nations*, IV, 2, 207.

Europe at the time of British ascendancy we see the influence of Cobden's ideas. Metternich was a man with his eyes on the past. He was on guard for the old order, trying to keep intact an Empire that was poised uneasily on the slowly rising passions of nationality. But all the statesmen who had plans for the future had learnt from Cobden. This was true of Napoleon the Third who was a Free Trader at the head of a Protectionist people;[1] of Cavour who wished to mould Italy on the English model; of the Tsar Alexander the Second under whose rule the movement towards freer trade in Russia which had begun in 1850 quickened its pace and widened its outlook,[2] and even of Bismarck who disarmed the hostility of the moderate Liberals by accepting an economic policy of which Zimmermann afterwards complained that it was a slavish imitation of Great Britain.[3] The results are seen in the commercial history of the fifties and sixties. In 1857 Russia negotiated treaties with France, Great Britain, and Belgium; in the following year with Austria, and in 1860 with other Western Governments. In 1860 Napoleon the Third concluded with Cobden the famous Commercial Treaty of that year, and this was followed by a series of commercial treaties in which Belgium, Holland, Sweden, Norway, Italy, Austria, Hungary, and the German Zollverein, paid honour to the new principles. The tariff level of Europe was being steadily lowered. Even more striking was the treatment of the Far East by European nations. When Japan was opened to Western civilization for the second time by the United States in the fifties, the privileges obtained by American diplomacy, the right to anchor in certain ports

[1] There is a *Punch* cartoon of January 1860 representing Cobden as an old dame teaching Napoleon at her knee. In 1842 Napoleon had written strongly against Free Trade, arguing that if France adopted it she would throw two million of her work-people out of employment. Morley, *Cobden*, II, 353.

[2] Knowles, *Economic Development in the Nineteenth Century*, p. 279.

[3] Ashley, *Modern Tariff History*, p. 41.

and to trade in the port of Yokohama, were not reserved to American citizens but were extended to Great Britain, Russia, Holland, and France. In the same way the wars waged by Great Britain and France against China in 1840 and in 1856 were followed by low tariffs for all foreign trade and by commercial facilities that were enjoyed by all Europeans.[1] Those wars were contrary to Cobden's principles, but the doors that were pushed open were pushed open for all and not merely for the Powers that had used their military force. Thus the ideas of Free Trade were guiding the peoples of Europe both in their treatment of each other and in their treatment of the East. Cobden and Cavour both predicted that the rest of the world would be immensely influenced by the British example. Cavour died in 1861 and Cobden in 1865. At the time of their death that belief was not unreasonable.

Yet the tide was already turning. The Morrill Tariff which started the United States on Protection had been adopted in 1861, and when the Civil War was over Free Trade went down. The War for the maintenance of the Union was probably the only war that Cobden approved, but like most wars it ended in Protection and high armaments. The Franco-German War of 1870 had similar results. France, disgusted with everything that reminded her of her luckless ruler and sceptical from the first of his Free Trade ideas (it was said that nine Frenchmen out of ten were hostile to the Treaty), denounced the Cobden Treaty in 1872 and reverted to a system of full tariffs. Bismarck, having to meet the growing expenses of his new Empire, preferred customs duties to heavier direct taxation. Italy, Austria, Hungary, and Russia, all moved away from Free Trade. With this change in fashion, the argument from example went over to the enemy. For if Free Trade was the policy of the industrial State that had achieved the greatest success in industry, States that were now pushing their way to the front with great energy and success were

[1] Binkley, *Realism and Nationalism*, p. 70.

using tariffs.[1] This was a condition very dangerous for Free Trade, because the chief critic of Free Trade, Frederick List, had contended that Free Trade suited England but that any State that wanted to copy and to rival her success would need the help of Protection. We can see the effect of the changing conditions in the mind of Bismarck. In 1878, when justifying his proposal to increase customs duties, he wrote: " I leave undecided the question whether complete mutual freedom of international commerce, such as is contemplated by the theory of Free Trade, would not serve the interests of Germany." [2] But four years later he wrote:

" I believe the whole theory of Free Trade to be wrong. England abolished Protection after she had benefited by it to the full extent. . . . That country used to have the strongest protective tariffs until it had become so powerful under their protection that it could step out of these barriers like a gigantic athlete and challenge the world. Free Trade is the weapon of the strongest nation, and England has become the strongest nation owing to her capital, her iron, her coal and her harbours and owing to her favourable geographical position; nevertheless she protected herself against foreign competition with exorbitant protective tariffs until her industries became so powerful."

The advantages that Bismarck named as giving Great Britain her success as the pioneer of the Industrial Revolution have been described in this volume. At the time he spoke similar advantages were falling to Germany and the United States from the development of the new railway power. The railways did two things for Germany. They brought her iron and coal into easy touch with each other, and they put her in the centre of Europe, as conveniently placed for distributing its commerce by land as England was for distributing it by sea. Of the effect of the new power on the United States Professor Clapham has said: " If a single national contribution towards the making of

[1] In 1880–4 German exports of manufactures were worth £91 million and in 1900–4 £154 million; the figures for the United Kingdom were £200 million and £224 million.
[2] Ashley, *Modern Tariff History*, p. 45.

the new era had to be selected for its world-wide economic importance, it would probably be this." [1] The United States resembled the Roman Empire in the variety of climate and natural resources within its frontiers ; the railway gave what the Roman Empire never possessed, the means of abolishing distance. Thus two powerful and energetic peoples came into a fortune ; the railway gave to Germany and the United States the same kind of help and confidence that Great Britain had enjoyed as the leading sea power, eager to find customers all over the world. But Great Britain had enjoyed a monopoly. The newcomers arrived after she had established her position, and they soon made up their minds that they could not hope to make their way against so strong a competitor under Free Trade. Thus, as each nation became an industrial nation, it turned to Protection. The most striking case was that of Russia, for Russia adopted high tariffs when her cotton industry was still young against the opposition of her landowners.[2]

The railways, by making continental States industrial, encouraged them to adopt Protection. They had a similar effect in a different way on the agricultural interests. Down to the Franco-German War German agriculture was an exporting industry and Free Trade in outlook. But as the German railways were helping Germany to sell her metals all over Europe, the American railways were enabling the United States to sell their grain in Germany. It was the invasion of American corn that drove the peoples of Europe, with a few distinguished exceptions (Denmark, Belgium, and the Netherlands), to protect their peasant agriculture by high tariffs. Now that the American farmer could reap the prairie and send his harvests, first across his huge continent, and then across the wide Atlantic, with such fatal ease, all Europe was thrown into confusion. This was a

[1] Clapham, *Economic History of Modern Britain. Free Trade and Steel*, p. 213.
[2] Knowles, *Economic Development in the Nineteenth Century*, p. 282.

phenomenon that Cobden had never foreseen, for he had argued that the British farmer would always have a protective tariff on corn of 10*s.* a quarter ; the cost of moving wheat from Danzig to London.[1] McCulloch, with what Mr. Fay calls the " classical economist's sure instinct for the short run," observed in 1841 that there was no prospect of any considerable supplies from the United States, and that European wheat had been shipped across the Atlantic in considerable quantities. The Repeal of the Corn Laws was not followed by any hardships to British agriculture for twenty years.[2] It was not till the seventies that the American Revolution brought the dreaded calamity. Most European States, putting a value on their peasants for one reason or other, took measures to protect themselves. Great Britain, though she was ruled at this moment by Disraeli, kept the Free Trade policy which he had denounced when it was harmless. One of the consequences was the ruin of Gladstone's great Land Act as an immediate measure of conciliation in Ireland, because prices fell faster than his Land Courts could adjust the new rents.

Free Trade was, of course, only one part of Cobden's plan for saving the world. Peace and disarmament were essential to his scheme. Here his ideas suffered defeat equally severe. The settlement that followed the Franco-German War left the two leading peoples of the Continent of Europe with a stupendous military burden and a haunting anxiety. With Germany determined to keep, and France to regain, the provinces that had changed masters, an atmosphere was created that was fatal to his hopes. Europe started on fifty years of fear.

Of the sixty or seventy fully self-governing States that make up the modern world, the great majority have followed the Protectionist example of the United States and Germany rather than the Free Trade example of Great Britain. Instead of living in the practice and spirit of arbitration as

[1] Knowles, *Industrial and Commercial Revolutions*, p. 186.
[2] Fay, *The Corn Laws and Social England*, p. 119.

Cobden hoped, the world began soon after his death to live in all the discomfort of an armed peace. Yet in considering where his teaching fell short, and why it failed, we must not forget the importance of the successes it achieved. Two large facts must strike the observer as he reflects on the history of the nineteenth century. The first is that the British Empire acquired for her possession or her tutelage an immense area of the world's surface without provoking war with any European power. Between the Crimean War and the Great War Great Britain, alone among the Great Powers, kept the peace with all her European neighbours. Would that have been possible if the Empire had not been administered on Cobden's principles ? The German statesman Zimmermann, speaking of the success of Germany as an industrial and commercial power, declared : " Our rise depended essentially on the English policy of the Open Door." [1] Would the great rulers of Europe have allowed one State to collect all this power and prestige in its hands if they had been shut out from its raw materials and its markets ?

The second fact is a contrast between the development of the New World in the sixteenth, seventeenth, and eighteenth centuries, and that of tropical Africa in the nineteenth. The discovery of America was followed by incessant war between the peoples of Europe. The development of Africa has been stained with cruelty and crime, but so far as the mutual relations of the peoples of Europe are concerned it has been peaceful. The Great Powers were afraid of letting these adventures draw Europe into war. The Berlin Conference in 1885 laid it down that no Power should extend its African territory without giving notice, that disputes should be settled by arbitration, and that territories annexed must be effectively occupied. The Brussels Conference in 1890 drew up a General Act to suppress the Slave Trade and the importation of arms within a fixed Mid-African zone. The

[1] E. Zimmermann, *The German Empire of Central Africa*, 1917 (translated Bevan), p. 2.

teaching of Adam Smith and Cobden had not been thrown away outside of Europe even if within Europe it had ceased to command respect. The last half of the nineteenth century was marked by a great deal of expansion and energy outside Europe. Almost all the wars of that time were concerned with issues that arose inside Europe.

The conversion of the world to Protection and large armaments, to economic nationalism and political rivalry, was deplored by its wisest statesmen, but few realized its full significance. For there was a widespread belief that the economic welfare of the world depended on technical progress. Science seemed able to correct the follies of mankind, and invention to spread power and happiness faster than economic nationalism could destroy them. The world seemed to be growing richer even though it did not seem to be growing wiser. This general optimism blinded men to the truth that every day the world was coming to depend more on this elaborate economic world system, and every day the forces that threatened to disturb and upset it were growing stronger. Hence, though efforts were made to organize international co-operation by arbitration treaties and the Hague Court, this was not the main and absorbing purpose of the leading statesmen of the time. The peace of the world came more and more to depend on an uneasy equilibrium of forces. Those who hoped that so doubtful a peace would last, put their faith in the belief that the great financial interests that demanded peace were strong enough to prevent a general outbreak. The task of organizing a political world order that would enable this economic world order to maintain itself seemed beyond human power. The Great War itself, strangely enough, added to the false confidence of mankind, for its remarkable history seemed to confirm the belief in the self-acting virtues of an economic system which had enabled large societies to feed and clothe themselves in the anarchy of universal war. Consequently, when the war was over, the efforts of the constructive minds of the time, whether statesmen or thinkers, to build up a system of public law and international co-operation, were spoilt by the economic optimism that cast its fatal spell over Versailles. At a time when economic confusion was threatening Europe with another Black Death, politicians believed that the economic system that had survived the war contained in itself such power of recovery, such a reservoir of strength, that its problems could be left largely to themselves. They did not see that the political restoration of Europe and her economic restoration were indissolubly connected. The politicians who discussed indemnities and colonies put national desires first and world needs second. In one room they created the League of Nations; in another the forces of revolution and disorder.

It is obvious that the task set to the twentieth century is much harder than the task set to the Roman Empire. The Romans solved their problem by imposing the will of one people on the whole of the rest of the society to which they belonged. The world to-day has to find some method of order, some principle of unity, for the common life of sixty or seventy States. Cobden's belief that Free Trade would of itself provide that unifying force seems to-day a strange illusion. But it seems less strange when we remember that he lived in the first flush of nineteenth-century optimism, in the days of the " march of mind," and that as a great traveller in backward Europe he had been able to contrast the stagnant poverty that active trade could dispel with the false ideas of prestige by which diplomatists still fed the quarrels of the world. The new truth would put an end to these superstitions, and commerce, as he believed, would teach Europe the lessons that she had never learnt from Pope or Emperor. This illusion explains the fallacy of the Manchester School. For that school combined Free Trade and non-intervention in the affairs of Europe as the true policy for the British people. Yet the mutual dependence of peoples, of which Cobden was so conscious, was the strongest argument against this conclusion. If the political order and the world economic order are so closely related that the collapse of one has been followed by the collapse of the other, no philosophy which encouraged or permitted the isolation of a powerful State could serve the cause that Cobden had at heart when preaching Free Trade. To Europe there was not unnaturally something cold and inhuman in this British detachment, and the gratitude with which the world might have accepted our open door was checked by the reflection that our motives were selfish even when our actions were generous. At the time of the Indian Mutiny De Tocqueville had a conversation with Nassau Senior, the economist, on this point.

" Your loss of India would have served no cause but that of barbarism, yet I venture to affirm that the whole of the Continent, though it detested the cruelties of your enemies, did not wish you to triumph. Much of this is to be attributed to the evil passions which make men always desire the fall of the prosperous and strong, but much belongs to a less dishonourable cause, the conviction of all nations that England considers them only with reference to her own greatness, that she is less sympathetic than any other modern nation, that she never notices what they think, feel, suffer or do but with relation to the use which England can make of their actions, their feelings, their sufferings or their thoughts, and that when she seems most to care for them she really only cares for herself. All this is exaggerated but not without truth." [1]

At the time De Tocqueville said this, England had only just emerged from the Crimean War, so that the impression given of her selfishness was due at least as much to the policy that the Manchester School attacked as to that which it recommended. But there certainly grew up a belief, both abroad and in England, that the non-intervention preached by the thinkers of the new school meant, not merely that we wished to stand aside from Europe's quarrels, but that we wished to stand aside from Europe's difficulties.

This was not true of Cobden himself, for he hoped to spread treaties of commerce and arbitration all over the world, and in this way to create a new spirit and habit of unity.

[1] *De Tocqueville's Conversations,* II, 191.

He sought by constant visits to encourage these ideas and these methods in the minds of the rulers of Europe. If Palmerston had agreed, he would have negotiated a treaty with France for the restriction of armaments. But Cobden was a Free Trader whose driving power came from his strong sense of the unity of civilization, and his followers were for the most part Free Traders whose strongest motive was their intelligent regard for the special interests of their own nation. So they were apt to give a selfish reading to his philosophy, and the Manchester School came to stand both in England and abroad for an ungenerous and almost cynical isolation; as a school that thanked God that England could keep out of Europe's expensive follies, and continue with business as usual. It was blind to the truth that the creation of a new political order was essential for the safety of the economic order from which England had derived wealth and power, and that that task demanded the active co-operation of every leading people.

Gladstone's strong European sense enabled him to grasp this neglected truth. He wrote at the time of the Franco-German War that the establishment of a system of public law was the first need of the age. He acted in this spirit over the Alabama dispute and the Majuba defeat; he took action to protect Belgium in 1870, and he tried to persuade his Cabinet to invite a general protest from the neutral Powers against the annexation of Alsace-Lorraine. But neither his own country nor Europe understood the importance of his principles, and he never designed or suggested any effective plan for giving them form and force in the politics of the world. He died lamenting the prospect of disaster which he saw to be inevitable in an age when the ambitions of the Great Powers were subject to no discipline or control.

The place Great Britain held after the Napoleonic Wars is held to-day by the United States. Her technique and invention, her engineers and her bankers, are forming and transforming the fortunes and habits of mankind. Russia and Japan are as much her pupils as France and Germany were the pupils of industrial Britain a century ago. Her obligations to Europe do not end, any more than did those of Great Britain, with such services, but this truth struggles slowly against the habits of mind that are fostered by her history. For the present state of Europe, with its dark face of passion, discourages and repels men and women of American instincts, as the state of Europe in the middle of last century discouraged and repelled men and women of British instincts. There is the same temptation to stand aside from Europe's difficulties on the plea that Europe's difficulties are Europe's quarrels. The conquest of her great continent was an absorbing and exciting adventure, diverting her mind from her relations with the outside world, flattering her pride with an illusion of economic independence, and obscuring the sense both of her debts and of her gifts to the politics and the culture of Europe. When a people with such a history steps into the first place as a world power, it is not easy to acquire at once a world outlook. The future of mankind seems to depend to-day on the answer that the United States gives to that sudden and disturbing summons.

INDEX

Aberdare, 78
Aberman, 146 n.
Achin, 179
Acre, 25
Actium, battle of, 269
Addenbroke, 150
Aden, 179 n.
Æthiopians, 9 n.
Africa, 8, 9, 13, 26 n., 39, (West) 180, 247
Africa, 265, 267; development of, 279
African Company, and slavery, 192
Agriculture, Annals of, 74, 86, 139 n., 148 n., 198 n., 211
Agriculture, Board of, 198 n., 211
Agriculture, Chapter VI *passim*; *see also* Village
    Danish, 89, 90
    French, 88, 89, 90 n.
    Roman, 5, 10
" Aidôs," 243
Aikin, 69
Aire, 77
Alabama dispute, 283
Albion Mills, 128
Albuquerque, 239
Alcock, 45
Alexander Severus, 5, 235 n.
Alexander the Great, 265
Alexander II (Tsar), 274
Alexander VI (Pope), 26, 236
Alexandria, 6; culture, 10, 11–12; fall of, 24
Allotments, 92, 93
Alsace, 47
Alsace-Lorraine, 283
America, 66; discovery of, 16, 212, 235 ff.; 270, 271, 272; development of, 266, 279; commerce with, 21; *see also* United States
    North, French and English in, 34, 38, 42, 239, 240 n.; iron from, 31, 33, 135 n., 146 n.; market for iron goods, 143; cotton industry in, 184, 185, 208, 209; slavery in, 190 ff., 198, 199, 249 n.; *see also* Slave Trade and Cotton, and United States
    South, 42, 185; as a market, 36, 37
American Congress (prohibition of slavery in 1776), 193
Amiens, Peace of, 46, 220
Amis des Noirs, 255
Amphictyonic Council, 236
Amsterdam, 49, 57, 62 n., 219; Bank of, 50
Amusements, English love of, 230
Annual Register, 118 n.; on ironworkers, 143 n., 144 n.
Anson, Lord, 78
Antioch, 16, 18, 209
Antonines, the, 229, 235 n.
Antoninus Pius, 12
Antony, Mark, 233
Antwerp, 57, 180, 219
Apprentices, in guilds, 99, 101, 196; and Statute of Artificers, 101, 108; decay of system, 228; parish, 198–201, 243
Aquileia, 6
Arabia, 6, 19, 178
Arabs, and trade, 264, 265, **270**
Aradus, 264
Aratus, 11
Archimedes, 10, 11, 65
Arezzo, 6
Argentine, 36 n., 66
Aristocracy, French, 59; English, and commerce, 60, 61; and canals, 78; and agriculture, 88–9; recruited from trade, 147; taste of, 219
Aristotle, 195
Arkwright, R., 3, 185, 211, 221; his water frame, 182; introduced into France, 45; into United States, 184
Artificers, Statute of, 101, 108

285

THE RISE OF MODERN INDUSTRY

Artistic power, lack of at Ind. Rev., 251, 251 n.
Ashby, A. W., 93 n.
Ashley, Lord, 226 ; *see* Shaftesbury
Ashley, P., 274 n., 276 n.
Ashley, Sir William, 53 n., 61 n., 90 n., 220 n.; on internal free trade, 58 n.
Ashton, T. S., 31 n., 77 n., 121 n., 136, 220 n., and Chapter IX *passim*
Ashton, 224 n., 231
Ashtons, the, 243
Asia, trade with, 6, 18, 23, 24, 27 ; skilled slaves from, 61 ; commerce in, 179, 180 ; Central, 265
Asia Minor, 265, 267
Assiento, the, 193, 199
Assistants, Court of, 100
Assize of Bread, 108
Astbury, J., 165, 166, **168**
Aston, Joseph, 76 n.
Athens, 229
Atlantic Routes, discovery of, **4**, 21, 24, 27, 38, 53, 54, 235
Atticus, Marcus, 12, 16, 220
Attwood, Thomas, 147 n.
Augsburg, 21, 24, 180
Augustine, St., 253, 259, 267 n.
Augustus (Emperor), 5, 12 ; arrest of abuses, 8, 9, 233 ; and food gratuities, 13 n.; and public games, 14 n.
Austen, Miss, 250 n.
Austerlitz, 193
Australia, 66, 95, 271
Austria, 85, 274, 275
Averia, the, 29, 30 n.
Avon, the, 77

Babylon, 6, 23
Bacon, Anthony, 138, 146 n.
Bacon, Francis, on Spain, 27 n., 28 n.; on plantations, 31 n.; his *Novum Organum*, 64 ; and enclosures, 84 ; on truth, 249
Baines, Sir E., 180 n., 184 ns., 185 n., 186 n.
Baines, E., 75, 76, 204 n.
Bakewell, R., 86
Baltic, the trade with, 6, 9 n., 25, 52
Bancroft, 193
Bank of England, 57
Bank of France, 57 n.
Banking, development of, 49, 56, 57, 68
Bantam, 179

Barcelona, 17
Barkham, 92, 93
Barnard Castle, 76
Bateson, M., 240 n.
Bavaria, 85
Baxter's *Christian Directory*, 196 n.
Beche, de la, 257 n.
Bedford, Duke of, 86
Belgium, 58, 66, 269, 273, 274, 277, 283 ; industrialization of, 46, 47 ; cotton manufacture, 188
Bell, Henry, 129
Bengal, 185
Benians, E. A., 239 n.
Bennett, Arnold, 167. *See also* Clayhanger
Benson, Thomas, 167
Bentham, J., 215, 254, 255 ; his Industry Houses, 197, 198 ; his influence, 216 n., 225
Berkshire, 94, 95
Berlin, 66
Berlin Conference (1885), **279**
Berlin Decrees, 43, 49 n.
Bermuda, 54
Beverley, 17, **68**
Bewdley, 77
Beyrut, 264
Bible, the, 252
Bingley, 78 n.
Binkley, 275 n.
Binning, Lord, 44 n.
Birmingham, 68, 116, 118, 126, 130, 147, 172 ; canal to, 78 ; Boulton's Works, 118 ; ironworks near, 135, 144, 152 ; growth of population, 152, **153** ; holidays and hours, 158
Bismarck, 274, 275, 276
Black, Dr., 116, 117
Black Country, 131
Black Sea, 19, 265 ; slaves from, 190, 191
Blackburn, 211
Blackpool, 230
Blacksmiths, 69
Blake, William, 247
Blenheim, 193
Blockade, continental, 47
Bloomfield Colliery, 122
Bologna, 18
Bolshevik revolution, 250
Bolton, 6, 211 ; its economy, 67 ; communications, 75, 76 ; population, 222
Booth, Enoch, 167, 168
Bootle, Wilbraham, 200

INDEX

Bordeaux, 220
Borgia, Alexander, 26, **236**
Boroughs, English, 98
Boston (Lincs), 68
Botsford, J. B., 21 n., 22 n.
Boulton, Matthew, early life and character, 118, 119; scientific management, 119; association with Watt, 120, 121 ff.; financial troubles, 125, 128; on rotary power, 126, 127, 212; coining, 128; old age, 129; death, 130
Bow china, 165 n.
Bow engine, 122, 123
Bradford, 68, 76; population, 223
Bradwell, 165
Brassey, Thomas, 273
Brazil, 26 n., 36, 180; raw cotton from, 184
Breconshire, 151 n.
Bridges, Dr., 196
Bridgewater, Duke of, 78
Bright, John, 243 n., 253
Brindley, James, 78
Bristol, commercial port, 7, 58, 68, 77, 80, 169; turnpike riots, 73; mail coach, 75; merchants and S. Wales mines, 146 n.
Britain, Roman, exports to, 9
Brontë, Charlotte, 106
Broseley, 122
Brougham, Lord, and education, 231, 254, 259
Bruges, 21, 24, 25, 219
Brussels Conference (1890), 279
Brutus, Marcus, 12
Buccaneers, suppression of, 239. *See also* Piracy
Bucks, 95
Bulow, 273
Burke, Edmund, 239; on American taxation, 33; on importance of England, 51 n.; on E. India Company, 65 n.; and minimum wage, 92; and Watt's patent, 121; and Watt's son, 129; on slavery, 205; on capital, 218 n.; and India, 253
Burley, 197 n.
Burns, C. Delisle, 219 n.
Burslem, 163, 166, 172 n.
Bury, Prof., 20 n., 215 n.
Bury, 76
Bute, Lord, 154
Byron, Lord, 106, 219, **255**

Caerphilly, 154
Cæsar, Julius, 7, **233**
Caffa, 190
Cairnes, J. E., 184 n., 249 n.
Cairo, 17, 24
Calcutta, 18
Calder, the, **77**
Calonne, 45
Calvin, 53
Cambridge Modern History, quoted on Egypt, 42 n.; on Napoleon, 46 n.; on Spaniards and natives, 239 n.; on textiles, 251 n.
Camden, 56
Canada, 34, **66**. *See also* America, North
Canals, Napoleon's, 46; Early French, 77; English, 77, 78; Ellesmere, 75; Grand Trunk, Bridgewater, Glamorgan, 78; Monkland, 117; Trent and Mersey, 169; and potteries, 173
Canaries, the, 54
Canning, George, 153, 156
Capitalism, in Roman Empire, 5, 12, 13; in Middle Ages, 16, 17, 240, 247; in Tudor England, 56; early eighteenth century, 68; in agriculture, 82; commercial in guilds, 17, 99; complete victory, 108; benefit to consumers, 210 and note, and Chapter XIII *passim*
Caracalla, 269
Cardiff, 70, 78, 79; cavalry, **155**
Cardwell, E., 204
Carlisle, 75
Carlyle, Thomas, 255
Carnarvonshire, 151 n.
Carolina, South, 193
Carron Iron Works, 116, 117, 138, 748
Carthage, 7, 10, 20, 265, 266
Cartwright, E. (power loom), **182**
Cartwright, Major, 182
Caste system, 214, 215
Catherine of Russia, 119, **162**
Cavour, 274, 275
Caxton, 249
Cecil, Lord Hugh, 214
Cesena, 52
Cette, 77
Ceylon, 6, 19
Chadwick, E., **226, 227**
Chalons, 17

288 THE RISE OF MODERN INDUSTRY

Chamberlayne, 230 n.
Chapman, Sir S., 181 n.
Chaptal, 48 n.
Chardin, 62 n.
Charité sur Loire, 45
Charles I, 102
Charles II, 106
Charles V, 27, 30 n., 252 n.
Charlesworth, M.P., quoted, 9 n., 268 n., 269 n.
Charlotte, Queen, 119
Chartered Companies, rise of, 54, 55. *See also* under Company
Chartists, the, 226, 256, 258, 259, 260
Chatham, Lord, 203, 253 ; on trade with America, 32
Chaucer, 215
Chelsea china, 165 n.
Chersonese, Tauric, 9 n.
Cheshire, 80 ; cotton factories, 189
Chester, 206
Chesterton, G. K., 249
Children, in ironworks, 133–4, 149–52 ; in potteries, 175–7 ; in cotton, 183, 197 ff., 201 ff.
Children's Employment Commission, on ironworks, 149–53 ; on social conditions of ironworkers, 156–8 ; on potteries, 175–7
Chili, 36 n.
China (porcelain), 165 ; production cheapened, 171
China (country), 268, 275 ; trade with, 19, 20, 23, 66, 185, 186, 187 ; home of silk industry, 178, 187 ; cotton manufacture, 188 ; child labour, 208 n.
Chinese traders, 9 n., 179
Chorley, 76
Christianity, mediæval, 253, 254, 260
Church, mediæval, 51, 53, 64, 212, 215 ; property of, 85 ; Councils of, 236 ; of eighteenth century, 212, 253, 254
Cicero, 195, 242, 253, 254 ; on commerce, 5 ; *De Officiis*, 232–5
Civil Service, as civilizing force, 255–7
Clapham, J. H., 45 n., 47 n., 48 ns., 90 n., 130 n., 273 n., 276, 277 n. ; on London finance, 49 n. ; on German life, 66, 67
Clark, Alice, 242 n.
Classics, advantages of study of, 251–3

Claudian, 14 n.
Clayhanger, 170 n., **176, 177**
Clement VII, Pope, 52
Climate, importance of, 218
Cloth industry (British), effect of growth on villeinage, 82 ; statistics of expansion in sixteenth century, 56 ; debt to the religious refugees, 62
Clutton-Brock, A., 245 n.
Clyde, the, 129
Coal, in Belgium and France, 47, 48 ; in England, 62 ; early transport of, 70 ; canals and, 77, 78, 79 ; and cotton industry, 181. *See also* Chapter IX
Coal mines, steam engines in, 112, 113
Coalbrookdale Works, 147, 148 n., 149, 150 ; described, 136–8
Coalfields and iron industry, 144
Cobbett, William, 21, 261 ; and agriculture, 90 n., 91, 93 ; and factories, 203
Cobden, Richard, and Free Trade, 271 and *passim*
Cœur, Jacque, 16
Coining, Boulton and, 128, 154
Coke of Norfolk, 86
Colbert, and colonists, 34 ; his economic policy, 40, 41, 59 ; and foreign workmen, 61, 62 ; and guilds, 101
Colchester, 17
Cole, G. D. H., 258 n.
Coleridge, S. T., 255
Colombia, 36 n.
Colonies, British, settled on soil that needed work, 31 ; conflict of interest between mainland colonies and sugar islands, 32 ; commercial restrictions, 33 ; liberty in other respects, 33 ; prosperity of, 34
Columbus, Bartholomew, 27
Columbus, Christopher, discovery of New World, 26, 27, 236, 237 n., 243, 249 ; on uses of gold, 221
Combination Acts, 207, 250 n.
Commerce, early, 4 ; mediæval, 16, 18–20 ; change in character, 21–3 ; Spanish regulation of colonial commerce, 30 ; British regulation of colonial commerce, 32, 33 ; British commerce with America after

INDEX

separation, 35; Dutch commerce, 39; French, 41, 45; effect of French wars on French and British commerce, 42–7; Chartered Companies for, 54; English aristocracy interested in, 60; English commerce slight in Middle Ages, 25; reasons for expansion after discovery of America, 25, 60–5; Burke on, 51 n., 65 n.; Napoleon's interest in, 46

Comum, 9
Condorcet, 231, 239
Conservatives, and new system, 213, 214, 217
Constance, Council of, 50 n.
Constantine, 214
Constantinople, 20; fall of, 24, 191, 237, 270
Corinth, 19, 229
Corn Laws, 108; repeal of, 273, 278
Corn prices, 88
Corn supply, of Rome, 6, 13, 29
Cornford, F. M., 61 n.
Cornishmen, Watt on, 124
Cornwall, steam engines in, 124–7; clay from, 168, 173 n.
Corsairs, 28
Cort, Henry, 136, 142, 147; his inventions, 138, 139; financial failure, 139
Cortes, 27
Cotton (raw material) from America and West Indies, 32, 44, 183, 184, 186; Sea Island cotton, 183, 184 n.; importance of saw gin, 183, 184, 249 n.; figures of imports, 184; cost, 186
Cotton clothing, 187
Cotton Exchange, 57, 187
Cotton industry, Napoleon and, 47; French compared to English, 48; English climate, 63; developed before railways, 79; concentration in Lancs, 80, 163; Luddites in, 107; Arbitration Act, 107; and steam power, 127, 182; individualism of, 145; in India, 178, 179, 180, 186; introduced into Europe, 180; development in England, 181; flying shuttle, spinning jenny, water frame and mule, 181, 182; power loom, 182, 183; as factory industry, 182, 183; increased production, 183; sources of raw material, 183, 184; development in United States, 184, 185; in Egypt, 184 n.; Indian market, 185, 186; organization of industry, 186, 211; figures of comparative progress, numbers employed and factories, 188, 189; pioneer of improvement, 256

Coupland, R., 192 n., 255 n.
Crassus, 16
Crawshay, W., 146 n.
Cretans, and trade, 264
Crompton, Samuel, 3, 46, 185, 211, 221; his mule, 182
Cromwell, Oliver, 39, 52
Cronstadt, 121
Cross, Sir Richard, 227
Crowley, Ambrose, 146 n., 148; works, 135 n. (spelt Crawley), 153
Crusades, the, 16, 222, 247, 270; and commerce, 18, 25
Ctesibius, 11
Cunningham, Dr., 194 n., 243 n.
Curriers Company, The, 102
Cuthbert of Kendal, 17 n.
Cyfarthfa, 146 n., 159

Da Gama, Vasco, 236, 243
Dalmatia, 267
Damascus, 6, 18, 23
Daniels, Professor, 44 n., 69 n., 76 n., 185 n., 186 n.; quoted on mule, 182 n.; researches of, 189
Danish Companies, 54 n.
Dante, 260
Danube, 6
Darby, Abiah, 136, 137
Darby, Abraham, the first and second, 136, 138, 142
Darby, Alfred, 158
Darby, Henry, 146 n.
Darwen, 223
Dauphiné, 45
Davies, Rev. David, 91, 92, 93
Davy, Sir Humphry, 249 n.
Debts, of landlord class, 84 n.
Defoe, on cloth merchants, 68; on transport, 70; on clothiers, 197
Deir, 264
Delos, 194, 195, 237
Delphi, 229
Denmark, 277; and agrarian reform, 82, 89–90

De Officiis, 233
Deptford, 127
De Quincey, 196 n.
Derby, 77; china, 165 n.
Derbyshire pedlars, 69; iron industry, 144; pottery wages, 177; cotton factories, 189
Derwent, the, 77
De Suffren, 42
De Tocqueville, 282
Devonshire, clay from, 166, 168, 173 n.
Diaz, 236
Dickens, Charles, 226, 244, 261
Diffusion of Useful Knowledge, Society for, 210
Dill, Dr. Samuel, 215 n., 220 n., 253 n.; on games, 14 n.; on public amenities, 228, 229
Disraeli, Benjamin, 278
Diocletian, 15; and caste system, 214
Doherty, J., 174, 258
Domitian, 235 n.
Dorset, 95, 173 n.
Douai, 17
Dowlais, 70, 146 n.
Drainage, 223, 227 n., 232 n.
Drake, Sir Francis, 236, 238, 239, 244
Drogheda, 52
Dryden, 64
Dudley, Dud, 136
Dunmow, 92
Dupleix, 42
Durham, 76, 94, 158, 222
Dutch, The, and commerce in East, 21, 179, 180, 243; commerce in West, 26; capitalists, 30; as a commercial power, 32, 38, 39, 40, 50; effect of Napoleonic wars on, 49; reasons of success, 58; population, 40 n.; Chartered Companies, 54; as bankers, 57; as immigrants, 62, 165; and *Assiento*, 193

East India Company, English, 21, 42, 54, 62 n., 135 n., 185, 186; Burke on, 65 n.; Dutch, 54; constitution of, 55 n.; French, 55
Edinburgh, 75
Education, importance and deficiency of, at Industrial Revolution, 228-32, 248; classical, of governing class, 251-3; zeal for, 259

Education in Wales, Commission on, 156-8, 231, 248 n.
Edward III, 61
Edwards, Ness, 148 n., 159 n., 223 n., 231 n., 232 n.; on capital for S. Wales, 146 n.
Egypt, and commerce, 7, 18, 20, 24, 178, 264, 267, 270; Napoleon and, 42; Leibnitz on, 42 n.; raw cotton from, 66, 184, 184 n., 186; and mediæval slave trade, 190, 191, 238
Elers, the brothers, 165, 166 n., 167
Elizabeth, Queen, 83; and immigrants, 61; industrial legislation, 91, 101; and forests, 134; slave trade, 192
" Elizabethan," 236
Ellesmere Canal, 75
Empire, Eastern, 19; fall of, 24, 191, 237; Roman, Spanish, etc., see *under* Countries
Enclosures, in sixteenth and seventeenth centuries, 83, 84, 103, 254; in eighteenth century, 84-8, 103; procedure, 87; in Denmark, 89, 90
Encyclopædia, French, 261
Engineering, 79
Engineers, Society of, 122
Epictetus, 267
Erasmus, 53
Ernle, Lord, *see* Prothero
Essex, 95
Ethelred, Statute of, 25
Etienne, St., 48 n.
Etruria, 13, 163
Etruria (Wedgwood's), 173 n.
Etruscans, 265
Euclid, 10
Euphrates, 264, 267
Euripides, 256
Evangelicals, 239
Evans, Sir Arthur, 264

Factories in India, 180; for cotton, 182, 188, 189; discipline in, 207, 208
Factory Acts, observance of, in Manchester, 158; and Potteries, 173, 177; early legislation, 201-2; as civilizing force, 255-8; inspection, 255, 256
Factory system, 248; in Potteries, 168
Faustus (Marlowe's), 244

INDEX

Fay, C. R., 181 n., 225 n., 273 n., 278, 278 n.
Ferdinand and Isabella, 27
Ferrero, Guglielmo, 9 n., 235 n.; on dealings of Rome with the East, 7, 8 n.
Fielden, John, 203, 243; and minimum wage, 107; on apprentice children, 197; on factory conditions, 201, 208, 209
Fieldings, the, 198
Five Towns, 163, and Chapter X *passim*
Flanders, social war in, 17; commerce, 24, 54; cotton industry, 180
Flemish immigrants, 61
Fletcher, J. S., 73 n., 75 n., 76 n.; on roads, 69 n., 71 n.; on opening of canal, 78 n.
Florence, cloth, 17, 65; silk, 18; guilds, 97
Florida Blanca, 36 n.
Foley, Lord, 147 n.
Fothergill, 119, 121, 125
Fox, C. J., 239; and minimum wage, 92; and slave trade, 193, 194, 203; and India, 253
Fox, Henry, 140 n.
Framework knitters, 106
France, 265, 278, 284; modern, 4; and early commerce, 20; and New World, 26; capitalists, 30; and colonies, 33, 34; and natives, 33 n., 239, 240; rivalry with England, 38, 40 ff., 50, 186, 239, 240; Colbert's policy, 41; effect of Napoleonic wars on industry, 42-4; taxation in 1815, 44 n.; industrial progress before war, 45; population, 40 n., 45; exports, 45; in India, 38, 55 n., 179, 185, 186; internal customs regulations, 59; agriculture, 82, 88, 89; aristocracy, 59, 60, 85, 88, 89; guilds in, 97, 101; metal workers, 142; cotton industry, 183, 184, 188; and Assiento, 193; abolitionist movement in, 255; and equality, 240; taste in textiles, 251 n.; intellectual relations with England, 254, 255; railways in, 273; and Free Trade, 273-5
Francis, St., 254

Franco-German War, 271, 275, 277, 278, 283
Frank, Tenney, 269 n.
Franklin, Benjamin, 239; and steam engine, 119
Free Trade, internal, in England, 46, 58, 59, 71; in France, 46; in Roman Empire, 269, 270; in Britain, 272 ff.; in Europe, 273 ff.
French Chartered Companies, **54, 55**
French India Company, 42
French peasant, 230
Friends, Society of, 239
Fuggers, The, 29, 50, 54 **n.**

Galileo, 249, 260
Galloway, R. L., 113 n.
Game Laws, The, 256
Gas, introduction of, **138, 220**
Gaul, 8, 247, 267; industry in, 6, 9, 10 n.
Genoa, 219; silk mills, 16, **18**; and commerce, 17, 18, 24, 25, 180; and slave trade, 190, 191, 243; and piracy, 238
George, M. Dorothy, 187 n., 196 n.
George II, 91
George III, 86, 198 n.
Germany, 278, 284; social strife in Middle Ages, 17; commerce, 24, 25; capitalists, 30; thirty years' war, 39, 53 n.; Germans as money lenders, 52, 56; Huguenots and, 62; economic life a century ago, 66, 67; effect of railways on, 1, 79; agricultural revolution in, 82; peasants in, 83 n.; aristocracy, 85; textile taste, 251 n.; mystics, 255; and Free Trade, 273, 276; railways, 276-7; and Protection, 276 f.
Gibbins, H. de B., 47 n.
Gibbon, Edward, on Roman commerce, 6; on national status in 1414, 50 n.; on Justinian and silk, 187
Giddy, D., 232 n.
Gig mills, 105
Ginghis Khan, 28 n., 246
Gladstone, W. E., 257 n., 278, 283
Glamorganshire, 151 n., 153, 154; militia, 155; population, 223
Glasgow, 76; Watt and, 114, **115, 116**; University, **115**; **Corporation, 115**

Gloucester, 72, 80, 95; magistrates and wages, 105
Good Hope, Cape of, 22
Gould, Nathaniel, 158, 201
Gower, Lord, 167
Gracchi, The, 5
Graham, Sir James, 204, 205
Grand National Consolidated Trades Union, 155
Grant, I. F., 86 n.
Grant, Professor A. J., on guilds, 101 n.
Gravesend, 173 n.
Greece, and arts of East, 6; and industry, 10, 11; and tyrants, 11 n.; civilization, 52; quarrels, 52, 236; immigrants into, 61; intellectual speculation, 63; simple habits, 218; views of life, 222, 235, 251; public buildings, 228
Greeks, their trade, 265–6; quarrels, 266
Greenock, 114
Gregs, the, 243
Gretton, R. H., 99 n., 220 n.; on Gild merchants, 100 n.
Grey, Charles, 92
Guest family, 146 n., 147 n.
Guiana, 54
Guild, commonly found in Western Europe in Middle Ages, 97; guild merchant, 97; history of English guilds like that of English town, 98; internal struggles, 98, 99; defeat of small master by commercial capitalist, 99; craft guild superseded by bodies like Livery Companies, 99; references to mediæval guilds in other chapters, 17, 23, 51, 52, 65, 196, 212, 215, 240; of merchants, 54; of Hammermen, 115
Guinea Coast, 199, 203
Gujarat, 179, 243

Hadrian, 5, 15, 235 n.
Halifax, 68, 76, 211
Hamilton, Alexander, 239
Hammermen, Guild of, 115
Hampshire, 95
Hanley, 163
Hannibal, 234 n.
Hanseatic League, 21, 25, 179
Hanse Towns, 24, 52

Hanway, Jonas, on tea, 22; and pauper children, 198
Hardy, Thomas, 3
Hargreaves, James, 46, 211; his jenny, 181, 182
Haring, C., 28 n., 29 n., 30 n.
Harrogate, 72
Hastings, Warren, 239
Hawkins, Sir John, 192
Hayes, Carlton, 20 n., 26 n., 30 n., 193 n.; on banking families, 54 n.
Hayti, 237 n.
Health, Board of, 226
Health, Public, Acts, 227
Health of Towns Commission (1884), 156, 223, 224
Health of Towns Committee (1840), 226
Hecksher, 44 n.
Heitland, W. E., 14 n., 214 n.; on reaping machine, 10 n.; on extortions of officials, 15 n.
Helens, St., 76, 78
Hellenistic kingdoms, 265
Hellespont, 264
Helps, Sir Arthur, on Peru, 30 n.; on wars in New World, 252 n.
Henry IV (of France), 4, 55 n.; and customs regulations, 59; and immigrants, 61
Henry VII, 27
Henry VIII, and Church lands, 60, 85
Herefordshire, 70, 72
Hero of Alexandria, 11, 12, 110
Herodes Atticus, 220, 229
Herodotus, 235 n.
Hewins, W. A. S., on Dutch East India Company, 55 n.
Heyd, W., 17 n., 18 n., 20 n., 25 n., 190 n., 191 n.; on Jacques Cœur, 16 n.
Hiero, 11
Highlanders, 93rd, 155
Highlands, 86 n.
Hispaniola, 237
Hobhouse, L. T., 216 n.
Hobson, J. A., 18 n., 63 n.
Hodder, E., 245 n.
Holidays, in Rome, 14 n.; in Middle Ages, 229
Holker, John, 45
Holland, 273, 274, 275, 277; and Berlin Decrees, 49 n. *See also* Dutch
Holyhead, 75

INDEX

Home Office Papers, 154 n., 174 n., 202 n.
Homfray, 146 n.
Horner, Francis, 199
Horner, Leonard, 231, 257 n.
Horrocks, H., 183
Horsehay Works, 148 n., 150
Horwich, 223
Housing. *See* Towns
Howlett, Rev. John, 92
Huddersfield, 68
Hudson, G. F., 268 n.
Hudson Bay, 42, 54
Huguenot immigrants, 61, 62
Hull, 77, 78, 169
Hume, Joseph, 207
Hume, Martin, 27 n., 30 n.
Hunts, 95
Hungary, 274, 275
Huntsman, Benjamin, 141, 142, 143
Hurst, G. B., on American trade, 34 n.
Hutchins and Harrison, 188 n.
Hyde, 224 n.

Immigrants, and industry, 61, 62, 165, 180
India, 265, 282; commerce, 6, 8, 9 n., 19, 23, 66; British Empire in, 15, 31 n., 38, 185, 186, 240; tea from, 21, 22; Portuguese and, 39, 180; rivalry of French and English in, 38, 42, 55 n., 179, 185, 186; home of cotton industry, 178, 179, 180, 182 n.; market for English cotton, 185-7; pillage in, 237, 253
Indians (American), 33 n.; cruelties to, 192, 237, 252
Indies, East, raw cotton from, 184
  West, 31, 32, 42; cotton from, 32, 184; slavery, 193, 194, 198, 199, 201, 203; conflict of interest between British West Indies and colonies on mainland, 32
Inquests, absence of, 152, 158, 159, 243
Inventions, outburst of, 63-5
Invergarry, 134 n.
Ipswich, 98
Irenæus, 267
Ireland, 9 n., 51 n.; immigrants from, in Lancs, 107; in S. Wales, 156
Irish Commercial Propositions, 145

Irish peasant, 230
Iron industry, and America, 31, 33, 135 n., 146 n.; and Severn, 77, 134, 136; and Russia, 123 n.; decline in early eighteenth century, 132; production of pig and bar iron, 132, 133; workers, 133; districts, 79, 80, 131, 134, 135; Darby's discoveries, 136-8; cast iron goods, increase in, 138, 220; Cort's inventions, 139, 140; steam power, 141; rapid expansion, 143; stimulus of war and slump, 143; misery of workers, 143 n.; concentration and large-scale organization, 144; ironmasters, political power and character, 145, 146, 147; new types of workers, 147, 148; wages and hours, 148, 149; conditions in Staffs and Shropshire, 149, 150; in S. Wales, 151; in Scotland, 152; Canning on ironworks, 153; life in new districts, 153-9; Truck system, 154, 155; masters as magistrates, 154; figures of production and distribution, 160, 161
Irwell, the, 77
Isabella, Queen, 237 n.
Italian, City States and commerce, 18, 54; and Guilds, 97; money lenders, 52, 56; bankers, 56, 57; cotton industry, 47, 180; mediæval slave trade, 191, 238; wars, 237
Italy, 265, 266, 274, 275

Jacquard's loom, 45; Napoleon and, 46
Jamaica, as slave market, 193, 195
James I, 56, 91
Japan, 274, 284; trade with, 179
Java, 22
Javan merchants, 179
Jefferson, Thomas, 239
Jellicoe, Adam, 140
Jellicoe, Samuel, 140
Jenny spinning, in France, 45; invention of, 181
Jerome, St., 253
Jerusalem, 18
"Jesus," The, 192
Jevons, H. S., 70 n., 79 n.

Jews, 269; as traders, 20; financiers, 49 n.; money lenders, 52, 56; expelled by Spaniards, 62
John of Newbury, 17 n.
Johnson, A. H., 83 n.
Johnson, Dr., 5
Joint Stock Companies, 55, 102
Jones, Stuart, 14 n.
Jones, W. H. S., 15 n.
Junot, 36
Justinian, and silk, 16 n., 187
Juvenal, 13; on commerce, 6

Kay, John, 46; flying shuttle, 181
Kendal, 17 n., 76
Kensington, 70
Kent, 95
Kent, Nathaniel, 91, 93
Kidderminster, 6
Kinneil House, 117, 120, 121
Kirkby Lonsdale, 76
Kirkcaldy, A. W., 37 n., 39 n.
Knaresborough, 74
Knowles, L. C. A., 34 n., 45 n., 181 n., 183 n., 274 n., 277 n., 278 n.; on British shipping, 37 n.; on population, 40 n.; on German economic life, 53 n.

Laistner, J., 11 n.
Lancashire, 219; Luddites, 104, 107; climate suitable for cotton industry, 181 n.; cotton factories, 189, 199; population, 80, 223; magistrates and concerts, 229; education in, 248; improvement in, 256
Lancaster, 76
Lanchester, H. V., 221 n.
Las Casas, 237, 239, 254; on Peru, 30 n.; and slavery, 192
Laski, H. J., 214 n.
Latimer, Bishop, 254
Lead poisoning, 168
Leathes, Stanley, Sir, 227 n.
Lecky, W. E. H., 21 n., 34 n., 36 n., 193 n., 235 n.; on American Indians, 33 n.
Leeds, 68, 91, 211; communications, 75, 76, 77; gas in, 220; population, 222
Leibnitz, 42 n.
Leipsic fair, 68
Levant, trade with, 24, 54, 55, 180; pirates, 238
Levasseur, E., 215 n.

Liability, Limited, 222 n.
Liberalism, and new system, 214–17
Liège, 148
Lille, 48 n.
Lima, 30
Lincoln, 17
Lipson, E., 17 n.
Lisbon, 36
List, Frederick, 276
Liverpool, commercial centre, 7, 10, 58, 68, 80; cotton exchange, 57; communications, 76, 77, 78, 79; and Potteries, 169, 172; slave trade, 203, 204 n.; death rate, 223
Livery Companies, 99, 101
Lloyd, G. I. H., 138 n.
Lloyds, the, 147
Locke, John, 53, 215, 241; on children's work, 197
Loire, the, 77
London, commerce, 19, 25; financial centre, 48, 49, 58; Stock Exchange, 57; communications with provinces, 68, 69, 70, 76, 77, 172
Longton, 163
Lord, J., 129 n.
Louis Bonaparte, King of Holland, 49 n.
Louis XI (of France), 4; and silk industry, 18; and immigrants, 61
Louis XIV, 241; his wars, 39, 40; his policy, 40–2
Louis XV, 34
Louvois, 41
Lovett, William, 259, 261
Lowe, Vere and Williams, 125
Lucca, 18, 65
Lucretius, 234 n.
Lucullus, 13, 236
Luddite Riots, 104–7
Luther, 53
Lyons, 269

Maassen, 273
Macadam, J. L., 75
Macaulay, T. B., on Baconian philosophy, 64 n.; on Southey, 225; on his classical education, 253 n.; and Civil Service, 257 n.
Macedon, 7, 8 n., 30
Mackintosh, Sir James, 254
Madeley Iron Works, 150
Madras, cotton from, 186

INDEX

Magellan, 236, 243
Magistrates, scarcity in S. Wales, 154
Mahomet Ali, 184 n.
Majuba, 283
Malabar, 6
Malaria, 15 n.
Malplaquet, 193
Manchester, 91, 126, 127, 172, 174; cotton industry, 23, 44, 163, 180; chapmen, 69; communications, 76, 77, 78, 79; population, 153, 222; death-rate, 223; public spirit, 158; squalor, 219, 221, 224, 229; gas, 220
Manor system, 81, 104, 215, 240
Manorial Courts, 81, 82, 83, 85, 104
Mantoux, P., 17 n., 77 n., 78 n., 145 n.
Marburg, 111
Marcus Aurelius, 14 n., 229
Markham, Sir C. R., 27 n.
Marlborough, Duke of, 193
Marlowe, C., 238, 244
Marseilles, 220, 265
Marshall, T. H., 130 n.
Marvin, F. S., 196 n.
Massey, 174
Mauritius, 184
McCulloch, J. R., 278
Mechanics, Watt's difficulties with, 122, 123, 127 n.
Mechanics' Magazine, 160 n.
Medici, Cosimo dei, 16
Medici, the, 54 n.
Melbourne, Lord, 155, 225, 227
Meredith, H. O., 185 n.
Merlin, Monmouth, 159 n.
Mersey, the, 77, 169, 181
Merthyr Tydfil, transport of coal, 70; canal, 78; ironworks, 134, 138, 146 n., 154; riots, 155; conditions, 159, 229, 232 n.; water supply, 159, 220; population, 223
Mesopotamia, 264, 270
Mesta, the, 30 n.
Metcalfe, J., 74
Meteyard, E., 163 n., 167 n.
Methodist movement, 260, 261
Metternich, 274
Mexico, 27, 30, 36 n., 185, 237
Middle Ages, commerce in, 16–21; as civilization, 51 ff.; changes, 54; peasant life, 81, 82

Middlesex, 80
Midlands, coal and iron, 58, 80, 148, 155; enclosures, 84; migration of ironworks to, 134, 144
Milan, Duchy of, 59
Mill, J. S., 255
Mines, Cornish, 124–7
Mining, capitalism in, 240; connexion with development of ironworks, 144, 147, 151, 153, 156
Mint, Royal, 128
Mirabeau, 239
Missionaries in New World, 236, 239
Mithridates, 269, 272
Moffitt, L. W., 223 n.
Monmouthshire, numbers employed in iron industry, 151 n.; social conditions, 156–9, 248, 256; population, 223
Monroe, President, 35 n.
Montcalm, 42
Monton, 223
Montpellier, 16 n., 17
Moors, 180, 191
More, Sir Thomas, 224, 254; *Utopia*, 237
Morland, W. H., 27 n., 39 n., 179 n.
Morley, Anthony, 134
Morley, John, 274 n.
Morocco, 54
Morrill Tariff, 275
Muirhead, J. P., 115 n., 120 n., 130 n.
Muir, Ramsay, 203 n.; on colonial rivalry, 26 n.
Mule, invention and importance of, 182
Mulhausen, cotton statistics, 48, 188
Municipal Corporations Act (1835), 225
Municipal Corporations Commission, 98
Murdock, William, wages, 123 n.; inventions, 126, 129
Murray, Gilbert, 243 n.
Mutiny, Indian, 54
Mycenae, 264
Myos, Harmos, 6
Myres, J. L., 264

Nantes, Revocation of Edict of, 61
Napoleon, 96, 271, 273; his wars, 42; Berlin Decrees, 43; economic policy, 46, 47; Bank of France, 57 n.

Napoleon III, 274, 275
Narbonne, 17
National Association for the Protection of Labour, 155
Navigation Acts, 39, 40
Navigation Laws, 273
Navy Board, 127, 140
Needles, the, 19
Nero, 9, 14 n., 235 n., 268
Nerva, 5
Nestor, 265
Netherlands, Spain and, 27; religious differences, 58
Newcastle (Staffs), 172
Newcastle-on-Tyne; communications, 76, 77; Gild merchant, 100 n.; ironworks, 135 n.
Newcomen, Thomas, his engine, 115, 119, 122, 124; described, 112, 113
Newhaven, 173 n.
Newton, Sir Isaac, 64, 65, 249, 260
Nile, the, 6, 264
Nonconformists, ironmasters as, 146. *See also* Methodists and Quakers
Norfolk, 80, 95
Normanby, Lord, 226
Normandy, 9
Normans, 19, 270
Northamptonshire, 80
Northumberland, 94, 158
Norway, 66, 274
Norwich, 68, 97, 219
Nottingham, 77; Luddites, 104, 106
Novgorod, 20
Nuremberg, 18

Oastler, R., 201, 203
Oldham, 67; population, 223; and schools, 231
Oldknow, Samuel, 189
Orders in Council, 43, 44, 47
Ordnance, Office of, 138
Orleans Canal, 77
Ostia, 6, 10, 16
Owen, H., 166 n., 172 n.
Owen, Robert, 261; national movements, 155, 226, 258, 260; factory legislation, 201, 243; education, 259
Oxford, 95

Paine, Tom, 231
Palestine, 9, 24
Palladius, 10 n.

Papin, Dionysius, 111
Papplewick, 127 n.
Paraguay, 36 n.
Paris, 97, 118, 218
Parliament, reformed, and abuses, 225; anomalies in eighteenth century, 213; Liberals and, 216
Parliamentary Inquiries and Reports, 3, 226
Parma, Duke of, 58
Parthenon, the, 247
Parthia, 269
Passy, 46
Paul, St., 246
Paul's, St., Cathedral, 222
Paulus, 7
Pedlars, 68, 69
Peel, Sir Robert (first Baronet), estate at death, 49 n.; and turnpike road, 73 n.; factory legislation, 173, 201; slave trade, 203
Peel, Sir Robert (second Baronet), 227
Pembrokeshire, 151 n.
Pepper, as article of commerce, 19, 20, 21, 22, 23, 179
Percival, Dr., 158, 201, 223, 226 n.
Pericles, 61 n., 246
Persia, 270; commerce with, 19, 178, 179
Peru, mineral treasures, 27; Las Casas on, 30 n.; liberation, 36 n.; cruelties in, 237
Peruzzi, the, 54 n.
Peter the Great, 123 n.
Peterloo, 44
Petty, Sir William, on Dutch, 57, 58
Philip II (of Spain), 27, 30 n., 241
Phillipps, L. March, 222 n.
Phœnicians and trade, 264, 265
Piacenza, 180
Piece Halls, 68
Piracy, 238, 239, 265, 266
Pisa, and commerce, 18, 25
Pitt, William (the younger), 239; and industry, 40; Board of Agriculture, 74; minimum wage, 92, 214 n.; Cotton Arbitration Act, 107; Irish Commercial Propositions, 145; taxation of iron, 145; slave trade, 193; on children's labour, 197; Combination Act, 207; and classics, 253
Pitts, the, and commerce, 60

Pizarro, 27, 237, 244
Place, Francis, and cotton clothing, 187; and Combination Laws, 207; and education, 259
Plague, The Great, 82
Playfair, Lyon, 257 n.
Pliny the Elder, 10 n., 268; on agriculture, 5; luxuries, 13; and sails, 63
Pliny the Younger, public gifts, 229
Plutarch, on Pompey, 8 n.; on Archimedes, 11 n.; on Sulla, 234 n.
Plymouth, 98
Po, Valley of the, 6, 9
Polo, Marco, 16, 191
Pompeius, Sextus, 269
Pompey, his spoils, 8 n., 236; his slaves, 196 n.
Ponsonby, Arthur, 133 n.
Poor Law system, 94, 95
Populations, in eighteenth century, 40 n., 45; changes of distribution in England, 80
Porter, G. R. (*Progress of the Nation*), 48 n.; iron figures, 161; cotton figures, 188, 189
Portland Vase, 170
Portugal, 265
Portuguese, and New World, 24, 26, 27, 180, 191; break up of empire, 36, 37; Regent, 36; in India, 39, 178, 179, 180, 181; in Africa, 39, 180, 191; slave labour, 191
Postlethwayt, 194 n.
Potter, Humphrey, 113
Potteries, the, early transport in, 70; nature of district, 163, 164; early peasant industry, 164; changes, 164; the Elers, 165; salt glazed ware, 166; Astbury and whitened body, 166; potters' rot, 166; Benson's water mill, 167; introduction of moulds, 167; Booth and fluid glaze, 167, 168; lead poison, 168; importation of clay, 168; growth of capitalism, 168; improvements in transport, 169, 170; Wedgwood's improvements, 170, 171; blue printing, 171; cheap china, 171; absence of mechanical power, 172; division of labour, 172; Wedgwood on condition of workers, 173; Unions and strikes, 174, 175; revelations of Children's Employment Commission, 175-7; wages, 175; Factory Acts, 177
Potter's Examiner, 175
Potters' rot, 166
Power, E., 86 n.
Power looms, in France, 48; in England, 107, 108; invention of, 182, 183; numbers, 183
Prescot, 76
Press gangs, 114
Preston, 76, 97, 211; housing, 223, 224
Prestonpans, 118
Pretender's Raid, 72
Price, Dr., 231
Protection, growth of, 275-80
Prothero, R. E. (Lord Ernle), 88 n.; on Tull, 86 n.
Prussia, 188, 273
Prussian Companies, 54 n.
Punch, 274 n.
Puritans, 212; cruelties to natives, 237, 252

Quaker, ironmasters, 137, 141, 147
Quebec Act, 34
Quesnai, 254

Rackham and Read, on Wedgwood, 170 n.
Radcliffe, William, 183
Radicals, and new system, 213; and natural rights, 216; early, 230, 260
Railways, introduced after textile revolution, 2, 79, 80; and Potteries, 170; in England, 273; in France, 273; in Germany, 276, 277; in Russia, 273 n.; in the United States, 276, 277; and Protection, 277
Raleigh, Sir Walter (1552-1618), 236; on Spanish treasure, 29 n.; on English trade, 39 n.
Raleigh, Sir Walter (professor), 27 n., 29 n., 221 n.; on Hispaniola massacres, 237
Ramillies, 193
Rathbone, E. F., 242 n.
Rathbone, W., 203
Raynal, 239
Reaping machine (Roman), 10 n.
Redmayne, Sir R., 48 n.
Red Sea, 6, 179 n.

Reform, Parliamentary, 174
Reformation, the, 4, 53; refugees, 61
Reid, J. S., 234 n.
Religion, wars of, 38, 40, 55 n.; importance in mediæval commerce, 20; object of munificence, 220 n., 221; Columbus on, 221
Renaissance, the, 53; intellectual activity, 64, 110; art, 222
Renard, G., 18 n.
Rennie, John, 128 n.
Restoration, English, and physical science, 64
Results of Machinery, The, 210
Revolt of 1830, 95
Revolution, agrarian, Chapter VI *passim*; changes before sixteenth century, 82, 83; enclosures of sixteenth century, 84; of eighteenth century, 87–8; compared with French agrarian revolution, 89; with Danish, 89, 90; social consequences, 91–6
— commercial, 21–3
— French, 4, 241; effects on French industry, 46; on agriculture, 88, 89; panic in England, 207, 250; Code of, 254; influence on English thought, 258, 259, 261
— Whig, 60, 85
Reynolds, Richard, 146 n., 147
Rheims, 17
Rhine Valley, 9
Ribble, the, 181
Rice, introduction of, 22
Richelieu, 4, 59
Rio de Janeiro, 36
Risca, 146 n.
Roads, condition of, 70, 71; improvements, 71–6; French, 71
Roanne, 45
Robert of Geneva, 52
Robison, Dr., 121
Rochdale, 69, 76, 211
Rodney, Admiral, 203
Roebuck, Dr., connexion with Watt, 116, 117; bankruptcy, 120, 124, 126
Roman Empire, political order of, 266–8, 270, 281; economic order of, 263, 267–9, 270
Rome, economic life, 5–16; capitalism in, 5, 12, 13; commerce in, 6, 7, 9 ff.; its limited character, 10; industrial development, 8, 9–16; absence of mechanical invention, 10 ff., 63; usury, 12; corn dole, 13; rifling of Mediterranean and East, 7, 8, 233, 236, 237; recovery under Augustus, 8, 233–5, 255 n.; slavery in, 5, 61, 194, 196; architecture, 8; roads, 8, 70; public games, 13, 14; care for towns and amenities, 220, 221, 228, 229; simplicity of food and clothing, 218; use of Greek teaching, 235, 251; influence of Roman literature, 252, 253
Rome (the town), 218, 221; sack of, 237
Romilly, Sir Samuel, 254; on apprentice children, 199, 200
Roscoe, William, 203
Rose, George, 203
Rostovtzeff, M., 9 n., 10 n., 13, 16 n., 269 n., 270
Rotary motion, 126, 130, 141
Rotherham, 144
Rothschilds, the, 49
Roubaix, 48 n.
Rouen, 45
Roundsman system, 94
Runcorn, 77
Royal Society, 64
Russell, Charles, 248 n.
Russia, 283; commerce, 20, 54; and mechanics, 123; iron industry, 123 n.; and railways, 273 n.; tariffs, 274, 275, 277
Ryswyk, Peace of, 239 n.

Saddler and Green, 171
Saddlers Company, 102
Saddleworth, 69
Sadler, 129
Sadler, M. T., 202, 203
Sagnac, M., 45 n.
Salford, 224 n.
Salonica, 62
Salvioli, 12 n., 218 n.; on Roman doles, 13 n.
Samos, 163
San Domingo, 192, 237 n.
Sandwich, 19, 25
Saracens, 18
Sardinia, 264, 265
Savery, Thomas, his steam engine, 111–12

INDEX

Saw-gin, invention of, 183, 249 n.
Saxony, 188
Schelt, the, 47
"Scotch Cattle," the, 155, 156
Scotland, 59, 68, 71; cattle from, 69; iron industry, 131, 134 n., 138, 148; conditions in ironworks, 152, 153; cotton factories, 189
Scotsmen as mechanics, Watt on, 122
Scott, Sir Walter, 219
Scott, W. R., on stockbroking, 55 n.
Scottish companies, 54 n.
  peasant, 230
Scrivenor, on ironmasters, 146 n.; ironworks, 160, 161
Scythia, 6
Seducing of artisans, 123, 206, 207
Seine, the, 77
Selby, 72
Seneca, 5
Sepulveda, 252 n.
Severn, the, 136, 169; highway for iron industry, 77, 134; cast-iron bridge over, 138
Seville, 30
Shaftesbury, Lord, 203, 254, 261; on industrial system, 247. See also Ashley, Lord
Shakespeare, William, 244, 256, 260; definition of man quoted by Burke, 205, 246
Shanghai, 208 n.
Sharp, Granville, 194
Sheffield, 6, 174; ironworks, 135, 144; cutlers, 68, 138, 142
Shelley, P. B., 219, 255
Shipley, 78 n.
Shoemakers Company, 102
Shops, early, 68, 69; and agrarian changes, 91
Shropshire, iron industry, 146 n., 148; conditions in, 149-50
Sicily, 18, 265, 266, 267, 270
Sidmouth, Lord, 108
Sierra Leone, 192
Sidon, 264
Silk, introduction of industry into Europe, 16, 187; development in Europe, 16, 18; in France, 18, 45; from India, 185. See also Spitalfields
Silk mills, in East, 16, 209, 247; in Genoa, 16
Simon, Sir John, 257 n.
Simon Stylites, St., 222

Simpson, F. A., on Holland and Berlin Decrees, 49 n.
Sinclair, Sir John, 74
Slaney, R. A., 226
Slavery, Roman, 5, 194, 195, 196 n., 247; protection of slaves, 235 n.; mediæval, 16 n., 190, 191, 238; forbidden in England, 194; American, 249 n. See also Slave Trade
Slave Trade, African, 208, 237, 243, 247; Bristol merchants and, 146 n.; origin and growth, 191, 192; England's share, 192; her monopoly after 1713, 193; prohibited by American Congress, 193; abolition of, by Fox, 194; Liverpool and, 203, 204; agitation against, 239, 254, 255
Smart, William, 35 n., 49 n.
Smeaton, John, 122, 127
Smiles, Samuel, 120 n., 130 n., 138 n., 140 n.
Smith, Adam, 53, 215, 280; on Spain, 27, 28 n., 31; on colonists, 33; on Navigation Acts, 40; on Dutch taxes, 40; on free trade, 59; on division of labour, 228, 231, 248; and Quesnai, 254; teaching of, 271 f.; pupils of, 273
Smith, General, 197 n.
Smith, Dr. Southwood, 226
Smithfield, 69
Smoke, nuisance of, 119, 187 n.; in Burslem, 166
Smollett, Tobias, 71
Socialists, 230
Soho Works, 118 and Chapter VIII passim; lit with gas, 138 n., 220
Solon, 61
Somerset, 72, 80
Somerset, Duke of, 84
Sophocles, 235
Southampton, 19, 25
Southey, Robert, 255; and housing, 224, 225; and factory children, 245
Southport, 76 n.
South Sea Bubble, 55
South Seas Company, 193
Spain, 17, 50, 265, 267, 268, 270; in Roman times, 8, 9; and New World, 24, 26-31, 212, 221; use of opportunities,

27; concentration on precious metals, 28; effect on politics and industry of Spain, 28–30; colonists strictly regulated by Spanish Government, 33; break up of empire, 36, 37; religious wars, 40; population, 40 n.; cotton industry, 180; African slave trade, 191, 192, 198; cruelties in New World, 237; regulations to protect natives, 239
Specialization, industrial, early, 5, 6; in Middle Ages, 16, 17, 18
Speenhamland system, 94
Spice Islands, 19, 31 n., 39, 179, 243, 256; early importance, 21
Spices, 25, 27. *See also* Pepper
Spinoza, 211
Spitalfields regulations, 107
Spode, brothers, 165, 171
Staffordshire, 80, 146 n., 148; ironworkers' misery at peace, 143 n.; conditions in ironworks, 149–50, 158; potteries, 163 and Chapter X *passim*
Stage coaches, 71, 75–6
Stalybridge, 224 n.
Stamford, 17
Stamp Act, 34
Steam engine, pioneers, 111; Savery's, 111, 112; Newcomen's, 112, 113; Watt's discovery of separate condenser, 110, 113; distribution of engines, 129 n.; used for iron industry, 136, 141, 142; for cotton mills, 127 n., 182; Dr. Bridges on, 196. *See also* Watt
Steam navigation, 129
Steel, 131; Huntsman's process, 141, 142
Stein, 273
Stephenson, George, 3, 80
Stockbroking, 55
Stock Exchange, 57
Stockholm, 218
Stockport, 224 n.
Stocks, M. D., 71 n.
Stockton and Darlington Railway, 79
Stoke, 163, 173 n.
Stour, the, 77
Stourbridge fair, 68
Stow, John, 238
Streeter, Canon, 64 **n.**
Strutts, the, 243

Stuarts, the, industrial policy, **60**, 61, 102, 103
Sturt, George, 248 n.
Suessa Senonum, 220
Suetonius, 10 n., 14 n.
Suez, 264
Suffolk, 92, 95
Sugar, increased consumption of, 22
Sugar Islands, 32
Sulla, 61, 234
Sully, 41
Sumatra, 19
Sunderland, 148
Sussex, 95; iron industry, 80, 134; charcoal burners, 133
Swansea cavalry, 155
Sweden, 274; iron from, 135 n., 140, 142
Swedish Companies, 54 n.
Switzerland, 188
Symington, 129
Syracuse, 7, 11
Syria, 267, 270; and Roman commerce, 8, 9; weavers, 18; mediæval commerce, 20, 24 capitalists, 247

Tacitus, 13, 253 n.
Taff Valley, 70
Talents, Ministry of all the, 145
Tamburlaine, 238, 244, 246
Tana, 190
Tartars, the, 28
Taskurgan, 9 n.
Tawney, J., 196 n.
Tawney, R. H., 53 n., 99 n., 241 n.; on German peasants, 83 n.; on landlords' debts, 84 n.
Tea, importance of, 21, 22, 23
Telemachus, 265
Telford, Thomas, 74, 75
Ten Hours Bill, 202, 203, 204
Thrace, 247
Thucydides, 253
Tiberius, 5
Tigris, 264
Tilley, A., 41 n., 89 n.
Tingtang mine, 124
Tobacco trade, 116
Tories, 60
Toulouse, 77
Tours, 18
Toutain, J., 266, 267 n., 269 n.
Townshend, Lord, 86
Towns (including Housing), Town-planning in earlier times, 218; lack of, in Industrial Revolu-

tion, 219 ; neglect of problem compared with Roman Empire, 220, 221 ; its significance, 222 ; urgency of problem, 222, 223 ; example from Preston in 1844, 223 ; great increase of town population, 223 ; new evils, 224 ; government of towns before 1835, 225 ; Improvement Commissioners set up by private legislation, 225 ; Parliamentary Committee of 1840 and its proposals, 226 ; Normanby's Bill of 1840, 226 ; disclosures before Commissions of 1867 and 1884, 227 ; lack of amenities, 229 ; comparison with Roman towns, 229 ; curse of Midas on new town, 232

Toynbee, A. J., 234 n., 252 n., 266, 269 ; on Greek thought, 63 n.
Tractarian movement, 254
Trade Unions, as civilizing force, 255, 258
Trajan, 5, 12, 14 n. ; vigorous administration, 9, 15
Transport ; Chapter V *passim*, in Potteries, 169, 170, 171, 172 ; development of, 271. *See also* Railways
Tredegar, 146 n.
Trent, the, 77
Trentham, 167
Trevelyan, Sir Charles, and Civil Service, 257 n.
Trevelyan, Sir George, 253 n.
Trevelyan, G. M., 75 n. ; on roads to London, 69
Truck system, in ironworks, 154 ; in potteries, 175
Trusts. *See* Turnpike
Tucker, Dean, 58
Tudors, the, 39, 99 ; and industry, 59 ; and boroughs, 98
Tull, Jethro, 85, 86
Tunstall, 163
Turgot, 41, 215, 273 ; on America, 34, 35 ; on internal customs regulations, 46, 59 ; and education, 231 n.
Turkey, cotton from, 184
Turks, 24
Turner of Worcester, 171
Turnpike Trusts, 71–6
Two Seas Canal, 77
Twyford, J., 165
Tyldesley, 207

Tyranny, Greek, 11 n.
Tyre, 264, 265 ; silk mills, 16, 209 ; commerce, 18, 219
Tysoe, 93 n.

Ulm, 180
Union Clubs, 155
Union, the, with Scotland, 59, 116
Unitarians, 239
United States, 1, 37, 181 ; War of Independence, 33, 35, 37 ; War of 1812, 35, 44 ; policy of Protection, 35 ; raw cotton supply from, 32, 44, 66, 183, 184 ; cotton industry, 181, 184, 185, 188 ; effects of Whitney's invention, 183, 184, 249 n. ; and Japan, 274 ; position to-day, 283–4 ; and Protection, 275 ff. ; railways in, 276–7 ; *see also* America
University of Glasgow, and Watt, 115
Unwin, Professor George, 59 n., 60 n., 101 n., 102 n., 180 n., 189 ; on social conflicts in fifteenth century, 17 n. ; on journeyman class, 99 n. ; on craftsmen, 100 ; on quarrels, 203
Upholsterers, London, 102
Ure, A., 45 n., 48 n., 185 n., 188 ; on cost of spinning, 186 n.
Ure, P. N., 11 n.
Usury, 53 n.
Utrecht, Treaty of, 40, 42 ; and slave trade, 193
Uttoxeter, 164

Valladolid, 252 n.
Varro, 6, 15 n.
Vauban, 59, 62
Vaucanson, 45
Venice, 219 ; as commercial power, 4, 17, 18, 19, 20, 24, 25, 32 ; and silk, 18 ; slave trade, 191, 243 ; and piracy, 238
Verona, 9
Versailles, Treaty of, 281
Vespasian, 10, 220
Vienna, Peace of, 47
Village, destruction of, Chapter VI, 2, 213 ; village life in Middle Ages, 81, 82 ; changes in English village after Great Plague and growth of cloth industry, 83 ; villeinage loses

servile character, 83; enclosures of sixteenth century, 84; of eighteenth century, 87; new problem of village after enclosures, 91; proposal for minimum wage, 91; for allotments, 92; Speenhamland system, 93; village riots of 1830, 95; auction of labourers, 96
Villeinage, 81, 82, 83
Virgil, 5
Virginia, 31, 193
Vitruvius, 221
Vivians, the, 147 n.
Voltaire, 239; on English aristocracy and trade, 60

Wages, minimum, legislation, 91, 105, 108; proposals, 92, 106, 107, 214 n.
Wakefield, 68, 77
Wales, South, iron industry, 79, 131, 144, 147 n., 148; capital for, 146 n.; conditions in ironworks, 151; truck system, 154; social conditions, 156–9, 248, 256; towns, 220; illiteracy, 231
Walker, Aaron, 146 n.
Walker's Iron Works, 138, 144, 148 n.
Walker, Samuel, 142
Walpole, Sir Robert, 40, 60
War of American Independence, 33, 35, 37, 116, 220; and iron trade, 138, 143, 147
American (1812), 35, 44
Dutch (1652), 39
French (1793–1802, 1803–15), 145, 147, 193; effects on Industrial Revolution, 43, 249, 250; on enclosures, 88; on condition of labourers, 93; on iron trade, 143; on French industry, 44 f.; on English financial capitalism, 49
Great (1914–18), 93, 250
Hundred Years (1338–1453), 52
of Louis XIV, 40, 41, 42
Thirty Years (1618–48), 39, 53 n.
Peloponnesian (431–404 B.C.), 247
Warmington, E. H., 269 n.
Warwick, Earl of, 84
Warwickshire, 80, 148
Washington, George, 239
Water pipes, 138, 220

Water supply, Roman, 221, 228; South Wales, 159, 220
Watt, James, 3, 12, 211, 249; his invention of separate condenser, 110, 113; early history, 114; life at Glasgow, 115; association with Roebuck, 116–18; with Boulton, 118 ff.; settles in England, 122; first successful engine, 122; difficulties with workmen, 122, 123; goes to Cornwall, 124; financial troubles, 124, 125; rotary motion, 126; scepticism about it, 127; other inventions, 127; improved financial position, 128; on steam navigation, 129; old age, 129, 130; importance of invention to iron industry, 136, 141, 142; on Cort, 140 n.; invention used for cotton mills, 127 n., 182; author of modern civilization, 130
Watt, James, junior, 129 n.
Weaver, the, 77, 169
Weavers, Cotton, petition, 108
Webb, Sidney, and Beatrice, 71 n.; on Turnpike Trusts, 72, 73 n.; on capitalism, 210 n.; on towns, 224 n., 229
Wedgwood, Francis, 177
Wedgwood, Josiah, dinner service for Catherine of Russia, 162; his improvements in pottery, 165, 170, 171, 172 n.; his energy over roads and canals, 169, 170; on improved conditions, 173
Wedgwood, Josiah (the second), 173
Wedgwood, J. C., 169 n., 173
Wedgwood, Dr. Thomas, 165
Wells, H. G., 12 n.
West India Company, Dutch, 54; French, 55
West Riding, 69, 80; cotton factories, 189
Wharfedale, 72
Wheal Busy mine, 124
Whigs, 60; and State control of industry, 61, 103
Whitbread, Samuel, on Orders in Council, 43; on minimum wage, 92, 214 n.; and education, 231
Whitney, Eli, his saw-gin, 183, 184, 249 n.
Wigan, 76, 78; Factory Acts disregarded in, 202 n.

INDEX

Wilberforce, William, 239 ; on iron districts, 131 ; on iron workers, 148 n. ; and slave trade, 193, 254 ; and Combination Act, 207 ; on working classes, 250
Wilkins, C., 146 n., 159 n., 160 n.
Wilkinson, John, in France, 45 ; and steam engine, 121, 122, 124, 141, 143 ; his character, 147 ; his assignats, 154
William III, 62, 165
Willington, 169
Wiltshire, 80, 95
Winchelsea, Lord, 93
Winchester, 68
Windham, William, 205
Winsford, 169
Wiss, Mr., 125
Wolsey, Cardinal, 84
Wolverhampton, 152, 153
Woman, effect of Industrial Revolution on, 187 n., 242
Wood, John, 243
Wool, early export of, 178
Woollen industry, early specialization, 17 ; organization of, 68, 69, 211 ; gradual changes, 79 ; shifting of centre, 80 ; regulations, 105 ; repealed, 108 ; Luddites, 105, 106 ; fear of Indian fabrics, 180. *See also* Cloth

Woolley, Sir Leonard, 267
Worcester, 77 ; china, 165 n., 171
Worcester, Marquis of, 111
Wordsworth, William, 219, 255
Worsley, 78
Worsted Acts, 104 n.
Worsted industry, 79, 80
Wortley, Mr., 200
Wrottersley, Sir J., on iron industry, 137 n.
Wyatt, J. and Paul, L., 182

Xenophon, 11

Yarranton, A., 77
Yokohama, 275
York, 17, 97 ; communications, 71, 74, 75, 76
Yorkshire, Luddites, 104–6 ; ironworks, 134, 144, 148 ; cotton factories, 199
Young, Arthur, 74, 90 n., 108 ; and minimum wage, 91, 92 ; and allotments, 92 ; on ironworks, 135 n., 137, 144, 148 n. ; on potteries, 172 n.
Ypres, 97

Zimmermann, E., 274, 279
Zimmern, A. E., 11 n., 187 n., 218 n.
Zollverein, German, 273, 274